PENGUIN ENGLISH LIBRARY
EL 38

NORTH AMERICA

ANTHONY TROLLOPE

ANTHONY TROLLOPE

NORTH AMERICA

Edited by Robert Mason,
with an introduction by
John William Ward

PENGUIN BOOKS

Penguin Books Ltd, Harmondsworth, Middlesex, England
Penguin Books Inc., 7110 Ambassador Road, Baltimore, Maryland 21207, U.S.A.
Penguin Books Australia Ltd, Ringwood, Victoria, Australia

—

First published 1862
Published in Penguin English Library 1968

—

Introduction copyright © John William Ward, 1968
Notes copyright © Robert Mason, 1968

—

Made and printed in Great Britain
by Hazell Watson & Viney Ltd
Aylesbury, Bucks
Set in Linotype Juliana

Contents

Introduction

BY J. W. WARD

THERE were considerable obstacles in Trollope's way when he came to write a book about the United States. The first was the simple one that his audience had come to expect a great deal of him. When, in the opening sentence of his introduction, Trollope said, 'It has been the ambition of my literary life to write a book about the United States,' he was quite self-conscious that his life was a literary life, even if it was leave from his official duties in the Post Office which made his trip to America possible. By 1861, when he was in the United States, *Barchester Towers* and *The Warden* had already appeared and Trollope had a considerable literary reputation to keep. But that was simply the inevitable and general hazard of any successful writer's career. There were two more particular obstacles in his way which, again, Trollope points to in his introduction. The first was personal, the memory of his mother's book, *Domestic Manners of the Americans* (1832), which had made the Trollope family name an epithet in American English. The second was historical; there was a civil war going on when Trollope landed in the United States and the time was hardly auspicious for travel.

Frances Trollope's book had been an acid portrait of the vulgarity and crudity of young America at a moment when the national pride of the United States was especially tender. It was an unbalanced book, but it was not a false book, although it took some years before Americans could bring themselves to say so. Anthony's judgement on his mother was diplomatic and just at one and the same moment. *Domestic Manners of the Americans* was, he wrote,

essentially a woman's book. She saw with a woman's keen eye, and described with a woman's light but graphic pen, the social defects and absurdities which our near relatives had adopted into their domestic life. All that she told was worth the telling .... But she did

not regard it as part of her work to dilate on the nature and operation of those political arrangements which had produced the social
absurdities which she saw, or to explain that though such absurdities were the natural result of those arrangements in their newness,
the defects would certainly pass away, while the political arrangements, if good, would remain.

Thus, without betraying his mother, Trollope deftly allowed
for American opinion of her and then went on to claim a different
intention for himself. 'If I could do anything to mitigate the soreness,' he insisted, 'if I could in any small degree add to the good
feeling which should exist between two nations which ought to
love each other so well ... I should think that I had cause to
be proud of my work.'

Yet, by the end of North America, Trollope was uneasy that
he had been too harsh, that he had not lived up to his generous
intention. Perhaps, but fortunately the historical moment provided
a different reception for his book than for his mother's. Mrs Trollope's criticism of democracy found an inevitably hostile audience
in Jacksonian America with its celebration of the dignity and
worth of the common man, but it found a quick and appreciative
one in England. The Reform Bills were before Parliament and
there were many in England only too glad to attend to any
criticism of the culture of democracy. North America, despite
points which at another moment might have stung, was well received in the United States, that is, the North, simply because
Americans were delighted to find one important Englishman, at
least, who defended the Union and the North's right to fight to
preserve it. But the English establishment had little sympathy
for the industrial and capitalistic North and Trollope met some
hostility at home, although the critic for Blackwood's Magazine
was candid enough to admit that his target was not so much
Trollope's book but rather the people of the North, whose politics
'we', he assumed, disliked extremely.

But if Trollope's attitude towards the rightness of the northern
cause won him a favourable audience when North America was
published, the war itself was no small obstacle to writing his book
in the first place. In contrast to his mother's concentration on the
'domestic' manners of the Americans, Trollope, as he insisted from

the outset, wished to describe 'the present social and political state of the country'. But the present state of the country was internecine war, so Trollope saw the political state of the country under rather special conditions. This may account for the fact that he actually had little to say by way of analysis of American political institutions and one may amend his statements of intention to read 'the present social state of the country'. That was Trollope's field. He had a fine eye for the revelatory human gesture and the social significance of a scene, and his skill there led him safely past all the other obstacles which lay in his way.

There is one incident in *North America* which may stand for Trollope's special strength and the worth of the whole book. A writer, Trollope lugged a portable writing-desk with him wherever he went in America (along with a tin tub), and once it came to grief. He wrote,

I shall never forget my agony as I saw and heard my desk fall from a porter's hand on a railway station, as he tossed it from him seven yards off on to the hard pavement. I heard its poor weak intestines rattle in their death-struggle, and knowing that it was smashed I forgot my position on American soil and remonstrated. 'It's my desk, and you've utterly destroyed it,' I said. 'Ha! Ha! Ha!' laughed the porter. 'You've destroyed my property,' I rejoined, 'and it's no laughing matter.' And then all the crowd laughed. 'Guess you'd better git it glued,' said one. So I gathered up the broken article and retired mournfully and crestfallen into a coach. This was very sad, and for the moment I deplored the ill-luck which had brought me to so savage a country.

If Trollope had gone no further, if he had stopped there with his justifiable despair at finding himself in so savage a country, one would accept the judgement Trollope himself made on *North America*. In *An Autobiography*, looking back on the book, Trollope decided *North America* was not a 'good book. I can recommend no one to read it now in order that he may be instructed or amused', Trollope was wrong. *North America* may not be, in the usual critical sense of the word, a 'good' book. It lacks form; it has little or no organization. It is hard to say what the point of the book is, what *North America* is about. Yet it is a fine example of a book which triumphs over its petty faults because of one

great, overriding virtue. That virtue is implicit in what follows
Trollope's lament over his shattered desk.

But though I was badly off on that railway platform, worse off than
I should have been in England – all that crowd of porters around
me were better off than our English porters. They had a 'good time'
of it.... They are arguing in their minds that civility to you will be
taken by you for subservience, or for an acknowledgment of super-
iority; and looking at your habits of life, – yours and mine together,
– I am not quite sure that they are altogether wrong. Have you ever
realized to yourself as a fact that the porter who carries your box
has not made himself inferior to you by the very act of carrying that
box? If not, that is the very lesson the man wishes to teach you.

If Trollope had not gone beyond simple chagrin at the heavy-
handed treatment he and his desk had from barbarous Americans,
we would count him only one more in that large number of educated and intelligent and self-satisfied Englishmen who came to
the United States to measure the decline of the West. But with
that wonderful question ('Have you ever realized to yourself *as
a fact* ... ?'), Trollope transcends the stereotype of the Englishman abroad and the limitations of the conventional travel
book.

Despite his own low opinion of the book, *North America* is
still well worth reading simply because Anthony Trollope was a
civilized man, civilized in the most exacting sense of the word.
He was a man thoroughly committed to his own way of life and
its values. Yet he was also a man fully aware that his values were
the result of his particular way of life, that they were, as he was
ready to admit, prejudices, the relative values of a certain kind
of society, not the expression of eternal verities (although he
was no more ready to surrender them because of that). The result
gave Trollope a secure vantage point from which to survey the
different kind of society he discovered in the United States and,
at the same time, the capacity to empathize with the new and the
unaccustomed, even when it violated his own preferences. A lesser man would have sulked in his coach, furious with the manners of a poorly disciplined working-class and the destruction of
his property, but Trollope, irritated and angry as he was, went

on to ask the more interesting question. What do those manners represent? What do they say about the strength as well as the weakness of the society which produced men with those manners? Trollope was, to put it shortly, admirably equipped to be an intelligent and sympathetic observer of American, or any other, culture.

The praise is more than a puff for a new edition of Trollope's observations on American society a hundred years ago. Trollope had a tolerance for ways of life other than his own which was remarkable for his time. In the middle of the nineteenth century, the conventional view was that society moved through a series of stages of development and that particular societies could be ranked as 'higher' or 'lower' on the scale by the degree to which they approximated the conditions and the values of the most 'civilized' society, usually that of the traveller, especially England during the years of its hegemony. When visitors, say, Anthony's mother, Frances Trollope, or Matthew Arnold, came to the United States, their criticism was that the United States lacked 'culture', that is, that it was not accomplished in the graces and achievements of English society. Trollope was not so foolish as to think that American society was, but he was intelligent enough to know that to say so did not say much about American society. If he found himself at home in Baltimore because it was 'more English', he did not conclude that the people of Baltimore were 'on this account better'. New York, he knew, was more characteristic, more American, 'the most thoroughly American of all American cities', but because he could not himself be happy there, Trollope did not 'on that account condemn it'.

The point is worth insisting on because there is more here than simply good-natured tolerance. At one point, discussing the causes of the Civil War in America, Trollope wrote:

The South is seceding from the North because the two are not homogeneous. They have different instincts, different appetites, different morals, and a different culture. It is well for one man to say that slavery has caused the separation; and for another to say that slavery has not caused it. Each in so saying speaks the truth. Slavery has caused it, seeing that slavery is the great point on which the two have agreed to differ. But slavery has not caused it, seeing that other points of difference are to be found in every circumstance and feature of the two people.

Even one only slightly acquainted with the massive historical literature on the causes of the American Civil War will recognize the modern accent of Trollope's concise statement that the conflict was a conflict between two cultures as well as a conflict over the moral issue of slavery. What is important, though, is not to give Trollope high grades for his interpretation of the American Civil War. He was actually not much interested in the war. What is important is to define clearly the kind of social imagination which makes Trollope still so interesting and which is implicit in the way he used the word, 'culture'.

In the history of the concept of 'culture', two quite different meanings have attached to the word. One is the honorific sense, as when one says, 'He is a cultured man'. This is the literary and humanistic meaning of the word and is the meaning Arnold had in view in *Culture and Anarchy*. Culture becomes a measure of intellectual and moral achievement and implies a hierarchy of personal and social values. It is apparent that Trollope is not using the word in that sense. He refers to the fact that the North and the South each have a different culture in order to describe, not to judge. He uses the word to differentiate, not to evaluate. Culture, in Trollope's usage, is simply a synonym for an entire way of life. The first usage of the word culture, in the same sense Trollope used it, is usually attributed to E. B. Tylor in *Primitive Culture* (1871), eight years after Trollope, where Tylor sets out to define the subject matter of the nascent discipline of anthropology. Again, what is important is not to score points for Trollope by arguing precedence for him in the evolution of the modern relativistic concept of culture, but to catch the quality of his vision. Trollope did not look down on what he saw. He looked at it. Trollope was capable of seeing something for what it was, not for what he thought it should be. Without surrendering his own standards, Trollope did not impose his standards on others. If one wishes, one might even compare Trollope on his travels with the cultural anthropologist in the field. But that puts rather a heavy burden on Trollope. One might better simply remember that he was a good novelist, able to imagine himself into the lives of others.

Before the extended stay which provided the material for *North America*, Trollope had been to the United States briefly once before. Then he wrote,

The government and social life of the people there ... afford the most interesting phenomena which we find as to the new world; – the best means of prophesying, if I may say so, what the world will next be, and what men will next do.

Much like Tocqueville, whose intelligence and style were in every other way so dissimilar, Trollope looked to the United States to discover what the world might become, not to insist that it remain the world he had always known. He had no cause, he wrote, ever to wish that he had been born an American, and he warned any other Englishman that if he came to America 'he will be pelted with the braggadocio of equality. The corns of his Old-World conservatism will be trampled on hourly by the purposely vicious herd of uncouth democracy'. But the intentional rudeness of the uncouth did not blind Trollope to the simple fact that the great mass of the people were far better off in America than in England and that their rudeness was the rough side of their sense of their equal worth. Trollope told his countrymen,

With us there is no level of society. Men stand on a long staircase, but the crowd congregates near the bottom, and the lower steps are very broad. In America men stand upon a common platform, but the platform is raised above the ground, though it does not approach in height the top of our staircase. If we take the average altitude in the two countries, we shall find that the American heads are the more elevated of the two.

The result, Trollope saw, was the pervasive sense in American democratic society that each man was on his own. It led to the remarkable energy, the expansiveness of a society where, ideally if not in fact, no obstacle stood in the way. It led to what Trollope called 'frontier men', by which he did not mean Americans who lived out on the physical edge of the forest. He meant all those Americans vigorously at work in the present for the future. He summed them all up in 'Monroe P. Jones, the speculator', who joined to a love of money to come 'a strong disregard for money made', and restlessly drove himself for more when he already had enough. As Trollope said, 'As an individual I differ very much from Monroe P. Jones,' but he was still able to recognize the romance which underlay the aggressive materialism of the type: 'Monroe P. Jones would be a great man to all posterity, if only he had a poet to sing of his valour.'

Trollope's ultimate strength was that he never lost sight of the romance which lay below the vulgar surface of American society. He could be wonderfully caustic about the pushiness of American women, could shrink from the frenetic movement and rootlessness of Americans constantly on the make, and could recognize that the new world being made was not the world he would have fashioned for himself. But he was imaginative enough to see, as he said in his last paragraph, that the 'self-asserting, obtrusive independence which so often wounds us is, if viewed aright, but an outward sign of those good things which a new country has produced for its people'. Among nineteenth-century travellers, few were as able as Trollope to see beneath the outward surface. With the result that North America is still an immensely readable book, the urbane reflections of a civilized man on the making of the American character.

J.W.W.

A Note on the Text

ANTHONY TROLLOPE spent nine months in the United States and Canada between August 1861 ad May 1862. He was writing industriously all the time, and the first of the two long volumes of *North America* was published by Chapman and Hall a few months after his return; the second followed later the same year. Unlike most of Trollope's other works, *North America* was never reprinted in England.

For the present edition the original two-volume work has been reduced to one volume of just over a third of the size. I have not altered any of the text and what appears here is exactly as Trollope wrote it, except that here and there his punctuation has been brought into conformity with modern practice. In deciding what to leave in and what to cut out, my aim was as far as possible to choose those extracts which were likely to be of interest to today's reader, both English and American. Many passages immediately commended themselves because of their topicality, others because they were good examples of Trollope at his most entertaining. On the other hand there were long dull areas and technical discourses of little interest now, and numerous repetitions, and it is in this latter category that I have made the most substantial cuts.

The Notes presented a problem. In 1862 the principal figures of recent American history were familiar to all American and to most English readers. At least Trollope thought so, for he wrote: 'Of Jefferson, Franklin and Madison we have all heard; our children speak of them and they are household words in the nursery of history.' Whether or not this was true then, it is not true today for many English readers, and since the present volume is intended for an English as much as for an American readership I have given brief notes to identify the men to whom Trollope refers. Otherwise I have provided notes when they seemed necessary for the understanding of the story, or are of some historical interest.

I should like to acknowledge my gratitude to Mr Clifton Child, O.B.E., my successor as Librarian of the Foreign Office, whose advice has been most valuable since the beginning of the project, and to others of my former colleagues in the library. In collecting material for the notes I have had useful information from Miss Everil Jones, of the British Embassy, Washington; Mr J. W. Mahoney of the Wine and Spirit Association; Mr John R. Murray; and Miss Stephanie Howell of Fortnum and Mason.

R.M.

A facsimile of the title page of Volume I of the first edition.

NORTH AMERICA.

BY

ANTHONY TROLLOPE,

AUTHOR OF

"THE WEST INDIES AND THE SPANISH MAIN," "DOCTOR THORNE,"
"ORLEY FARM," ETC.

IN TWO VOLUMES.

VOL. I.

LONDON:
CHAPMAN & HALL, 193 PICCADILLY.
1862.

Introduction

It has been the ambition of my literary life to write a book about the United States, and I had made up my mind to visit the country with this object before the intestine troubles of the United States Government had commenced. I have not allowed the division among the States and the breaking out of civil war to interfere with my intention; but I should not purposely have chosen this period either for my book or for my visit. I say so much, in order that it may not be supposed that it is my special purpose to write an account of the struggle as far as it has yet been carried.

My wish is to describe as well as I can the present social and political state of the country. This I should have attempted, with more personal satisfaction in the work, had there been no disruption between the North and South; but I have not allowed that disruption to deter me from an object which, if it were delayed, might probably never be carried out. I am therefore forced to take the subject in its present condition, and being so forced I must write of the war, of the causes which have led to it, and of its probable termination.

Thirty years ago my mother wrote a book about the Americans,[1] to which I believe I may allude as a well known and successful work without being guilty of any undue family conceit. That was essentially a woman's book. She saw with a woman's keen eye, and described with a woman's light but graphic pen, the social defects and absurdities which our near relatives had adopted into their domestic life. All that she told was worth the telling, and the telling, if done successfully, was sure to produce a good result. I am satisfied that it did so.

But she did not regard it as a part of her work to dilate on the nature and operation of those political arrangements which had produced the social absurdities which she saw, or to explain that though such absurdities were the natural result of those arrangements in their newness, the defects would certainly pass away, while the political arrangements, if good, would remain. Such a work is fitter for a man than for a woman.

I am very far from thinking that it is a task which I can perform with satisfaction either to myself or to others. It is a work which some man will do who has earned a right by education, study, and success to rank himself among the political sages of his age. But I may perhaps be able to add something to the familiarity of Englishmen with Americans. The writings which have been most popular in England on the subject of the United States have hitherto dealt chiefly with social details; and though in most cases true and useful, have created laughter on one side of the Atlantic, and soreness on the other. If I could do anything to mitigate the soreness, if I could in any small degree add to the good feeling which should exist between two nations which ought to love each other so well, and which do hang upon each other so constantly, I should think that I had cause to be proud of my work.

And now touching this war which had broken out between the North and South before I left England. I would wish to explain what my feelings were; or rather what I believe the general feelings of England to have been before I found myself among the people by whom it was being waged. It is very difficult for the people of any one nation to realize the political relations of another, and to chew the cud and digest the bearings of these internal politics. But it is unjust in the one to decide upon the political aspirations and doings of that other without such understanding.

I left England in August last – August 1861. At that time, and for some months previous, I think that the general English feeling on the American question was as follows: 'This widespread nationality of the United States, with its enormous territorial possessions and increasing population, has fallen asunder, torn to pieces by the weight of its own discordant parts – as a congregation when its size has become unwieldy will separate, and reform itself into two wholesome wholes. It is well that this should be so, for the people are not homogeneous as a people should be who are called to live together as one nation. They have attempted to combine free-soil sentiments with the practice of slavery, and to make these two antagonists live together in peace and unity under the same roof; but as we have long expected they have failed.

'Now has come the period for separation; and if the people would only see this, and act in accordance with the circumstances which Providence and the inevitable hand of the world's ruler has prepared for them, all would be well. But they will not do this. They will go to war with each other. The South will make her demands for secession with an arrogance and instant pressure which exasperates the North; and the North, forgetting that an equable temper in such matters is the most powerful of all weapons, will not recognize the strength of its own position. It allows itself to be exasperated and goes to war for that which if regained would only be injurious to it.

'Thus millions on millions sterling will be spent. A heavy debt will be incurred; and the North, which divided from the South might take its place among the greatest of nations, will throw itself back for half a century, and perhaps injure the splendour of its ultimate prospects. If only they would be wise, throw down their arms and agree to part! But they will not.'

This was, I think, the general opinion when I left England. It would not, however, be necessary to go back many months to reach the time when Englishmen were saying how impossible it was that so great a national power should ignore its own greatness, and destroy its own power by internecine separation. But in August last all that had gone by, and we in England had realized the probability of actual secession. I certainly did think that the northern States, if wise, would have let the southern States go. I had blamed Buchanan as a traitor for allowing the germ of secession to make any growth – and as I thought of him as a traitor then, so do I think of him as a traitor now. But I had also blamed Lincoln, or rather the Government of which Mr Lincoln in this matter is no more than the exponent, for his efforts to avoid that which is inevitable. In this I think that I – or as I believe I may say we, we Englishmen – were wrong. I do not see how the North, created as it was and had been, could have submitted to secession without resistance.

Had the southern States sought to obtain secession by constitutional means, they might or might not have been successful; but if successful there would have been no war. I do not mean to brand all the southern States with treason, nor do I intend to say that having secession at heart they could have obtained it by constitutional means. But I do intend to say that acting as they did, demanding secession not constitutionally but in opposition to the constitution, taking upon themselves the right of breaking up a nationality of which they formed only a part, and doing that without consent of the other party, opposition from the North and war was an inevitable consequence.

It is, I think, only necessary to look back to the revolution by which the United States separated themselves from England to see this. There is hardly to be met, here and there, an Englishman who now regrets the loss of the revolted American colonies – who now thinks that civilization was retarded and the world injured by that revolt; who now conceives that England should have expended more treasures and more lives in the hope of retaining those colonies. It is agreed that the revolt was a good thing; that those who were then rebels became patriots by success, and that they deserved well of all coming ages of mankind. But not the less absolutely necessary was it that England should endeavour to hold her own. She was as the mother bird when the young bird will fly alone. She suffered those pangs which Nature calls upon mothers to endure.

As was the necessity of British opposition to American independence, so was the necessity of northern opposition to southern secession. I do not say that in other respects the cases were parallel. The States separated from us because they would not endure taxation without representation – in other words because they were big enough and old enough to go alone.

The South is seceding from the North because the two are not homogeneous. They have different instincts, different appetites, different morals, and a different culture. It is well for one man to say that slavery has caused the separation; and for another to say that slavery has not caused it. Each in so saying speaks the truth. Slavery has caused it, seeing that slavery is the great point on which the two have agreed to differ. But slavery has not caused it, seeing that other points of difference are to be found in every circumstance and feature of the two people.

The North and South must ever be dissimilar. In the North labour has always been honourable, and because honourable successful. In the South labour has ever been servile – at least in some senses, and therefore dishonourable; and because dishonourable has not, to itself, been successful. In the South, I say, labour has ever been dishonourable; and I am driven to confess that I have not hitherto seen a sign of any change in the Creator's fiat in this matter. That labour will be honourable all the world over, as years advance and the millenium draws nigh, I for one never doubt.

So much for English opinion about America in August last. And now I will venture to say a word or two as to American feeling respecting this English opinion at that period. It will of course be remembered by all my readers that at the beginning of the war Lord Russell, who was then in the lower House, declared as Foreign Secretary of State that England would regard both North and South as belligerents, and would remain neutral as to both of them. This declaration gave violent offence to the North, and has been taken as indicating British sympathy with the cause of the seceders.

'What would you in England have thought,' a gentleman of much weight in Boston said to me, 'if when you were in trouble in India, we had openly declared that we regarded your opponents there as belligerents on equal terms with yourselves?'

I was forced to say that, as far as I could see, there was no analogy between the two cases. In India an army had mutinied, and that an army composed of a subdued, if not a servile race. The analogy would have been fairer had it referred to any sympathy shown by us to insurgent Negroes.

'But,' said my friend, 'we should not have proclaimed to the world that we regarded you and them as standing on an equal footing.'

But the fairer analogy lies between Ireland and the southern States. The monster meetings and O'Connell's triumphs are not so long gone by but that many of us can remember the first demand for secession made by Ireland, and the line which was then taken by American sympathies. It is not too much to say that America then believed that Ireland would secure secession, and that the great trust of the Irish repealers was in the moral aid which she did and would receive from America.

'But our Government proclaimed no sympathy with Ireland,' said my friend. No. The American Government is not called on to make such proclamations; nor had Ireland ever taken upon herself the nature and labours of a belligerent.

That this anger on the part of the North is unreasonable I cannot doubt. That it is unfortunate, grievous and very bitter, I am quite sure. But I do not think it is in any degree surprising. I am inclined to think that did I belong to Boston as I do belong to London. I should share in the feeling, and rage as loudly as all men there have raged against the coldness of England. When men have on hand such a job of work as the North has now undertaken they are always guided by their feelings rather than their reason. What two men ever had a quarrel in which each did not think that all the world, if just, would espouse his own side of the dispute?

'We have worked for them, and fought for them, and paid for them,' says the North. 'By our labour we have raised their indolence to a par with our energy. While we have worked like men, we have allowed them to talk and bluster. We have warmed them in our bosom, and now they have turned against us and sting us. The world sees that this is so. England, above all, must see it, and seeing it should speak out her true opinion.'

Mr and Mrs Jones are the dearly beloved friends of my family. My wife and I have lived with Mrs Jones on terms of intimacy which have been quite endearing. Jones has the run of my house with perfect freedom, and in Mrs Jones' drawing-room I have always had my own armchair, and have been quite regaled with large breakfast-cups of tea, quite as though I were at home. But of a sudden Jones and his wife have fallen out, and there is for a while in Jones' Hall a cat and dog life that may end – in one hardly dare to surmise what calamity. Mrs Jones begs that I will interfere with her husband, and Jones entreats the good offices of my wife in moderating the hot temper of his own.

But we know better than that. If we interfere, the chances are that our dear friends will make it up and turn against us. I grieve beyond measure in a general way at the temporary break-up of the Jones' Hall happiness. I express general wishes that it may be temporary. But as far as saying which is right or wrong – as to expressing special sympathy on either side in such a quarrel – it is out of the question. 'My dear Jones, you must excuse me. Any news in the City today? Sugars have fell; how are teas?' Of course, Jones thinks I'm a brute; but what can I do?

I have been somewhat surprised to find the trouble that has been taken by American authors, statesmen and logicians to prove that this secession on the part of the South has been revolutionary. Of course the movement has been revolutionary and anti-constitutional. Nobody, no single Southerner, can really believe that the Constitution of the United States as framed in 1787, or altered since, intended to give to the separate States the power of seceding as they pleased. Such licence would have been destructive to the very idea of a great nationality. Where would New England have been as part of the United States, if New York, which stretches from the Atlantic to the borders of Canada, had been endowed with the power of cutting off the six northern States from the rest of the Union?

It is revolutionary, but what then? Have the northern States of the American Union taken upon themselves in 1861 to proclaim their opinion that revolution is a sin? Are they going back to the divine right of any sovereignty? Are they going to tell the world that a nation or a people is bound to remain in any political status, because that status is the recognized form of government under which such a people have lived? Is this to be the doctrine of United States citizens – of all people? Of course, the movement is revolutionary and why not? It is agreed now among all men and all nations that any people may change its form of government to another, if it wills to do so – and if it can do so.

There are two other points on which these northern statesmen and logicians also insist. It being settled that secession on the part of the Southerners is revolution, it is argued firstly, that no occasion for revolution had been given by the North to the South; and, secondly, that the South has been dishonest in its revolutionary tactics. Men certainly should not raise a revolution for nothing; and it may certainly be declared that whatever men do, they should do so honestly.

But in that matter of cause and ground for revolution, it is so very easy for either party to put in a plea that shall be satisfactory to itself! Mr and Mrs Jones each had a separate story. Mr Jones was sure that the right lay with him; but Mrs Jones was no less sure. No doubt the North had done much for the South – had earned money for it; had fed it – and had moreover in a great measure fostered all its bad habits. It had not only been generous to the South, but over-indulgent. But also it had continually irritated the South by meddling with that which the Southerners believed to be a question absolutely private to themselves.

The matter was illustrated to me by a New Hampshire man who was conversant with black bears. These bears are caught among the hills, and are thus imprisoned for the amusement of hotel guests.

'Them Southerners,' said my friend, 'are jist as one as that 'ere bear. We feeds him and gives him a house and his belly is always full. But then, jist because he's a black bear, we're ollers a poking him with sticks, and o' course the beast is kinder riled. He wants to be back to the mountains. He wouldn't have his belly filled, but he'd have his own way. It's jist so with them Southerners.'

It is of no use proving to any man or to any nation that they have got all they should want, if they have not got all that they do want. If a servant desires to go, it is of no avail to show him that he has all he can desire in his present place. The Northerners say that they have given no offence to the Southerners, and that therefore the South is wrong to raise a revolution. The very fact that the North is the North, is an offence to the South. As long as Mr and Mrs Jones were one in heart and one in feeling, having the same hopes and the same joys, it was well that they should remain together. But when it is proved that they cannot so live without tearing out each other's eyes, Sir Cresswell Cresswell, the revolutionary institution of domestic life, interferes and separates them.

This is the age of such separations. I do not wonder that the North should use its logic to show that it has received cause of offence but given none. But I do think that such logic is thrown away. The matter is not one for argument. The South has thought that it can do better without the North than with it; and if it has the power to separate itself, it must be conceded that it has the right.

And then as to that question of honesty. Whatever men do they should certainly do honestly. Speaking broadly one may say that the rule applies to nations as strongly as to individuals, and should be observed in politics as accurately as in other matters. We must, however, confess that men who are scrupulous in their private dealings do too constantly drop these scruples when they handle public affairs. The name of Napoleon III stands fair now before Europe, and yet he filched the French Empire with a falsehood. The union of England and Ireland is a successful fact, but nevertheless it can hardly be said that it was honestly achieved. I heartily believe that the whole of Texas is improved in every sense by having been taken from Mexico and added to the southern States, but I much doubt whether that annexation was accomplished with absolute honesty. We all reverence the name of Cavour but Cavour did not consent to abandon Nice to France with clean hands.

When men have political ends to gain they regard their opponents as adversaries, and then that old rule of war is brought to bear. Deceit or valour – either may be used against a foe. Would it were not so! The rascally rule – rascally in reference to all political contests – is becoming less universal than it was. But it still exists with sufficient force to be urged as an excuse; and while it does exist it seems almost needless to show that a certain amount of fraud has been used by a certain party in a revolution. If the South be ultimately successful, the fraud of which it may have been guilty will be condoned by the world.

The southern or democratic party of the United States had, as all men know, been in power for many years. Either southern Presidents had been elected, or northern Presidents with southern politics. The South for many years had had the disposition of military matters, and the power of distributing military appliances of all descriptions. It is now alleged by the North that a conspiracy had long been hatching in the South with the view of giving to the southern States the power of secession whenever they might think fit to secede; and it is further alleged that President after President for years back has unduly sent the military treasures of the nation away from the North down to the South, in order that the South might be prepared when the day should come.

That a President with southern instincts should unduly favour the South, that he should strengthen the South, and feel that arms and ammunition were stored there with better effect than they could be stored in the North, is very probable. We all understand what is the bias of a man's mind, and how strong that bias may become when the man is not especially scrupulous. But I do not believe that any President previous to Buchanan sent military materials to the South with the self-acknowledged purpose of using them against the Union. That Buchanan did so, or knowingly allowed this to be done, I do believe and I think that Buchanan was a traitor to the country whose servant he was and whose pay he received.

And now, having said so much in the way of introduction, I will begin my journey.

Chapter 1

WE – the we consisting of my wife and myself [2] – left Liverpool for Boston on the 24th August, 1861, in the *Arabia*, one of Cunard's North American mail packets. We had determined that my wife should return alone at the beginning of winter, when I intended to go to a part of the country in which, under the existing circumstances of the war, a lady might not feel herself altogether comfortable. I proposed staying in America over the winter, and returning in the spring; and this programme I have carried out with sufficient exactness.

The *Arabia* touched at Halifax; and as the touch extended from 11 a.m. to 6 p.m. we had an opportunity of seeing a good deal of that colony. At seven o'clock on the morning but one after that, we were landed at Boston.

At Boston I found friends ready to receive us with open arms, though they were friends we had never known before. I own that I felt myself burdened with much nervous anxiety at my first introduction to men and women in Boston. I knew what the feeling there was with reference to England, and I knew also how impossible it is for an Englishman to hold his tongue and submit to dispraise of England.

As for going among a people whose whole minds were filled with affairs of the war, and saying nothing about the war, I knew that no resolution to such an effect could be carried out. If one could not trust oneself to speak, one should have stayed at home in England. I will here state that I always did speak out openly what I thought and felt, and that though I encountered very strong – sometimes almost fierce – opposition, I never was subjected to anything that was personally disagreeable to me.

In September we did not stay above a week in Boston, having been fairly driven out of it by the mosquitoes. I had been told that I should find nobody in Boston whom I cared to see, as everybody was habitually out of town during the heat of the latter summer and early autumn; but this was not so. The war and attendant turmoils of war had made the season of vacation shorter than usual, and most of those for whom I asked were back at their posts.

I know no place at which an Englishman may drop down suddenly among a pleasanter circle of acquaintance, or find himself with a more clever set of men, than he can do at Boston. I confess that in this respect I think that but few towns are at present more fortunately circumstanced than the capital of the Bay State, as Massachusetts is called, and that very few towns make a better use of their advantages. Boston has a right to be proud of what it has done for the world of letters. It is proud; but I have not found that its pride was carried too far.

It is not specially interesting to the eye – what new town, or even what simply adult town, can be so? There is an Athenaeum, and a State Hall, and a fashionable street – Beacon Street, very like Piccadilly as it runs along the Green Park – and there is the Green Park opposite to this Piccadilly, called Boston Common. Beacon Street and Boston Common are very pleasant. Excellent houses there are, and large churches, and enormous hotels; but of such things as these a man can write nothing that is worth the reading. The traveller who desires to tell his experience of North America must write of people rather than of things.

I found myself instantly involved in discussions on American politics, and the bearing of England upon those politics.

'What do you think, you in England – what do you all believe will be the upshot of this war?' That was the question always asked in those or other words.

'Secession, certainly,' I always said, but not speaking quite with that abruptness.

'And you believe, then, that the South will beat the North?'

I explained that I, personally, had never so thought, and that I did not believe that to be the general idea. Men's opinions in England, however, were too divided to enable me to say that there was any prevailing conviction on the matter.

My own impression was, and is, that the North will, in a military point of view, have the best of the contest – will beat the South; but that the Northerners will not prevent secession, let their success be what it may. Should the North prevail after a two years' conflict, the North will not admit the South to an equal participation of good things with themselves, even though each separate rebellious State should return suppliant, like a prodigal son, kneeling on the floor of Congress, each with a separate rope of humiliation round its neck. Such was my idea as expressed then, and I do not know that I have since had much cause to change it.

'We will never give it up,' one gentleman said to me – and, indeed, many have said the same – 'till the whole territory is again united from the Bay to the Gulf ! It is impossible that we should allow of two nationalities within those limits.'

'And do you think it possible,' I asked, 'that you should receive back into your bosom this people which you now hate with so deep a hatred, and receive them again into your arms as brothers on equal terms? Is it in accordance with experience that a conquered people should be so treated – and that, too, a people whose very habit of life is at variance with the habits of their presumed conquerors? When you have flogged them into a return of fraternal affection, are they to keep their slaves or are they to abolish them?'

'No,' said my friend; 'it may not be practical to put those rebellious States at once on an equality with ourselves. For a time they will probably be treated as the Territories are now treated.' (The Territories are vast outlying districts belonging to the Union, but not as yet endowed with State governments, or a participation in the United States Congress.) 'For a time they must, perhaps, lose their full privileges; but the Union will be anxious to readmit them at the earliest possible period.'

'And as to the slaves?' I asked again.

'Let them emigrate to Liberia : back to their own country.'

I could not say that I thought much of the solution of the difficulty. It would, I suggested, overtask even the energy of America to send out an emigration of four million souls, to provide for their wants in a new and uncultivated country, and to provide after that for the terrible gap made in the labour market of the southern States.

'The Israelites went back from bondage,' said my friend. But a way was opened for them by a miracle across the sea, and food was sent to them from heaven, and they had among them a Moses for a leader and a Joshua to fight their battles.

I could not but express my fear that the days of such immigrations were over. This plan of sending back the Negroes to Africa did not reach me only from one or two mouths; and it was suggested by men whose opinions respecting their country have weight at home and are entitled to weight abroad. I mention this merely to show how insurmountable would be the difficulty of preventing secession, let which side win that may.

All the world has heard of Newport in Rhode Island as being the Brighton, and Tenby, and Scarborough of New England. And the glory of Newport is by no means confined to New England, but is shared by New York and Washington, and in ordinary years by the extreme South. It is the habit of Americans to go to some watering place every summer – that is, to some place either of sea water or of inland waters. This is done much in England; more in Ireland than in England – but, I think, more in the States than even in Ireland. But of all such summer haunts, Newport is supposed to be in many ways the most captivating. In the first place it is certainly the most fashionable, and in the next place it is said to be the most beautiful. We decided on going to Newport, led thither by the latter reputation rather than the former.

As we were still in the early part of September we expected to find the place full, but in this we were disappointed – disappointed, I say, rather than gratified, although a crowded house at such a place is certainly a nuisance. But a house which is prepared to make up six hundred beds, and which is called on to make up only twenty-five becomes, after a while, somewhat melancholy. The natural depression of the landlord communicates itself to his servants, and from the servants it descends to the twenty-five guests, who wander about the long passages and deserted balconies like the ghosts of those of the summer visitors who cannot rest quietly in their graves at home.

In England we know nothing of hotels prepared for six hundred visitors, all of whom are expected to live in common.

Domestic architects would be frightened at the dimensions which are needed, and at the number of apartments which are required to be clustered under one roof.

We went to the Ocean Hotel at Newport, and fancied, as we first entered the hall under a veranda as high as the house, and made our way into the passage, that we had been taken to a well-arranged barrack.

'Have you rooms?' I asked, as a man always does ask on first reaching his inn.

'Rooms enough,' the clerk said. 'We have only fifty here.' But that fifty dwindled down to twenty-five during the next day or two.

We were a melancholy set, the ladies appearing to be afflicted in this way worse than the gentlemen, on account of their enforced abstinence from tobacco. What can twelve ladies do scattered about a drawing-room, so-called, intended for the accommodation of two hundred? The drawing-room at the Ocean Hotel, Newport, is not as big as Westminster Hall, but would, I should think, make a very good House of Commons for the British nation.

Fancy the feelings of a lady when she walks into such a room intending to spend her evening there, and finds six or seven other ladies located on various sofas at terrible distances – all strangers to her. She has come to Newport probably to enjoy herself; and as, in accordance with the customs of the place, she has dined at two, she has nothing before her for the evening but the society of that huge furnished cavern.

Her husband, if she have one, or her father, or her lover, has probably entered the room with her. But a man has never the courage to endure such a position long. He sidles out with some muttered excuse, and seeks solace with a cigar. The lady, after half an hour of contemplation, creeps silently near some companion in the desert, and suggests in a whisper that Newport does not seem to be very full at present.

We stayed there for a week, and were very melancholy; but in our melancholy we still talked of the war. Americans are said to be given to bragging, and it is a sin of which I cannot altogether acquit them. But I have constantly been surprised at hearing the Northerners speak of their own military achievements with anything but self-praise.

'We've been whipped, sir; and we shall be whipped again before we've done; uncommon well whipped we shall be.'

'We began cowardly, and were afraid to send our own regiments through one of our own cities.' This alluded to a demand that had been made on the Government, that troops going to Washington should not be sent through Baltimore, because of the strong feeling for rebellion which was known to exist in that city. President Lincoln complied with this request, thinking it well to avoid a collision between the mob and the soldiers.

'We began cowardly, and now we're going on cowardly, and daren't attack them. Well; when we've been whipped often enough, then we shall learn the trade.'

Now all this – and I heard much of such a nature – could not be called boasting.

But yet with it all there was a substratum of confidence. I have heard northern gentlemen complaining of the President, complaining of all his ministers one after another, complaining of the contractors who were robbing the army, of the commanders who did not know how to command the army, and of the army itself which did not know how to obey; but I do not remember that I have discussed the matter with any Northerner who would admit a doubt as to ultimate success.

We were certainly rather melancholy at Newport, and the empty house may perhaps have given its tone to the discussions on the war. I confess that I could not stand the drawing-room, the ladies' drawing-room as such-like rooms are always called at the hotels, and that I basely deserted my wife. I could not stand it either here or elsewhere, and it seemed to me that other husbands – ay, and even lovers – were as hard pressed as myself.

I protest that there is no spot on the earth's surface so dear to me as my own drawing-room, or rather my wife's drawing-room at home; that I am not a man given hugely to clubs, but one rather rejoicing in the rustle of petticoats. I like to have women in the same room with me.

But at these hotels I found myself driven away – propelled as it were by some unknown force – to absent myself from the feminine haunts. Anything was more palatable than them; even 'liquoring up' at a nasty bar, or smoking in a comfortless reading-room among a deluge of American newspapers.

And I protest also – hoping as I do so that I may say much in these volumes to prove the truth of such protestation – that this comes from no fault of the American women.

They are as lovely as our own women. Taken generally, they are better instructed – though perhaps not better educated. They are seldom troubled with *mauvaise honte* – I do not say it in irony, but begging that the words may be taken at their proper meaning. They can always talk, and very often can talk well.

But when assembled together in these vast, cavernous, would-be luxurious, but in truth horribly comfortless hotel drawing-rooms – they are unapproachable. I have seen lovers, whom I have known to be lovers, unable to remain five minutes in the same cavern with their beloved ones.

And then the music. There is always a piano in an hotel drawing-room, on which, of course, some one of the forlorn ladies is generally employed. I do not suppose that these pianos are in fact, as a rule, louder and harsher, more violent and less musical, than other instruments of the kind. They seem to be so, but that, I take it, arises from the exceptional mental depression of those who have to listen to them.

Then the ladies, or probably some one lady, will sing, and as she hears her own voice ring and echo through the lofty corners and round the empty walls, she is surprised at her own force, and with increased efforts sings louder and still louder. She is tempted to fancy that she is suddenly gifted with some power of vocal melody unknown to her before, and filled with the glory of her own performance shouts till the whole house rings. At such moments she at least is happy, if no one else is so. Looking at the general sadness of her position, who can grudge her such happiness?

And then the children – babies, I should say if I were speaking of English bairns of their age; but seeing that they are Americans, I hardly dare to call them children. The actual age of these perfectly civilized and highly educated beings may be from three to four. One will often see five or six such seated at the long dinner-table of the hotel, breakfasting and dining with their elders, and going through the ceremony with all the gravity, and more than all the decorum, of the grandfathers.

When I was three years old I had not yet, as I imagine, been promoted beyond a silver spoon of my own wherewith to eat my bread and milk in the nursery, and I feel assured that I was under the immediate care of a nursemaid, as I gobbled up my minced mutton mixed with potatoes and gravy.

But at hotel life in the States the adult infant lisps to the waiter for everything at table, handles his fish with epicurean delicacy, is choice in his selection of pickles, very particular that his beefsteak at breakfast shall be hot, and is instant in his demand for fresh ice in his water. But perhaps, his or in this case her, retreat from the room when the meal is over, is the *chef d'œuvre* of the whole performance. The little precocious, full-blown beauty of four signifies that she has completed her meal – or is 'through' her dinner, as she would express it – by carefully extricating herself from the napkin which has been tucked around her. Then the waiter, ever attentive to her movements, draws back the chair on which she is seated, and the young lady glides to the floor.

A little girl in Old England would scramble down, but little girls in New England never scramble. Her father and mother, who are no more than her chief ministers, walk before her out of the saloon, and then – she swims after them. But swimming is not the proper word. Fishes in making their way through the water assist, or rather impede, their motion with no dorsal wriggle. No animal taught to move directly by its Creator adopts a gait so useless, and at the same time so graceless. Many women, having received their lessons in walking from a less eligible instructor, do move in this way, and such women this unfortunate little lady has been instructed to copy.

To me Newport could never be a place charming by reason of its own charms. That it is a very pleasant place when it is full of people and the people are in spirits and happy, I do not doubt. But then the visitors would bring, as far as I am concerned, the pleasantness with them.

The hotels are all built away from the sea; so that one cannot sit and watch the play of the waves from one's window. Nor are there pleasant rambling paths down among the rocks, and from one short strand to another.

There is excellent bathing for those who like bathing on shelving sand. I don't. The spot is about half a mile from the hotels, and to this the bathers are carried in omnibuses. Till one o'clock ladies bathe; – which operation, however, does not at all militate against the bathing of men, but rather necessitates it as regards those men who have ladies with them. For here ladies and gentlemen bathe in decorous dresses, and are very polite to each other. I must say that I think the ladies have the best of it. My idea of sea-bathing for my own gratification is not compatible with a full suit of clothing. I own that my tastes are vulgar and perhaps indecent; but I love to jump into the deep clear sea from off a rock, and I love to be hampered by no outward impediments as I do so. For ordinary bathers, for all ladies, and for men less savage in their instincts than I am, the bathing at Newport is very good.

The private houses – villa residences as they would be termed by an auctioneer in England – are excellent. Many of them are, in fact, large mansions, and are surrounded with grounds, which, as the shrubs grow up, will be very beautiful. Some have large, well-kept lawns, stretching down to the rocks, and these to my taste give the charm to Newport.

We hired saddle-horses, and rode out nearly the length of the island. It was all very well, but there was little in it remarkable either as regards cultivation or scenery. We found nothing that it would be possible either to describe or remember. The Americans of the United States have had time to build and populate vast cities, but they have not yet had time to surround themselves with pretty scenery.

Outlying grand scenery is given by nature; but the prettiness of home scenery is a work of art. It comes from the thorough draining of land, from the planting and subsequent thinning of trees, from the controlling of waters, and constant use of minute patches of broken land. In another hundred years or so Rhode Island may be, perhaps, as pretty as the Isle of Wight.

Rhode Island has all the attributes of government in common

with her stouter and more famous sisters. She has a governor, and an upper house, and a lower house of legislature; and she is somewhat fantastic in the use of these constitutional powers, for she calls on them to sit now in one town and now in another. Providence is the capital of the State; but the Rhode Island parliament sits sometimes at Providence and sometimes at Newport.

I should think it would be well for all parties if the whole State could be swallowed up by Massachusetts or by Connecticut, either of which lies conveniently for the feat; but I presume that any suggestion of such a nature would be regarded as treason by the men of Providence Plantation.

Chapter 2

WE determined to go to Portland, in Maine, from thence to the White Mountains in New Hampshire – the American Alps, as they love to call themselves – and then on to Quebec and up through the two Canadas to Niagara; and this route we followed. From Boston to Portland we travelled by railroad, the carriages on which are in America always called cars.

And here I beg, once for all, to enter my protest loudly against the manner in which these conveyances are conducted. The one grand fault – there are other smaller faults – but the one grand fault is that they admit but one class. Two reasons for this are given. The first is that the finances of the companies will not admit of a divided accommodation; and the second is that the republican nature of the people will not brook a superior or aristocratic classification of travelling.

As regards the first, I do not in the least believe in it. If a more expensive manner of railway travelling will pay in England, it would surely do so here. Were a better class of carriages organized, as large a portion of the population would use them in the United States as in any country in Europe. And it seems to be evident that in arranging that there shall be only one rate of travelling, the price is enhanced on poor travellers exactly in proportion as it is made cheap to those who are not poor.

It will be said that the American cars are good enough for all purposes. The seats are not very hard, and the room for sitting is sufficient. Nevertheless I deny that they are good enough for all purposes. They are very long, and to enter them and find a place often requires a struggle and almost a fight. There is rarely any person to tell a stranger which car he should enter.

One never meets an uncivil or unruly man, but the women of the lower ranks are not courteous. American ladies love to lie at ease in their carriages, as thoroughly as do our women in Hyde Park, and to those who are used to such luxury, travelling by railroad in their own country must be grievous.

I would not wish to be thought a sybarite myself, or to be held as complaining because I have been compelled to give up my seat to women with babies and bandboxes who have accepted the courtesy with very scanty grace. I have borne worse things than these, and have roughed it much in my days from want of means and other reasons. Nor am I yet so old but what I can rough it still. Nevertheless I like to see things as well done as is practicable, and railway travelling in the States is not well done. I feel bound to say as much as this, and now I have said it, once for all.

Few cities, or localities for cities, have fairer natural advantages than Portland – and I am bound to say that the people of Portland have done much in turning them to account.

What must be the natural excellence of the harbour of Portland will be understood when it is borne in mind that the Great Eastern can enter it at all times, and that it can lie along the wharves at any hour of the tide. The wharves which have been prepared for her are joined to and in fact are a portion of the station of the Grand Trunk Railway, which runs from Portland up to Canada. So that passengers landing at Portland out of a vessel so large even as the Great Eastern can walk at once on shore, and goods can be passed on to the railway without any of the cost of removal. I will not say there is no other harbour in the world that would allow of this, but I do not know any other that would do so.

But the Great Eastern has never been to Portland, and as far as I know has no intention of going there. She was, I believe, built with that object.[3] At any rate it was proclaimed during her building that such was her destiny, and the Portlanders believed it with a perfect faith. They went to work and built wharves expressly for her; two wharves prepared to fit her two gangways, of ways of exit and entrance. They built a huge hotel to receive her passengers. They prepared for her advent with a full conviction that a millennium of trade was about to be wafted to their happy port.

'Sir, the town has expended two hundred thousand dollars in expectation of that ship and that ship has deceived us.' So was the matter spoken of to me by an intelligent Portlander. I explained to that intelligent gentleman that two hundred thousand dollars would go a very little way towards making up the loss which the ill-fortuned vessel had occasioned on the other side of the water. He did not in words express gratification at this information, but he looked it.

But there are still good days in store for the town. Though the Great Eastern has not gone there, other ships from Europe, more profitable if less in size, must eventually find their way thither. At present the Canada line of packets runs to Portland only during those months in which it is shut out from the St Lawrence and Quebec by ice. But the St Lawrence and Quebec cannot offer the advantages which Portland enjoys, and that big hotel and those new wharves will not have been built in vain.

I have said that a good time is coming, but I would by no means wish to signify that the present times in Portland are bad. So far from it, that I doubt whether I ever saw a town with more evident signs of prosperity. It has about every mark of ample means, and no mark of poverty.

It contains about 27,000 people, and for that population covers a very large space of ground. The streets are broad and well built, the main streets not running in those absolutely straight parallels which are so common in American towns, and are so distressing to English eyes and English feelings. All these, except the streets devoted exclusively to business, are shaded on both sides by trees – generally, if I remember rightly, by the beautiful American elm, whose drooping boughs have all the grace of the willow without its fantastic melancholy.

What the poorer streets of Portland may be like I cannot say. I saw no poor street. But in no town of 30,000 inhabitants did I ever see so many houses which must require an expenditure of from six to eight hundred[4] a year to maintain them.

The ways of the people seemed to be quiet, smooth, orderly and republican. There is nothing to drink in Portland of course, for, thanks to Mr Neal Dow,[5] the Maine Liquor Law is still in force in that State. There is nothing to drink, I should say, in such orderly houses as that I selected.

'People do drink some in the town, they say,' said my hostess to me; 'and liquor is to be got. But I never venture to sell any. An ill-natured person might turn on me, and where should I be then?'

I did not press her, and she was good enough to put a bottle of porter at my right hand at dinner, for which I observed she made no charge.

'But they advertise beer in the shop-windows,' I said to a man who was driving me.

'Scotch ale, and bitter beer.'

'A man can get drunk on them.'

'Wa'al, yes. If he goes to work hard, and drinks a bucketful,' said the driver, 'perhaps he may.'

From which and other things I gathered that the men of Maine drank bottle deep before Mr Neal Dow brought his exertions to a successful termination.

But if the men and women of Portland may not drink they may eat, and it is a place, I should say, in which good living on that side of the question is very rife. It has an air of supreme plenty, as though the agonies of an empty stomach were never known there. The faces of the people tell of three regular meals of meat a day, and of digestive powers in proportion.

Oh happy Portlanders, if they only knew their own good fortune! They get up early, and go to bed early. The women are comely and sturdy, about to take care of themselves without any fal-lal of chivalry; and the men are sedate, obliging, and industrious. I saw the young girls in the streets, coming home from their tea-parties at nine o'clock, many of them alone, and all with some basket in their hands which betokened an evening not passed absolutely in idleness. No fear there of unruly questions on the way, or of insolence from the ill-conducted of the other sex!

All was, or seemed to be, orderly, sleek and unobtrusive. Probably of all modes of life that are allotted to man by his Creator, life such as this is the most happy. One hint, however, for improvement I must give, even to Portland! It would be well if they could make their streets of some material harder than sand.

From Portland we made our way up to the White Mountains. Now I would ask any of my readers who are candid enough to expose their own ignorance whether they ever heard, or at any rate whether they know anything of the White Mountains. As regards myself I confess that the name had reached my ears; that I had an indefinite idea that they formed an intermediate stage between the Rocky Mountains and the Alleghenies, and that they were inhabited either by Mormons, Indians, or simply by black bears.

That there was a district in New England containing mountain scenery superior to much that is yearly crowded by tourists in Europe, that this is to be reached with ease by railways and stage-coaches, and that it is dotted with huge hotels almost as thickly as they lie in Switzerland, I had no idea. Much of this scenery, I say, is superior to the famed and classic lands of Europe. I know nothing, for instance, on the Rhine equal to the view from Mount Willard, down the mountain pass called the Notch.

The great beauty of the autumn, or fall, is in the brilliant hues which are then taken by the foliage. The autumnal tints are fine with us. They are lovely and bright wherever foliage and vegetation form a part of the beauty of scenery.

But in no other land do they approach the brilliancy of the fall in America. The bright rose colour, the rich bronze which is almost purple in its richness, and the glorious golden yellows must be seen to be understood. By me at any rate they cannot be described. These begin to show themselves in September, and perhaps I might name the latter half of that month as the best time for visiting the White Mountains.

I am not going to write a guide-book, feeling sure that Mr Murray[6] will do New England, and Canada, including Niagara and the Hudson river, with a peep into Boston and New York before many more seasons have passed by. But I cannot forbear to tell my countrymen that any enterprising individual with a hundred pounds to spend on his holiday – a hundred and twenty would make him more comfortable in regard to wine, washing, and other luxuries – and an absence of two months from his labours, may see as much and do as much here for the money as he can see or do elsewhere.

In some respects he may do more; for he will learn more of American nature in such a journey than he can ever learn of the nature of Frenchmen by such an excursion among them.

Some three weeks of the time, or perhaps a day or two over, he must be at sea, and that portion of his trip will cost him fifty pounds – presuming that he chooses to go in the most comfortable and costly way – but his time on board ship will not be lost. He will learn to know much of Americans there, and will perhaps form acquaintances of which he will not altogether lose sight of for many a year. He will land at Boston, and staying a day or two there will visit Cambridge, Lowell, and Bunker Hill; and, if he be that way given, will remember that here live, and occasionally are to be seen alive, men such as Longfellow, Emerson, Hawthorne, and a host of others whose names and fames have made Boston the throne of western literature. He will then – if he take my advice and follow my track – go by Portland up into the White Mountains.

At Gorham, a station on the Grand Trunk line, he will find an hotel as good as any of its kind, and from thence he will take a light waggon, so called in these countries – and here let me presume that the traveller is not alone; he has his wife or friend, or perhaps a pair of sisters – and in his waggon he will go up through primeval forests to the Glen House. When there he will ascend Mount Washington on a pony. That is de rigueur, and I do not, therefore, dare to recommend him to omit the ascent. I did not gain much myself by my labour.

He will not stay at the Glen House, but will go on to – Jackson's I think they call the next hotel; at which he will sleep. From thence he will take his waggon on through the Notch to the Crawford House, sleeping there again; and when here let him of all things remember to go up Mount Willard. It is but a walk of two hours, up and down, if so much.

When reaching the top he will be startled to find that he looks down into the ravine without an inch of foreground. He will come out suddenly on a ledge of rock, from whence, as it seems, he might leap down at once into the valley below.

Then going on from the Crawford House he will be driven through the woods of Cherry Mount, passing, I fear without toll of custom, the house of my excellent Mr Plaistead, who keeps an hotel at Jefferson.

'Sir,' said Mr Plaistead, 'I have everything here that a man ought to want; air, sir, that ain't to be got better nowhere; trout, chickens, beef, mutton, milk – and all that for a dollar a day. A' top of that hill, sir, there's a view that ain't to be beaten this side of the Atlantic, or I believe the other. And an echo, sir! We've an echo that comes back to us six times, sir; floating on the light wind, and wafted about from rock to rock till you would think the angels were talking to you. If I could raise that echo, sir, every day at command I'd give a thousand dollars for it. It would be worth all the money to a house like this.'

And he waved his hand about from hill to hill, pointing out in graceful curves the lines which the sounds would take. Had destiny not called on Mr Plaistead to keep an American hotel, he might have been a poet.

My traveller, however, unless time were plenty with him, would pass Mr Plaistead, merely lighting a friendly cigar, or perhaps breaking the Maine Liquor Law if the weather be warm, and would return to Gorham on the railway. All this mountain district is in New Hampshire, and presuming him to be capable of going about the world with his mouth, ears, and eyes open, he would learn much of the way in which men are settling themselves in this still sparsely populated country.

Here young farmers go into the woods, as they are doing far down west in the Territories, and buying some hundred acres at perhaps six shillings an acre, fell and burn the trees and build their huts, and take the first steps, as far as man's work is concerned, towards accomplishing the will of the Creator in those regions. For such pioneers of civilization there is still ample room even in the long settled States of New Hampshire and Vermont.

I cannot say that I like the hotels in those parts, or indeed the mode of life at American hotels in general. In order that I may not unjustly defame them, I will commence these observations by declaring that they are cheap to those who choose to practise the economy which they encourage, that the viands are profuse in quantity and wholesome in quality, that the attendance is quick and unsparing, and that travellers are never annoyed by that grasping greedy hunger and thirst after francs and shillings which disgrace in Europe many English and many continental inns. All this is, as much be admitted, great praise; and yet I do not like the American hotels.

One is in a free country and has come from a country in which one has been brought up to hug one's chains – so at least the English traveller is constantly assured – and yet in an American inn one can never do as one likes. A terrific gong sounds early in the morning, breaking one's sweet slumbers, and then a second gong sounding some thirty minutes later, makes you understand that you must proceed to breakfast, whether you be dressed or no. You certainly can go on with your toilet and obtain your meal after half an hour's delay. Nobody actually scolds you for so doing, but the breakfast is, as they say in this country, 'through'.

You sit down alone, and the attendant stands immediately over you. Probably there are two so standing. They fill your cup the instant it is empty. They tender you fresh food before that which has disappeared from your plate has been swallowed. They begrudge you no amount that you can eat or drink; but they begrudge you a single moment that you sit there neither eating nor drinking. This is your fate if you're too late, and therefore as a rule you are not late.

In that case you form one of a long row of eaters who proceed through their work with a solid energy that is past all praise. It is wrong to say that Americans will not talk at their meals. I never met but few who would not talk to me, at any rate till I got to the Far West; but I have rarely found that they would address me first.

The dinner comes early; at least it always does so in New England, and the ceremony is much of the same kind. You came there to eat, and the food is pressed on you almost ad nauseam. But as far as one can see there is no drinking. In these days, I am quite aware, that drinking has become improper, even in England. We are apt at home to speak of wine as a thing tabooed, wondering how our fathers lived and swilled. I believe that as a fact we drink as much as they did; but nevertheless that is our theory.

I confess, however, that I like wine. It is very wicked, but it seems to me that my dinner goes down better with a glass of sherry than without it. As a rule I always did get it at hotels in America. But I had no comfort with it. Sherry they do not understand at all. Of course I am only speaking of hotels. Their claret they get exclusively from Mr Gladstone,[7] and looking at the quality, have a right to quarrel even with Mr Gladstone's price.

But it is not the quality of the wine that I hereby intend to subject to ignominy, so much as the want of any opportunity for drinking it. After dinner, if all that I hear be true, the gentlemen occasionally drop into the hotel bar and 'liquor up'. Or rather this is not done specially after dinner, but without prejudice to the hour at any time that may be found desirable. I also have 'liquored up', but I cannot say that I enjoy the process. I do not intend hereby to accuse Americans of drinking too much, but I maintain that what they do drink, they drink in the most uncomfortable manner that the imagination can devise.

The farther that I got away from Boston the less strong did I find the feeling of anger against England. There, as I have said before, there was a bitter animosity against the mother country in that she had shown no open sympathy with the North. In Maine and New Hampshire I did not find this to be the case to any violent degree. Men spoke of the war as openly as they did at Boston, and in speaking to me generally connected England with the subject.

But they did so simply to ask questions as to England's policy. What will she do for cotton when her operatives are really pressed? Will she break the blockade? Will she insist on a right to trade with Charlestown and New Orleans?

I always answered that she would insist on no such right, if that right were denied to others and the denial enforced. England, I took upon myself to say, would not break a veritable blockade, let her be driven to what shifts she might in providing for her operatives. 'Ah; that's what we fear,' a very staunch patriot said to me, if words may be taken as a proof of staunchness. 'If England allies herself with the Southerners, all our trouble is for nothing.' It was impossible not to feel that all that was said was complimentary to England. It is her sympathy that the Northern men desire, to her co-operation that they would willingly trust, on her honesty that they would choose to depend. It is the same feeling whether it shows itself in anger or in curiosity. An American whether he be embarked in politics, in literature, or in commerce, desires English admiration, English appreciation of his energy, and English encouragement.

The anger of Boston is but a sign of its affectionate friendliness. What feeling is so hot as that of a friend when his dearest friend refuses to share his quarrel or to sympathize in his wrongs? To my thinking the men of Boston are wrong and unreasonable in their anger; but were I a man of Boston I should be as wrong and as unreasonable as any of them. All that, however, will come right. I will not believe it possible that there should in very truth be a quarrel between England and the northern States.

Chapter 3

THE Grand Trunk Railway runs directly from Portland to Montreal, which latter town is, in fact, the capital of Canada, though it has never been so exclusively and, as it seems, never is to be so, as regards authority, government, and official name. In such matters authorities and government often say one thing while commerce says another; but commerce always has the best of it and wins the game whatever government may decree.

Quebec is the present seat of Canadian Government, its turn for that honour having come round some two years ago; but it is about to be deserted in favour of Ottawa, a town which is, in fact, still to be built on the river of that name. The public edifices are, however, in a state of forwardness; and if all goes well the Governor, the two Councils, and the House of Representatives will be there before two years are over whether there will be a town to receive them or no. Who can think of Ottawa without bidding his brothers to row, and reminding them that the stream runs fast, that the rapids are near and the daylight past? I asked as a matter of course, whether Quebec was much disgusted at the proposed change, and I was told that the feeling was not now very strong. Had it been determined to make Montreal the permanent seat of Government Quebec and Toronto would both have been up in arms.

I must confess that in going from the States into Canada, an Englishman is struck by the feeling that he is going from a richer country into one that is poorer, and from a greater country into one that is less. An Englishman going from a foreign land into a land which is in one sense his own, of course finds much in the change to gratify him. He is able to speak as the master, instead of speaking as the visitor. His tongue becomes more free, and he is able to fall back to his national habits and national expressions. He no longer feels that he is admitted on sufferance, or that he must be careful to respect laws which he does not quite understand.

This feeling was naturally strong in an Englishman in passing from the States into Canada at the time of my visit. English policy at that moment was violently abused by Americans, and was upheld as violently in Canada. But, nevertheless, with all this, I could not enter Canada without seeing, and hearing, and feeling that there was less of enterprise around me there than in the States – less of general movement, and less of commercial success. To say why this is so would require a long and very difficult discussion, and one which I am not prepared to hold. It may be that a dependent country, let the feeling of independence be ever so much modified by powers of self-government, cannot hold its own against countries which are in all respects their own masters. Few, I believe, would now maintain that the northern States of America would have risen in commerce as they have risen, had they still remained attached to England as colonies. If this be so, that privilege of self-rule which they have acquired, has been the cause of their success. It does not follow as a consequence that the Canadas fighting their battle alone in the world would do as the States have done. Climate, or size, or geographical position might stand in their way. But I fear that it does not follow, if not as a logical conclusion at least as a natural result, that they never will do so well unless some day they shall so fight their battle.

The power of self-government is as thoroughly developed as perhaps may be possible in a colony. But after all it is a dependent form of government, and as such may perhaps not conduce to so thorough a development of the resources of the country as might be achieved under a ruling power of its own, to which the welfare of Canada itself would be the chief if not the only object.

I beg that it may not be considered from this that I would propose to Canada to set up for itself at once and declare itself independent. In the first place I do not wish to throw over Canada, and in the next place I do not wish to throw over England. If such a separation shall ever take place, I trust that it may be caused, not by Canadian violence but by British generosity. Such a separation, however, never can be good till Canada herself shall wish it.

Some years since the Americans thought that Canada might

shine in the Union firmament as a new star, but that delusion is, I think, over. Such annexation if ever made, must have been made not only against the arms of England but must also have been made in accordance with the wishes of the people so annexed. It was then believed that the Canadians were not averse to such a change, and there may possibly have been then among them the remnant of such a wish. There is certainly no such desire now, not even a remnant of such a desire; and the truth of this matter is, I think, generally acknowledged. The feeling in Canada is one of strong aversion to the United States Government, and of predilection for self-government under the English Crown. A fainéant Governor and the prestige of British power is now the political aspiration of the Canadians in general; and I think this is understood in the States. Moreover the States have a job of work on hand which, as they themselves are well aware, is taxing all their energies. Such being the case I do not think that England needs to fear any invasion of Canada, authorized by the States Government.

If the Canadians wished the change, in God's name let them go. But the Canadians are averse to such a change with a degree of feeling that amounts to national intensity. Their sympathies are with the southern States, not because they care for cotton, not because they are anti-abolitionists, not because they admire the hearty pluck of those who are endeavouring to work out for themselves a new revolution. They dislike Mr Everett's flattering hints to his countrymen as to the one nation that is to occupy the whole continent.[8] They dislike the Monroe doctrine. They wonder at the meekness with which England has endured the vauntings of the northern States, and are endued with no such meekness of their own. They would, I believe, be well prepared to meet and give an account of any filibusters who might visit them.

That it will never be the destiny [of the Canadas] to join themselves to the States of the Union, I feel fully convinced. In the first place it is becoming evident from the present circumstances of the Union – if it had never been made evident by history before – that different people with different habits living at long distances from each other cannot well be brought together in equal terms under one government. That noble ambition of the Americans that all the continent north of the isthmus should be united under one flag, has already been thrown from its saddle. The North and South are virtually separated, and the day will come in which the West will also secede. As population increases and trades arise peculiar to those different climates, the interests of the people will differ, and a new secession will take place beneficial to both parties. If this be so, if even there be any tendency this way, it affords the strongest argument against the probability of any future annexation of the Canadas. And then, in the second place, the feeling of Canada is not American, but British. If ever she be separated from Great Britain, she will be separated as the States were separated. She will desire to stand alone, and to enter herself as one among the nations of the earth.

How would England be affected by a union of the British North American colonies under one Federal Government? Before this question can be answered, he who prepares to answer it must consider what interest England has in her colonies, and for what purpose she holds them. Does she hold them for profit, or for glory, or for power; or does she hold them in order that she may carry out the duty which has devolved upon her of extending civilization, freedom, and well-being through the new uprising nations of the world? Does she hold them, in fact, for her own benefit, or does she hold them for theirs? I know nothing of the ethics of the Colonial Office, and not much perhaps of those of the House of Commons; but looking at what Great Britain has hitherto done in the way of colonization, I cannot but think that the national ambition looks to the welfare of the colonists, and not to home aggrandisement. That the two may run together is most probable. Indeed there can be no glory to a people so great or so readily recognized by mankind at large as that of spreading civilization from East to West, and from North to South. But the one object should be the prosperity of the colonists; and not profit, nor glory, nor even power to the parent country.

A wish that British North America should ever be severed from England, or that the Australian colonies should ever be so severed, will be by many Englishmen deemed unpatriotic. But I think that such severance is to be wished if it be the case that the colonies standing alone would become more prosperous than they are under British rule. We have before us an example in the United States of the prosperity which has attended the rupture of such old ties. I will not now contest the point with those who say that the present moment of an American civil war is ill chosen for vaunting that prosperity. There stand the cities which the people have built, and their power is attested by the world-wide importance of their present contest. And if the States have so risen since they left their parent's apron-string why should not British North America rise as high?

That the time has as yet come for such a rising I do not think; but that it will soon come I do most heartily hope. The making of the railway of which I have spoken,[9] and the amalgamation of the provinces would greatly tend to such an event. If, therefore, England desires to keep these colonies in a state of dependency; if it be more essential to her to maintain her power with regard to them than to increase their influence; if her main object be to keep the colonies, then I should say that an amalgamation of the Canadas with Nova Scotia and New Brunswick should not be regarded with favour by statesmen in Downing Street. But if, as I would fain hope, and do partly believe, such ideas of national power as these are now out of vogue with British statesmen, then I think that such an amalgamation should receive all the support which Downing Street can give it.[10]

The sending forth of a child-nation to take its own political status in the world has never yet been done by Great Britain. I cannot remember that such has been done by any power that was powerful enough to keep such dependency within its grasp. But a man thinking on these matters cannot but hope that a time will come when such amicable severance may be effected. Great Britain cannot think that through all coming ages she is to be the mistress of the vast continent of Australia, lying on the other side of the globe's surface; that she is to be the mistress of all South Africa, as civilization shall extend northwards; that the enormous territories of British North America are to be subject for ever to a veto from Downing Street. If the history of past empires does not teach her that this may not be so, at least the history of the United States might so teach her.

I do not think that the time has yet come in which Great Britain should desire the Canadians to start for themselves. But I think it would be well to be prepared for such a coming day. Great Britain, should she ever send forth her child alone into the world, must of course guarantee her security. Such guarantees are given by treaties; and in the wording of them it is presumed that such treaties will last for ever. It will be argued that in starting British North America as a political power on its own bottom, we should bind ourselves to all the expense of its defence, while we should give up all right to any interference in its concerns; and that from a state of things so unprofitable as this there would be no prospect of deliverance.

For a time, no doubt, Great Britain would be so hampered – if indeed she would feel herself hampered by extending her name and prestige to a country bound to her by ties such as those which would then exist between her and this new nation. Such treaties are not everlasting, nor can they be made to last even for ages. Those who word them seem to think that powers and dynasties will never pass away. But they do pass away, and the balance of power will not keep itself fixed for ever on the same pivot. The time may come – that it may not come soon we will all desire – but the time may come when the name and prestige of what we call British North America will be as serviceable to Great Britain as those of Great Britain are now serviceable to her colonies.

But what shall be the new form of government for the new kingdom? That is a speculation very interesting to a politician; though one which to follow out at great length in these early days would be rather premature. That it should be a kingdom – that the political arrangement should be one of which a crowned hereditary king should form a part, nineteen out of every twenty Englishmen would desire; and, as I fancy, so would nineteen out of every twenty Canadians. A king for the United States when they first established themselves was impossible. The name of a king, or monarch, or sovereign had become horrible to their ears. Even to this day they have not learned the difference between arbitrary power retained in the hand of one man, such as that now held by the Emperor over the French, and such hereditary headship in the State as that which belongs to the Crown in Great Britain. And this was necessary, seeing that their division from us was erected by strife, and carried out with war and bitter animosities.

In those days also there was a remnant, though but a small remnant, of the power of tyranny left within the scope of the British Crown. That small remnant has been removed; and to me it seems that no form of existing government – no form of government that ever did exist, gives or has given so large a measure of individual freedom to all who live under it as a constitutional monarchy in which the Crown is divested of direct political power.

I will venture to suggest a king for this new nation; and seeing that we are rich in princes there need be no difficulty in the selection. Would it not be beautiful to see a new nation established under such auspices, and to establish a people to whom their independence had been given – and to whom it had been freely surrendered as soon as they were capable of holding the position assigned to them?

Chapter 4

I FEEL bound to say that a stranger regarding Quebec mainly as a town, finds very much of which he cannot but complain. The footpaths through the streets are almost entirely of wood, as indeed seems to be general throughout Canada. Wood is of course the cheapest material, and although it may not be altogether good for such a purpose it would not create animadversion if it were kept in tolerable order. But in Quebec the paths are intolerably bad. They are full of holes. The boards are rotten and worn in some places to dirt. The nails have gone, and the broken planks go up and down under the feet, and in the dark they are absolutely dangerous. But if the paths are bad the roadways are worse. The street through the lower town along the quays is, I think, the most disgraceful thoroughfare I ever saw in any town. I believe the whole of it, or at any rate a great portion, has been paved with wood; but the boards have been worked into mud, and the ground under the boards has been worked into holes, till the street is more like the bottom of a filthy ditch than a roadway through one of the most thickly populated parts of a city.

Had Quebec in Wolfe's time been as it is now, Wolfe would have stuck in the mud between the river and the rock, before he reached the point which he desired to climb. In the upper town the roads are not so bad as they are below, but they are still very bad. I was told that this arose from disputes among the municipal corporations. It is made a subject of great boast in Canada that the communal authorities do carry on such a large part of the public business, and that they do it generally so well, and at so cheap a rate. I have nothing to say against this, and as a whole believe the boast is true. I must protest, however, that the streets of the greater cities – for Montreal is nearly as bad as Quebec – prove the rule by a very bad exception.

We learned while at Quebec that it behoved us not to leave the colony till we had seen the lake and mountains of Memphra-Magog. In order to do this we were obliged to choose the rail-

way, and to go back beyond Richmond to the station at Sherbrooke. Sherbrooke is a large village on the confines of Canada,
and as it is on the railway will no doubt become a large town.
It is very prettily situated on the meeting of two rivers, it has
three or four different churches, and intends to thrive.

At Sherbrooke we are still in Lower Canada. Indeed, as regards
distance, we are when there nearly as far removed from Upper
Canada as at Quebec. But the race of people here is very different.
The French population had made their way down into these town-
ships before the English and American war broke out, but had
not done so in great numbers. The country was then very unapproachable, being far to the south of the St Lawrence, and far
also from any great line of internal communication towards the
Atlantic. But, nevertheless, many settlers made their way in here
from the States; men who preferred to live under British rule,
and perhaps doubted the stability of the new order of things. They
or their children have remained here since, and as the whole
country has been opened up by the railway many others have
flocked in. Thus a better class of people than the French hold possession of the larger farms, and are on the whole doing well.

I am told that many Americans are now coming here, driven
over the borders from Maine, New Hampshire, and Vermont, by
fears of the war and the weight of taxation. I do not think that
fears of war or the paying of taxes drive many individuals away
from home. Men who would be so influenced have not the amount
of foresight which would induce them to avoid such evils; or
at any rate such fears would act slowly. Labourers, however, will
go where work is certain, where work is well paid, and where
the wages to be earned will give plenty in return. It may be that
work will become scarce in the States, and that food will become
dear. If this be so, labourers from the States will no doubt find
their way into Canada.

From Sherbrooke we went with the mails on a pair-horse waggon to Magog. Cross country mails are not interesting to the
generality of readers, but I have a professional liking [11] for them
myself. I have spent the best part of my life looking after and I
hope improving such mails and I always endeavour to do a stroke
of work when I come across them. I learned on this occasion that

the conveyance of mails with a pair of horses in Canada costs little more than half what is paid for the same work in England with one horse, and something less than is paid in Ireland, also for one horse. But in Canada the average pace is only five miles an hour. In Ireland it is seven, and the time is accurately kept, which does not seem to be the case in Canada. In England the pace is eight miles an hour. The cross mail conveyances in Canada did not seem to be very closely bound as to time; but they are regulated by clock-work in comparison with some of them in the United States.[12]

On the following day we crossed the lake to Georgeville, and drove around another lake called the Massawhippi back to Sherbrooke. This was all very well, for it showed us a part of the country which is comparatively well-tilled, and has long been settled. The people here are quiet, orderly, and I should say a little slow. It is manifest that a strong feeling against the northern States has lately sprung up. This is much to be deprecated, but I cannot but say that it is natural. It is not that the Canadians have any special secession feelings, or that they have entered with a peculiar warmth into the questions of American politics; but they have been vexed and acerbated by the braggadocio of the northern States. They constantly hear that they are to be invaded, and translated into citizens of the Union; that British rule is to be swept off the continent, and that the star-spangled banner is in fact a fine flag, and has waved to some purpose; but those who live near it, and not under it, fancy that they hear too much of it.

At the present moment the loyalty of both the Canadas to Great Britain is beyond all question. From all that I can hear I doubt whether this feeling in the Provinces was ever so strong, and under such circumstances American abuse of England and American braggadocio is more than usually distasteful. All this abuse and all this braggadocio comes to Canada from the northern States, and therefore the southern cause is at the present moment the more popular with them.

On the following day we reached Montreal, which is the commercial capital of the two Provinces. This question of the capitals is at the present moment a subject of great interest in Canada, but as I shall be driven to say something on the matter when I report myself as being in Ottawa, I will refrain now. Montreal is an exceedingly good commercial town, and business there is brisk. It has now 85,000 inhabitants. Having said that of it, I do not know what more there is left to say.

Ottawa is in Upper Canada, but crossing the suspension bridge from Ottawa into Hukk the traveller is in Lower Canada. It is therefore exactly in the confines, and has been chosen as the site of the new Government capital very much for this reason. Other reasons have, no doubt, had a share in this decision. At the time when the choice was made Ottawa was not large enough to create the jealousy of the more populous towns. Though not on the main line of railway, it was connected with it by a branch railway, and it is also connected with the St Lawrence by water communication. And then it stands nobly on a magnificent river, with high overhanging rock, and a natural grandeur of position which has perhaps gone far in recommending it to those whose voice in the matter has been potential. Having the world of Canada from whence to choose the site of a new town, the choosers have certainly chosen well. It is another question whether or no a new town should have been deemed necessary.

Be that as it may, I do not think that any unbiassed traveller will doubt that the best possible selection has been made, presuming always that Montreal could not be selected. I take for granted that the rejection of Montreal was regarded as a *sine qua non* in the decision. To me it appears grievous that this should have been so. It is a great thing for any country to have a large, leading, world-known city, and I think that the Government should combine with the commerce of the country in carrying out this object. But commerce can do a great deal more for Government than Government can do for commerce. Government has selected Ottawa as the capital of Canada; but commerce has already made Montreal the capital, and Montreal will be the chief city of Canada, let Government do what it may to foster the other town. Montreal is more centrical than Ottawa – nay, it is nearly as centrical as any town can be. It is easier to get to Montreal from Toronto, than to Ottawa – and if from Toronto, then from all that distant portion of Upper Canada, back to Toronto. To all of

Lower Canada Montreal is, as a matter of course, much easier of access than Ottawa. But having said so much in favour of Montreal, I will again admit that, putting aside Montreal, the best possible selection has been made.

We went up to the new town by boat, taking the course of the River Ottawa. We passed St Ann's, but no one at St Ann's seemed to know anything of the brothers who were to rest there on their weary oars. At Maxwellstown I could hear nothing of Annie Laurie or of her trysting place on the braes, and the turn-pike men at Tara could tell me nothing of the site of the hall, and had never even heard of the harp. When I go down South I shall expect to find that the Negro melodies have not yet reached 'Old Virginie'.

I said in the last chapter that the city of Ottawa was still to be built; but I must explain, lest I should draw down on my head the wrath of the Ottawaites, that the place already contains a population of 15,000 inhabitants. As, however, it is being prepared for four times that number – for eight times that number let us hope – and as it straggles over a vast extent of ground, it gives one the idea of a city in an active course of preparation. Ottawa is preparing for itself broad streets, and grand thorough-fares. The buildings already extend over a length considerably exceeding two miles, and half a dozen hotels have been opened, which, if I were writing a guide book in a complimentary tone, it would be my duty to describe as first-rate. But the half-dozen first-rate hotels, though open, as yet enjoy but a moderate amount of custom. All this justifies me, I think, in saying that the city has as yet to get itself built. The manner in which this is being done justifies me also in saying that the Ottawaites are going about their task with a worthy zeal.

To me I confess that the nature of the situation has great charms – regarding it as a site for a town. It is not on a plain, and from the form of the rock overhanging the river, and of the hill that falls from thence down to the water, it has been found impracticable to lay out the place in right-angled parallelograms. A right-angled parallelogramical city, such as are Philadelphia and the new portion of New York, is from its very nature odious to me. I know that much may be said in its favour – that drainage and gas pipes come easier to such a shape, and that ground can be better economized. Nevertheless I prefer a street that is forced to twist itself about. I enjoy the narrowness of Temple Bar, and the misshapen curvature of Pickett Street. The disreputable dinginess of Holywell Street is dear to me, and I love to thread my way up the Olympic to Covent Garden. Fifth Avenue in New York is as grand as paint and glass can make it, but I would not live in a palace in Fifth Avenue if the corporation of the city would pay my baker's and butcher's bills.

The glory of Ottawa will be – and, indeed, already is – the set of public buildings which is now being erected on the rock which guards as it were the town from the river. How much of the excellence of these buildings may be due to the taste of Sir Edmund Head,[13] the late Governor, I do not know. That he has greatly interested himself in the subject is well known. And as the style of the different buildings is so much alike as to make one whole, though the designs of different architects were selected, and these different architects employed, I imagine that considerable alterations must have been made in the original drawings. There are three buildings, forming three sides of a quadrangle; but they are not joined, the vacant spaces at the corner being of considerable extent. The fourth side of the quadrangle opens upon one of the principal streets of the town. The centre building is intended for Houses of Parliament, and the two side buildings for the Government offices.

Of the first Messrs Fuller and Jones are the architects, and of the latter Messrs Stent and Laver. I did not have the pleasure of meeting any of these gentlemen; but I take it upon myself to say that as regards purity of art and manliness of conception their joint work is entitled to the very highest praise. How far the buildings may be well arranged for the required purposes, how far they may be economical in construction, or specially adapted to the severe climate of country, I cannot say; but I have no hesitation in risking my reputation for judgement in giving my warmest commendation to them as regards beauty of outline and truthful nobility of detail.

I will not attempt to describe them, for I should interest no one in doing so, and should certainly fail in my attempt to make any reader understand me. I know no modern Gothic purer of its kind, or less sullied with fictitious ornamentation. Our own Houses of Parliament are very fine, but it is, I believe, generally felt that the ornamentation is too minute; and more particularly, it may be questioned whether perpendicular Gothic is capable of the highest nobility which architecture can achieve. I do not pretend to say that these Canadian public buildings will reach that highest nobility. They must be finished before any final judgement can be pronounced; but I do feel very certain that the final judgement will be greatly in their favour.

The buildings front on what will, I suppose, be the principal street of Ottawa, and they stand upon a rock looking immediately down upon the river. In this way they are blessed with a site peculiarly happy. Indeed I cannot at this moment remember any so much so. The castle of Edinburgh stands very well; but then, like many other castles, it stands upon a summit by itself, and can only be approached by a steep ascent. These buildings at Ottawa, though they look down from a grand eminence immediately on the river, are approached from the town without any ascent. The rock, though it falls almost precipitously down to the water, is covered with trees and shrubs, and then the river that runs beneath it is rapid, bright, and picturesque in the irregularity of all its lines. The view from the back of the library, up to the Chaudière falls, and to the saw-mills by which they are surrounded, is very lovely. So that I will say again, that I know of no site for such a set of buildings so happy as regards both beauty and grandeur.

The great trade of Canada is lumbering; and lumbering consists in cutting down pine trees up in the far distant forests, in hewing or sawing them into shape for market, and getting them down the rivers to Quebec, from whence they are exported to Europe, and chiefly to England. Timber in Canada is called lumber; those engaged in the trade are called lumbermen and the business itself is called lumbering.

The men for this purpose are hired in the fall of the year, and are sent up hundreds of miles away to the pine forests in strong gangs. Everything is there found for them. They make log huts for their shelter, and food of the best and strongest is taken up for their diet. But no strong drink of any kind is allowed, nor is it within reach of the men. There are no publics, no shebeen houses, no grog-shops. Sobriety is an enforced virtue; and so much is this considered by the masters, and understood by the men, that very little contraband work is done in the way of taking up spirits to these settlements. It may be said that work up in the forests is done with the assistance of no stronger drink than tea; and it is very hard work. There cannot be much work that is harder; and it is done amidst the snows and forests of a Canadian winter. A convict in Bermuda cannot get through his daily eight hours of light labour without an allowance of rum; but a Canadian labourer can manage to do his daily task on tea without milk. These men, however, are by no means teetotallers. When they come back to the towns they break out, and reward themselves for their long enforced moderation.

From Ottawa we went by rail to Prescott, which is surely one of the most wretched little places to be found in any country. Immediately opposite to it, on the other side of the St Lawrence, is the thriving town of Ogdenburgh. But Ogdenburgh is in the United States. Had we been able to learn at Ottawa any facts as to the hours of the river steamers and railways we might have saved time and have avoided Prescott; but this was out of the question.

I was much struck at Prescott – and indeed all through Canada, though more in the upper than the lower Province – by the sturdy roughness, some would call it insolence, of those of the lower classes of the people with whom I was brought into contact. If the words 'lower classes' give offence to any reader, I beg to apologize – to apologize and to assert that I am one of the last men to apply such a term in a sense of reproach to those who earn their bread by the labour of their hands. But it is hard to find terms which will be understood; and that term, whether it give offence or no, will be understood. Of course such a complaint as that I now make is very common as made against the States. Men in the States with horned hands and fustian coats are very often most unnecessarily insolent in asserting their independence. What I now mean to say is that precisely the same fault is to be found in Canada. I know very well what the men mean when they offend in this manner. And when I think on the subject with deliberation, at my own desk, I can not only excuse, but almost approve of them.

But when one personally encounters their corduroy braggadocio; when the man to whose services one is entitled answers one with determined insolence; when one is bidden to follow 'that young lady', meaning a chambermaid, or desired with a toss of the head, to wait for the 'gentleman who is coming', meaning the boots, the heart is sickened, and the Englishman pines for the civility – for the servility, if my American friends choose to call it so – of a well-ordered servant. But the whole scene is easily construed and turned into English. A man is asked by a stranger some question about his employment, and he replies in a tone which seems to imply anger, insolence, and a dishonest intention to evade the service for which he is paid. Or if there be no question of service or payment, that man's manner will be the same, and the stranger feels that he is slapped in the face and insulted.

The translation of it is this. The man questioned, who is aware that as regards coat, hat, boots, and outward cleanliness he is below him by whom he is questioned, unconsciously feels himself called upon to assert his political equality. It is his shibboleth that he is politically equal to the best, that he is independent, and that his labour, though it earn him but a dollar a day by porterage, places him as a citizen on an equal rank with the most wealthy fellow-man that may employ or accost him. But being so inferior in that coat, hat, and boots matter, he is forced to assert his equality by some effort. As he improves in externals he will diminish the roughness of his claim. As long as the man makes his claim with any roughness, so long does he acknowledge within himself some feeling of external inferiority. When that has gone – when the American has polished himself up by education and general well-being to a feeling of external equality with gentlemen, he shows, I think, no more of that outward braggadocio of independence than a Frenchman.

From Prescott we went by the Grand Trunk Railway to Toronto, and stayed there for a few days. Toronto is the capital of the province of Upper Canada, and I presume will in some degree remain so in spite of Ottawa and its pretensions. That is, the law courts will still be held there. I do not know that it will enjoy any other supremacy, unless it be that of trade and population. Some few years ago Toronto was advancing with rapid strides, and was bidding fair to rival Quebec, or even perhaps Montreal. Hamilton, also another town of Upper Canada, was going ahead in the true American style; but then reverses came in trade, and the towns were checked for a while. Toronto, with a neighbouring suburb which is a part of it, as Southwark is of London, contains now over 50,000 inhabitants. The streets are all parallelogramical, and there is not a single curvature to rest the eye. It is built down close to Lake Ontario; and as it is also on the Grand Trunk Railway it has all the aid which facility of traffic can give it.

The two sights of Toronto are the Osgood Hall and the University. The Osgood Hall is to Upper Canada what the Four Courts are to Ireland. The law courts are all held there. Exteriorly little can be said for Osgood Hall, whereas the exterior of the Four Courts in Dublin is very fine; but as an interior the temple of Themis at Toronto beats hollow that which the goddess owns in Dublin. In Dublin the Courts themselves are shabby, and the space under the dome is not so fine as the exterior seems to promise that it should be. In Toronto the Courts themselves are, I think, the most commodious that I ever saw, and the passages, vestibules, and hall are very handsome. In Upper Canada the common law judges and those in Chancery are divided as they are in England; but it is, as I was told, the opinion of Canadian lawyers that the work may be thrown together. Appeal is allowed in criminal cases; but as far as I could learn such power of appeal is held to be both troublesome and useless. In Lower Canada the old French laws are still administered.

But the University is the glory of Toronto. This is a Gothic building and will take rank after, but next to, the buildings at Ottawa. It will be the second piece of noble architecture in Canada, and as far as I know on the American continent. It is, I believe, intended to be purely Norman, though I doubt whether the received types of Norman architecture have not been departed from in many of the windows. Be that as it may the college is a manly, noble structure, free from false decoration, and infinitely creditable to those who projected it. I was informed by the head of the college that it has been open only two years, and here also I fancy that the colony has been much indebted to the taste of the late Governor, Sir Edmund Head.

Toronto as a city is not generally attractive to a traveller. The country around is flat; and although it stands on a lake, that lake has no attributes of beauty. Large inland seas such as are these great northern lakes of America never have such attributes of beauty. Picturesque mountains rise from narrow valleys, such as form the beds of lakes in Switzerland, Scotland and northern Italy. But from such broad waters as those of Lake Ontario, Lake Erie, and Lake Michigan, the shores shelve very gradually, and have none of the materials of lovely scenery.

From Toronto we went across to Niagara, re-entering the States at Lewiston in New York.

Chapter 5

OF all the sights on this earth of ours which tourists travel to see – at least of all those which I have seen – I am inclined to give the palm to the Falls of Niagara. In the catalogue of such sights I intend to include all buildings, pictures, statues, and wonders of art made by men's hands, and also all beauties of nature prepared by the Creator for the delight of his creatures. This is a long word: but as far as my taste and judgement go, it is justified.

I know no other one thing so beautiful, so glorious, and so powerful. I would not by this be understood as saying that a traveller wishing to do the best with his time should first of all places seek Niagara. In visiting Florence he may learn almost all that modern art can teach. At Rome he will be brought to understand the cold hearts, correct eyes, and cruel ambition of the old Latin race. In Switzerland he will surround himself with a flood of grandeur and liveliness, and fill himself, if he be capable of such filling, with a flood of romance. The Tropics will unfold to him all that vegetation in its greatest richness can produce. In Paris he will find the supreme of polish, the *ne plus ultra* of varnish according to the world's capability of varnishing. And in London he will find the supreme of power, the *ne plus ultra* of work according to the world's capability of working.

Any one of such journeys may be more valuable to a man – nay, any one such journey must be more valuable to a man, than a visit to Niagara. At Niagara there is that fall of waters alone. But that fall is more graceful than Giotto's tower, more noble than the Apollo. The peaks of the Alps are not so astounding in their solitude. The valleys of the Blue Mountains in Jamaica are less green. The finished glaze of life in Paris is less invariable and the full tide of trade round the Bank of England is not so inexorably powerful.

In visiting Niagara it always becomes a question on which side the visitor shall take up his quarters. On the Canada side there

is no town, but there is a large hotel, beautifully placed immediately opposite to the falls, and this is generally thought to
be the best locality for tourists. In the State of New York is the
town called Niagara Falls, and here there are two large hotels,
which, as to their immediate site, are not so well placed as that
in Canada.

My advice on the subject to any party starting for Niagara
would depend upon their habits, or on their nationality. I would
send Americans to the Canadian side, because they dislike walking; but English people I would locate on the American side,
seeing that they are generally accustomed to the frequent use
of their own legs.

The two sides are not very easily approached, one from the
other. Immediately below the falls there is a ferry, which may be
traversed at the expense of a shilling; but the labour of getting up
and down from the ferry is considerable, and the passage becomes wearisome. There is also a bridge, but it is two miles down
the river, making a walk or drive of four miles necessary, and
the toll for passing is four shillings or a dollar in a carriage, and
one shilling on foot. As the greater variety of prospect can be
had on the American side, as the island between the two falls is
approachable from the American side and not from the Canadian,
and as it is in this island that visitors will best love to linger
and learn to measure in their minds the vast triumph of waters
before them, I recommend such of my readers as can trust a little
– it need be but a little – to their own legs, to select their hotel
at Niagara Falls town.

The falls are made by a sudden breach in the level of the
river. All cataracts are, I presume, made by such breaches; but
generally the waters do not fall precipitously as they do at Niagara, and never elsewhere, as far as the world yet knows, has a
breach so sudden been made in a river carrying in its channel
such or any approach to such a body of water. Up above the falls,
for more than a mile, the waters leap and burst over rapids,
as though conscious of the destiny that awaits them.

Here the river is very broad, and comparatively shallow, but
from shore to shore it frets itself into little torrents, and begins
to assume the majesty of its power. Looking at it even here, in

the expanse which forms itself over the greater fall, one feels sure that no strongest swimmer could have a chance of saving himself, if fate had cast him in even among those petty whirl-pools. The waters, though so broken in their descent, are deliciously green. This colour as seen early in the morning, or just as the sun has set, is so bright as to give to the place one of its chiefest charms.

This will be best seen from the further end of the island – Goat Island, as it is called, which, as the reader will understand, divides the river immediately above the falls.

We will go at once on to the glory, and the thunder, and the majesty, and the wrath of that upper hell of waters. We are still, let the reader remember, on Goat Island, still in the States, and on what is called the American side of the main body of the river. Advancing beyond the path leading down to the lesser fall, we come to that point of the island at which the waters of the main river begin to descend.

From hence across to the Canadian side the cataract continues itself in one unabated line. But the line is very far from being direct or straight. After stretching for some little way from the shore, to a point in the river which is reached by a wooden bridge at the end of which stands a tower upon the rock – after stretching to this, the line of the ledge bends inwards against the flood – in, and in, and in, till one is led to think that the depth of that horseshoe is immeasurable. It has been cut with no stinting hand. A monstrous cantle has been worn back out of the centre of the rock, so that the fury of the waters converges, and the spectator as he gazes into the hollow with wishful eyes fancies that he can hardly trace out the centre of the abyss.

Go down to the end of that wooden bridge, seat yourself on the rail, and there sit till all the outer world is lost to you. There is no grander spot about Niagara than this. The waters are absolutely around you. If you have that power of eye-control which is so necessary to the full enjoyment of scenery you will see nothing but the water.

You will certainly hear nothing else; and the sound, I beg you to remember, is not an ear-cracking, agonizing crash and clang of noises; but is melodious, and soft withal, though as loud as thunder. It fills your ears, and as it were envelops them, but at the same time you can speak to your neighbour without an effort. But at this place, and in these moments, the less of speaking I should say the better. There is no grander spot than this.

Here, seated on the rail of the bridge, you will not see the whole depth of the fall. In looking at the grandest works of nature, and of art too, I fancy, it is never well to see all. There should be something left to the imagination, and much should be half-concealed in mystery. The greatest charm of a mountain range is the wild feeling that there must be strange unknown desolate worlds in those far-off valleys beyond.

And so here, at Niagara, that converging rush of waters may fall down, down at once into a hell of rivers as far as the eye can see.

It is glorious to watch them in the first curve over the rocks. They come green as a bank of emeralds; but with a fitful flying colour, as though conscious that in one moment more they would be dashed into spray and rise into air, pale as driven snow. The vapour rises high into the air, and is gathered there, visible always as a permanent white cloud over the cataract; but the bulk of the spray which fills the lower hollow of that horseshoe is like a tumult of snow.

This you will not fully see from your seat on the rail. The head of it rises ever and anon out of that cauldron below, but the cauldron itself will be invisible. It is ever so far down – far as your own imagination can sink it. But your eyes will rest full upon the curve of the waters. The shape you will be looking at is that of a horseshoe, but of a horseshoe miraculously deep from toe to heel – and this depth becomes greater as you sit there.

That which at first was only great and beautiful, becomes gigantic and sublime till the mind is at loss to find an epithet for its own use. To realize Niagara you must sit there till you see nothing else than that which you have come to see. You will hear nothing else, and think of nothing else.

At length you will be at one with the tumbling river before you. You will find yourself among the waters as though you belonged to them. The cool liquid will run through your veins, and the voice of the cataract will be the expression of your own heart. You will fall as the bright waters fall, rushing down into your new world with no hesitation and with no dismay; and you will rise again as the spray rises, bright, beautiful, and pure.

Then you will flow away in your course to the uncompassed, distant, and eternal ocean.

Chapter 6

FROM Niagara we went by the Canada Great Western Railway to Detroit, the big city of Michigan. It is an American institution that the States should have a commercial capital, or what I call their big city, as well as a political capital, which may as a rule be called the State's central city.

The object in choosing the political capital is average nearness of approach from the various confines of the States; but commerce submits to no such Procrustean laws in selecting her capitals, and consequently she has placed Detroit on the borders of Michigan, on the shore of the neck of water which joins Lake Huron to Lake Erie through which all the trade must flow which comes down from Lakes Michigan, Superior and Huron, on its way to the eastern States and to Europe.

We had thought of going from Buffalo across Lake Erie to Detroit; but we found that the better class of steamers had been taken off the waters for the winter. And we also found that navigation among these lakes is a mistake whenever the necessary journey can be taken by railway. The waters are by no means smooth; and then there is nothing to be seen. I do not know whether others may have a feeling, almost instinctive, that lake navigation must be pleasant – that lakes must of necessity be beautiful. I have such a feeling; but not now so strongly as formerly. Such an idea should be kept for use in Europe, and never brought over to America with other travelling gear. The lakes in America are cold, cumbrous, uncouth, and uninteresting; intended by nature for the conveyance of cereal produce, but not for the comfort of travelling men and women. So we gave up our plan of traversing the lake, and reached the Detroit river at Windsor by the Great Western line, and passed thence by the ferry into the city of Detroit.

In making this journey at night we introduced ourselves to the thoroughly American institution of sleeping-cars – that is, of cars in which beds are made up for travellers. The traveller may have a whole bed, or half a bed, or no bed at all as he pleases, paying a dollar or half a dollar extra should he choose the partial or full fruition of a couch.

I confess I have always taken a delight in seeing these beds made up, and consider that the operations of the change are generally as well executed as the manoeuvres of any pantomime at Drury Lane. The work is usually done by Negroes or coloured men; and the domestic Negroes of America are always light-handed and adroit.

The nature of an American car is no doubt known to all men. It looks as far removed from all bedroom accommodation, as the baker's barrow does from the steam-engine into which it is to be converted by harlequin's wand. But the Negro goes to work much more quietly than the harlequin, and for every four seats in the railway car he builds up four beds, almost as quickly as the hero of the pantomime goes through his performance.

The great glory of the Americans is in their wondrous contrivances – in their patent remedies for the usually troublous operations of life. In their huge hotels all the bell-ropes of each house ring on one bell only, but a patent indicator discloses a number, and the whereabouts of the ringer is shown. One fire heats every room, passage, hall, and cupboard – and does it so effectually that the inhabitants are all but stifled. Soda-water bottles open themselves without any trouble of wire or strings. Men and women go up and down stairs without motive power of their own. Hot and cold water are laid on to all the chambers – though it sometimes happens that the water from both taps is boiling, and that when once turned on it cannot be turned off again by any human energy. Everything is done by a new and wonderful patent contrivance; and of all their wonderful contrivances that of their railroad beds is by no means the least. Mattresses slip out from one nook and pillows from another. Blankets are added, and the bed is ready.

Any over-particular individual – an islander, for instance, who hugs his chains – will generally prefer to pay the dollar for the double accommodation. Looking at the bed in the light of a bed – taking as it were an abstract view of it – or comparing it with some other bed or beds with which the occupant may have acquaintance – I cannot say that it is in all respects perfect. But distances are long in America; and he who declines to travel by night will lose very much time. He who does so travel will find the railway bed a great relief. I must confess that the feeling of dirt on the following morning is rather oppressive.

From Windsor on the Canada side we passed over to Detroit in the State of Michigan by a steam ferry. But ferries in England and ferries in America are very different. Here on this Detroit ferry, some hundred of passengers who were going forward from the other side without delay, at once sat down to breakfast.

I may as well explain the way in which disposition is made of one's luggage as one takes these long journeys. The traveller when he starts has his baggage checked. He abandons his trunk – generally a box studded with nails, as long as a coffin and as high as a linen chest – and in return for this he receives an iron ticket with a number on it. As he approaches the end of his first instalment of travel, and while the engine is still working its hardest, a man comes up to him, bearing with him suspended on a circular bar an infinite variety of other checks. The traveller confides to this man his wishes; and if he be going further without delay, surrenders his check and receives a counter-check in return. Then while the train is still in motion, the new destiny of the trunk is imparted to it.

But another man, with another set of checks, also comes the way, walking leisurely through the train as he performs his work. This is the minister of the hotel-omnibus institution. His business is with those who do not travel beyond the next terminus. To him, if such be your intention, you make your confidence, giving up your tallies and taking other tallies, by way of receipt; and your luggage is afterwards found by you in the hall of your hotel.

There is undoubtedly very much of comfort in this; and the mind of the traveller is lost in amazement as he thinks of the futile efforts with which he would struggle to regain his luggage were there no such arrangement. Enormous piles of boxes are disclosed on the platform at all the larger stations, the numbers of which are roared forth with quick voice by some two or three railway denizens at once. A modest English voyager with six

or seven small packages, would stand no chance of getting anything if he were left to his own devices.

As it is I am bound to say that the thing is well done. I have
had my desk with all my money in it lost for a day, and my black
leather bag was on one occasion sent back over the line. They,
however, were recovered; and on the whole I feel grateful to the
check system of the American railways.

And then, too, one never hears of extra luggage. Of weight
they are quite regardless. On two or three occasions an over-
wrought official has muttered between his teeth that ten packages
were a great many, and that some of those 'light fixings' might
have been made up into one. And when I came to understand
that the number of every check was entered in a book, and
re-entered at every change, I did whisper to my wife that she
ought to do without a bonnet-box. The ten, however, went on,
and were always duly protected. I must add, however, that
articles requiring tender treatment will sometimes reappear a
little the worse from the hardships of their journey.

I have not much to say of Detroit; not much, that is, beyond
what I have to say of all the North. It is a large well-built half-
finished city, lying on a convenient waterway, and spreading
itself out with promises of a wide and still wider prosperity. It
has about it perhaps as little of intrinsic interest as any of those
large western towns which I visited. It is not so pleasant as
Milwaukee, nor so picturesque as St Paul, nor so grand as Chicago,
nor so civilized as Cleveland, nor so busy as Buffalo.

Indeed, Detroit is neither pleasant nor picturesque at all. I will
not say that it is uncivilized, but it has a harsh, crude, unpre-
possessing appearance. It has some 70,000 inhabitants, and good
accommodation for shipping. It was doing an enormous business
before the war began, and when these troublous times are over
will no doubt go ahead. I do not, however, think it well to recommend any Englishman to make a special visit to Detroit, who
may be wholly uncommercial in his views and travel in search
of that which is either beautiful or interesting.

From Detroit we continued our course westward across the
State of Michigan through a country that was absolutely wild
till the railway pierced it. Very much of it is still absolutely

wild. For miles upon miles the road passes the untouched forest, showing that even in Michigan the great work of civilization has hardly more than been commenced.

As one thinks of the all but countless population which is before long to be fed from these regions, of the cities which will grow here, and of the amount of government which in due time will be required, one can hardly fail to feel that the division of the United States into separate nationalities is merely a part of the ordained work of creation, as arranged for the well-being of mankind. The States already boast of thirty millions of inhabitants – not of unnoticed and unnoticeable beings, requiring little, knowing little, and doing little, such as are in the East hordes which may be counted by tens of millions, but of men and women who talk loudly and are ambitious, who eat beef, who read and write, and understand the dignity of manhood.

But these thirty millions are as nothing to the crowds which will grow sleek and talk loudly, and become aggressive on these wheat and meat producing levels. The country is as yet but touched by the pioneering hand of population. In the old countries agriculture, following on the heels of pastoral patriarchal life, preceded the birth of cities.

But in this young world the cities have come first. The new Jasons, blessed with the experience of the old world adventurers, have gone forth in search of their golden fleeces armed with all that the science and skill of the East had as yet produced, and in setting up their new Colchis have begun by the erection of firstclass hotels and the fabrication of railroads. Let the old world bid them God speed in their work. Only it would be well if they could be brought to acknowledge from whence they have learned all that they know.

Our route lay right across the State to a place called Grand Haven on Lake Michigan, from whence we were to take boat for Milwaukee, a town in Wisconsin on the opposite or western shore of the lake. On arriving at Grand Haven we found that there had been a storm on the lake, and that the passengers from the trains of the preceding day were still remaining there, waiting to be carried over to Milwaukee. The water, however – or the sea as they all call it – was still very high, and the captain declared his intention of remaining there that night. Whereupon all our fellow-travellers huddled themselves into the great lake steamboat, and proceeded to carry on life there as though they were quite at home. The men took themselves to the bar-room and smoked cigars and talked about the war with their feet upon the counter, and the women got themselves into rocking-chairs in the saloon and sat there listless and silent, but not more listless and silent than they usually are in the big drawing-rooms of the big hotels.

There was supper there, precisely at six o'clock, beefsteaks, and tea, and apple jam, and hot cakes, and light fixings, to all which luxuries an American deems himself entitled, let him have to seek his meal where he may. And I was soon informed with considerable energy, that let the boat be kept there as long as it might by stress of weather, the beefsteaks and apple jam, light fixings and heavy fixings, must be supplied at the cost of the owners of the ship.

'Your first supper you pay for,' my informant told me, 'because you eat that on your own account. What you consume after that comes of their doing, because they don't start; and if it's three meals a day for a week, it's their look out.' It occurred to me that under such circumstances a captain would be very apt to sail either in foul weather or in fair.

It was a bright moonlight night, moonlight such as we rarely have in England, and I started off by myself for a walk, that I might see of what nature were the environs of Grand Haven. A more melancholy place I have never beheld. Grand Haven itself is but a poor place, not having succeeded in catching much of the commerce which comes across the lake from Wisconsin, and which takes itself on eastwards by the railway. Altogether it is a dreary place, such as might break a man's heart, should he find that inexorable fate required him there to pitch his tent.

On my return I went down into the bar-room of the steamer, put my feet upon the counter, lit my cigar, and struck into the debate then proceeding on the subject of the war. I was getting West, and General Fremont[14] was the hero of the hour.

'He's a frontier man, and that's what we want. I guess he'll go through. Yes, sir.'

'As for relieving General Fre-mont,' – with the accent always strongly on the 'mont', – 'I guess you may as well talk of relieving the whole West. They won't meddle with Fre-mont. They are beginning to know in Washington what stuff he's made of.'

'Why, sir; there are 50,000 men in these States who will follow Fre-mont, who would not stir a foot after any other man.'

From which, and the like of it in many other places, I began to understand how difficult was the task which the statesmen in Washington had in hand.

I received no pecuniary advantage whatever from that law as to the steam-boat meals which my new friend had revealed to me. For my one supper of course I paid, looking forward to any amount of subsequent gratuitous provisions. But in the course of the night the ship sailed, and we found ourselves at Milwaukee in time for breakfast on the following morning.

Milwaukee is a pleasant town, a very pleasant town, containing 45,000 inhabitants. How many of my readers can boast that they know anything of Milwaukee, or even have heard of it? To me its name was unknown until I saw it on huge railway placards stuck up in the smoking-rooms and lounging halls of all American hotels. It is the big town of Wisconsin, whereas Madison is the capital. It stands immediately on the western shore of Lake Michigan, and is very pleasant.

Why it should be so, and why Detroit should be the contrary, I can hardly tell; only I think that the same verdict would be given by any English tourist. It must be always borne in mind that 10,000 or 40,000 inhabitants in an American town, and especially in any new western town, is a number which means much more than would be implied by any similar number as to an old town in Europe. Such a population in America consumes double the amount of beef which it would in England, wears double the amount of clothes, and demands double as much of the comforts of life. If a census could be taken of the watches it would be found, I take it, that the American population possessed among them nearly double as many as would the English; and I fear also that it would be found that many more of the Americans were readers and writers by habit.

In any large town in England it is probable that a higher

excellence of education would be found than in Milwaukee, and also a style of life into which more of refinement and more of luxury had found its way. But the general level of these things, of material and intellectual well-being – of beef, that is, and book learning – is no doubt infinitely higher in a new American than in an old European town. Such an animal as a beggar is as much unknown as a mastodon. Men out of work and in want are almost unknown.

I do not say that there are none of the hardships of life – and to them I will come by-and-by; but want is not known as a hardship in these towns, nor is that dense ignorance in which so large a proportion of our town populations is still steeped. And then the town of 40,000 inhabitants is spread over a surface which would suffice in England for a city of four times the size. Our towns in England – and the towns, indeed, of Europe generally – have been built as they have been wanted.

No aspiring ambition as to hundreds of thousands of people warmed the bosoms of their first founders. Two or three dozen men required habitations in the same locality, and clustered them together closely. Many such have failed and died out of the world's notice. Others have thriven, and houses have been packed on to houses till London and Manchester, Dublin and Glasgow have been produced. Poor men have built, or have had built for them, wretched lanes; and rich men have erected grand palaces. From the nature of their beginnings such has, of necessity, been the manner of their creation.

But in America, and especially in western America, there has been no such necessity and there is no such result. The founders of cities have had the experience of the world before them. They have known of sanitary laws as they began. That sewerage, and water, and gas, and good air would be needed for a thriving community has been to them as much a matter of fact as are the well understood combinations between timber and nails, and bricks and mortar. They have known that water carriage is almost a necessity for commercial success, and have chosen their sites accordingly.

Broad streets cost as little, while land by the foot is not as yet of value to be regarded, as those which are narrow; and therefore the sites of towns have been prepared with noble avenues, and imposing streets. A city at its commencement is laid out with an intention that it shall be populous. The houses are not all built at once, but there are the places allocated for them. The streets are not made, but there are the spaces.

Many an abortive attempt at municipal greatness has so been made and then all but abandoned. There are wretched villages with huge straggling parallel ways which will never grow into towns. They are the failures – failures in which the pioneers of civilization, frontier men as they call themselves, have lost their tens of thousands of dollars. But when the success comes, when the happy hit has been made, and the ways of commerce have been truly foreseen with a cunning eye, then a great and prosperous city springs up, ready made, as it were, from the earth.

Such a town is Milwaukee, now containing 45,000 inhabitants, but with room apparently for double that number; with room for four times that number, were men packed as closely there as they are with us.

In the principal business streets of all these towns one sees vast buildings. They are usually called blocks, and are often so denominated in large letters on their front, as Portland Block, Devereux Block, Buel's Block. Such a block may face to two, three, or even four streets, and, as I presume, has generally been a matter of one special speculation. It may be divided into separate houses, or kept for a single purpose, such as that of an hotel, or grouped into shops below, and into various sets of chambers above.

I have had occasion in various towns to mount the stairs within these blocks, and have generally found some portion of them vacant – have sometimes found the greater portion of them vacant. Men build on an enormous scale, three times, ten times as much as is wanted. The only measure of size is an increase on what men have built before.

Monroe P. Jones, the speculator, is very probably ruined, and then begins the world again, nothing daunted. But Jones' block remains, and gives to the city in its aggregate a certain amount of wealth. Or the block becomes at once of service and finds tenants.

In which case Jones probably sells it and immediately builds two others twice as big.

That Monroe P. Jones will encounter ruin is almost a matter of course; but then he is none the worse for being ruined. It hardly makes him unhappy. He is greedy of dollars with a terrible covetousness; but he is greedy in order that he may speculate more widely. He would sooner have built Jones' tenth block, with a prospect of completing a twentieth, than settle himself down at rest for life as the owner of a Chatsworth or a Woburn. As for his children he has no desire of leaving them money. Let the girls marry. And for the boys – for them it will be good to begin as he began. If they cannot build blocks for themselves, let them earn their bread in the blocks of other men.

So Monroe P. Jones, with his million of dollars accomplished, advances on to a new frontier, goes to work again on a new city, and loses it all. As an individual I differ very much from Monroe P. Jones. The first block accomplished, with an adequate rent accruing to me as the builder, I fancy that I should never try a second. But Jones is undoubtedly the man for the West. It is that love of money to come, joined to a strong disregard for money made, which constitutes the vigorous frontier mind, the true pioneering organization. Monroe P. Jones would be a great man to all posterity, if only he had a poet to sing of his valour.

It may be imagined how large in proportion to its inhabitants will be a town which spreads itself in this way. There are great houses left untenanted, and great gaps left unfilled. But if the place be successful – if it promise success, it will be seen at once that there is life all through it. Omnibuses, or street cars working on rails, run hither and thither. The shops that have been opened are well filled. The great hotels are thronged. The quays are crowded with vessels, and a general feeling of progress pervades the place. It is easy to perceive whether or no an American town is going ahead. The days of my visit to Milwaukee were days of civil war and national trouble, but in spite of civil war and national trouble Milwaukee looked healthy.

I have said that there was but little poverty – little to be seen of real want in these thriving towns, but that they who laboured in them had nevertheless their own hardships. This is so. I would not have any man believe that he can take himself to the western States of America – to those States of which I am now speaking – Michigan, Wisconsin, Minnesota, Iowa, or Illinois, and there by industry escape the ills to which flesh is heir.

The labouring Irish in these towns eat meat seven days a week, but I have met many a labouring Irishman among them who has wished himself back in his old cabin. Industry is a good thing, and there is no bread so sweet as that which is eaten in the sweat of a man's brow, but labour carried to excess wearies the mind as well as the body and the sweat that is ever running makes the bread bitter.

There is, I think, no task-master over free labour so exacting as an American. He knows nothing of hours, and seems to have that idea of a man which a lady always has of a horse. He thinks that he will go for ever. I wish those masons in London who strike for nine hours' work with ten hours' pay could be driven to the labour market of western America for a spell. And moreover, which astonished me, I have seen men driven and hurried, as it were, forced at their work, in a manner which to an English workman would be intolerable.

This surprised me much, as it was at variance with our – or perhaps I should say with my – preconceived ideas as to American freedom. I had fancied that an American citizen would not submit to be driven – that the spirit of the country if not the spirit of the individual would have made it impossible. I thought that the shoe would have pinched quite on the other foot. But I found that such driving did exist; and American masters in the West with whom I had an opportunity of discussing the subject all admitted it.

'Those men'll never half move unless they're driven,' a foreman said to me once as we stood together over some twenty men who were at their work. 'They kinder look for it, and don't well know how to get along when they miss it.'

But there is worse even than this. Wages in these regions are what we should call high. An agricultural labourer will earn perhaps fifteen dollars a month and his board and a town labourer will earn a dollar a day. A dollar may be taken as representing four shillings, though it is in fact more. Food in these parts is much cheaper than in England, and therefore the wages must be considered as very good.

In making, however, a just calculation it must be borne in mind that clothing is dearer than in England and that much more of it is necessary. The wages nevertheless are high, and will enable the labourer to save money – if only he can get them paid. The complaint that wages are held back and not even ultimately paid is very common. There is no fixed rule for satisfying all such claims once a week; and thus debts to labourers are contracted and when contracted are ignored.

With us there is a feeling that it is pitiful, mean almost beyond expression, to wrong a labourer of his hire. We have men who go in debt to tradesmen perhaps without a thought of paying them – but when we speak of such a one who has descended into the lowest mire of insolvency, we say that he has not paid his washerwoman. Out there in the West the washerwoman is as fair game as the tailor, the domestic servant as the wine merchant. If a man be honest he will not willingly take either goods or labour without payment and it may be hard to prove that he who takes the latter is more dishonest than he who takes the former; but with us there is a prejudice in favour of one's washerwoman by which the western mind is not weakened.

'They certainly have to be smart to get it,' a gentleman said to me whom I taxed on the subject. 'You see on the frontier a man is bound to be smart. If he ain't smart he'd better go back East – perhaps as far as Europe. He'll do there.'

I had got my answer, and my friend had turned the question. But the fact was admitted by him as it had been by many others.

We found a completed regiment consisting entirely of Germans. A thousand Germans had been collected in that State and brought together in one regiment, and I was informed by an officer on the ground that there are many Germans in sundry other of the Wisconsin regiments. It may be well to mention here that the number of Germans through all these western States is very great. That they form a great portion of the population of New York, making the German quarter of that city the third largest German town in the world, I have long known; but I had no previous idea of their expansion westward. In Detroit nearly every third shop bore a German name, and the same remark was to be made at Milwaukee and on all hands I heard praises of their morals, of their thrift, and of their new patriotism. I was continually told how far they exceeded the Irish settlers. To me in all parts of the world an Irishman is dear. When handled tenderly he becomes a creature most lovable. But with all my judgement in the Irishman's favour, and with my prejudices leaning the same way, I feel myself bound to state what I heard and what I saw as to the Germans.

But this regiment of Germans, and another not completed regiment, called from the State generally, were as yet without arms, accoutrements, or clothing. There was the raw material of the regiment, but there was nothing else. Winter was coming on – winter in which the mercury is commonly twenty degrees below zero – and the men were in tents with no provision against the cold. These tents held each two men, and were just large enough for two to lie. The canvas of which they were made seemed to me to be thin, but I think always double.

At this camp there was a house in which the men took their meals, but I visited other camps in which there was no such accommodation. I saw the German regiment called to its supper by tuck of drum, and the men marched in gallantly, armed each with a knife and spoon. I managed to make my way in at the door after them, and can testify to the excellence of the provisions of which their supper consisted. A poor diet never enters into any combination of circumstances contemplated by an American. Let him be where he will, animal food is, with him, the first necessary of life, and he is always provided accordingly.

The view from Milwaukee over Lake Michigan is very pleasing. One looks upon a vast expanse of water to which the eye finds no bounds, and therefore there are none of the common attributes of lake beauty; but the colour of the lake is bright, and within a walk of the city the traveller comes to the bluffs or low round-topped hills from which he can look down upon the shores. These bluffs form the beauty of Wisconsin and Minnesota, and relieve the eye after the flat level of Michigan. Round Detroit there is no rising ground, and therefore, perhaps, it is that Detroit is uninteresting.

I have said that those who are called on to labour in these States have their own hardships, and I have endeavoured to explain what are the sufferings to which the town labourer is subject. To escape from this is the labourer's great ambition, and his mode of doing so consists almost universally in the purchase of land. He saves up money in order that he may buy a section of an allotment, and thus become his own master.

All his savings are made with a view to this independence. Seated on his own land he will have to work probably harder than ever, but he will work for himself. No taskmaster can then stand over him and wound his pride with harsh words. He will be his own master, will eat the food which he himself has grown, and live in the cabin which his own hands have built. This is the object of his life and to secure this position he is content to work late and early and to undergo the indignities of previous servitude.

The Government price for land is about five shillings an acre – one dollar and a quarter – and the settler may get it for this price if he be contented to take it not only untouched as regards clearing, but also far removed from any completed road. The traffic in these lands has been the great speculating business of western men. Five or six years ago when the rage for such purchases was at its height land was becoming a scarce article in the market !

Individuals or companies bought it up with the object of re-selling it at a profit – and many no doubt did make money. Railway companies were, in fact, companies combined for the purchase of land. They purchased land, looking to increase the value of it five-fold by the opening of a railroad. It may easily be understood that a railway, which could not be in itself remunerative, might in this way become a lucrative speculation. No settler could dare to place himself absolutely at a distance from any thoroughfare. At first the margins of nature's highways, the navigable rivers and lakes, were cleared.

But as the railway system grew and expanded itself, it became manifest that lands might be rendered quickly available which were not so circumstanced by nature. A company which had purchased an enormous territory from the United States Government at five shillings an acre might well repay itself all the cost of a railway through that territory, even though the receipts of the railway should do no more than maintain the current expenses.

The settler must begin by making certain improvements on the selected land, clearing and cultivating some small portion, building a hut, and probably sinking a well. When this has been done, when he has thus given a pledge of his intentions by depositing on the land the value of a certain amount of labour, he cannot be removed.

The primary settler goes to work upon his land amidst all the wildness of nature. He levels and burns the first trees, and raises his first crop of corn amidst stumps still standing four or five feet above the soil; but he does not do so till some mode of conveyance has been found for him. So much I have said hoping to explain the mode in which the frontier speculator paves the way for the frontier agriculturist. But the permanent farmer very generally comes on the land as the third owner. The first settler is a rough fellow, and seems to be so wedded to his rough life that he leaves his land after his first wild work is done, and goes again further off to some untouched allotment.

He finds that he can sell his improvements at a profitable rate and takes the price. He is a preparer of farms rather than a farmer. He has no love for the soil which his hand has first turned. He regards it merely as an investment, and when things about him are beginning to wear an aspect of comfort, when his property has become valuable, he sells it, packs up his wife and little ones, and goes again into the woods.

The western American has no love for his own soil, or his own house. The matter with him is simply one of dollars. To keep a farm which he could sell at an advantage from any feeling of affection – from what we should call an association of ideas – would be to him as ridiculous as the keeping of a family pig would be in an English farmer's establishment. The pig is a part of the farmer's stock in trade, and must go the way of all pigs. And so is it with house and land in the life of the frontier man in the western States.

But yet this man has his romance, his high poetic feeling, and above all his manly dignity. Visit him, and you will find him without coat or waistcoat, unshorn, in ragged blue trousers and old flannel shirt, too often bearing on his lantern jaws the signs of ague and sickness; but he will stand upright before you and speak to you with all the ease of a lettered gentleman in his own library.

All the odious incivility of the republican servant has been banished. He is his own master, standing on his own threshold, and finds no need to assert his equality by rudeness. He is delighted to see you, and bids you sit down on his battered bench without dreaming of any such apology as an English cottier offers to a Lady Bountiful when she calls. He has worked out his independence, and shows it in every easy movement of his body. He tells you of it inconsciously in every tone of his voice. You will always find in his cabin some newspaper, some book, some token of advance in education.

When he questions you about the old country he astonishes you by the extent of his knowledge. I defy you not to feel that he is superior to the race from whence he has sprung in England or in Ireland. To me I confess that the manliness of such a man is very charming. He is dirty and perhaps squalid. His children are sick and he is without comforts. His wife is pale, and you think you see shortness of life written in the faces of all the family.

But over and above it all there is an independence which sits gracefully on their shoulders, and teaches you at the first glance that the man has a right to assume himself to be your equal.

Chapter 7

FROM Milwaukee we went across Wisconsin and reached the Mississippi at La Crosse, but on reaching La Crosse we found that the vessel destined to take us up the river had not yet come down. She was bringing a regiment from Minnesota, and under such circumstances some pardon might be extended to irregularities. The wonder was that at such a period all means of public conveyance were not put absolutely out of gear. One might surmise that when regiments were constantly being moved for the purposes of civil war, when the whole North had but one object of collecting together a sufficient number of men to crush the South, ordinary travelling for ordinary purposes would be difficult, slow, and subject to sudden stoppages.

Such, however, was not the case either in the northern or western States. The trains ran much as usual, and those connected with the boats and railways were just as anxious as ever to secure passengers. The boat clerk at La Crosse apologized amply for the delay, and we sat ourselves down with patience to await the arrival of the second Minnesota regiment on its way to Washington.

During the four hours that we were kept waiting we were harboured on board a small steamer, and at about eleven the terribly harsh whistle that is made by the Mississippi boats informed us that the regiment was arriving. It came up to the quay in two steamers, 750 being brought in that which was to take us back, and 250 in a smaller one. The moon was very bright, and great flaming torches were lit on the vessel's side, so that all the operations of the men were visible.

I got out upon the quay and stood close by the plank, watching each man as he left the vessel and walked across towards the railway. Those whom I had previously seen in tents were not equipped, but these men were in uniform and each bore his musket. Taking them all together they were as fine a set of men as I ever saw collected. No man could doubt on seeing them that they bore on their countenances the signs of higher breeding and better education than would be seen in a thousand men enlisted in England.

I do not mean to argue from this that Americans are better than English. I do not mean to argue here that they are even better educated. My assertion goes to show that the men generally were taken from a higher level in the community than that which fills our own ranks. In the old countries population is thick, and food sometimes scarce. Men can be spared, and any employment may be serviceable, even though that employment be in itself so unproductive as that of fighting battles or preparing for them. But in the western States of America every arm that can guide a plough is of incalculable value. Minnesota was admitted as a State about three years before this time, and its whole population is not much above 150,000. Of this number perhaps 40,000 may be working men. And now this infant State with its huge territory and scanty population is called upon to send its heart's blood out to the war. And it has sent its heart's best blood. Forth they came – fine, stalwart, well-grown fellows, looking to my eye as though they had as yet but faintly recognized the necessary severity of military discipline.

As soldiers fit, or capable of being made fit for the duties they had undertaken, I could find but one fault with them. Their average age was too high. There were men among them with grizzled beards, and many who had counted thirty, thirty-five and forty years. They had, I believe, devoted themselves with a true spirit of patriotism. No doubt each had some ulterior hope as to himself – as has every mortal patriot. Regulus, when he returned hopeless to Carthage, trusted that some Horace would tell his story. Each of these men from Minnesota looked probably forward to his reward; but the reward desired was of a high class.

The first great misery to be endured by these regiments will be the military lesson of obedience which they must learn before they can be of any service. It always seemed to me when I came near them that they had not as yet recognized the necessary austerity of an officer's duty. The idea of a captain was the stage idea of a leader of dramatic banditti, a man to be followed and

obeyed as a leader, but to be obeyed with that free and easy
obedience which is accorded to the reigning chief of the forty
thieves.

'Wa'll Captain,' I have heard a private say to his officer, as
he sat on one seat in a railway car with his feet upon the back of
another. And the captain has looked as though he did not like it.
The captain did not like it, but the poor private was being fast
carried to that destiny which he would like still less. From the
first I have had faith in the northern army, but from the first I
have felt that the suffering to be endured by these free and
independent volunteers would be very great. A man to be available as a private soldier must be compressed and belted in till he
be a machine.

From La Crosse to St Paul, the distance up the river is something over 200 miles, and from St Paul down to Dubuque, in
Iowa, to which we went on our return, the distance is 450 miles.
On the whole we slept on board four nights, and lived on board
as many days. I cannot say that the life was comfortable, though
I do not know that it could be made more so by any care on the
part of the boat-owners. My first complaint would be against the
great heat of the cabins. The Americans as a rule live in an
atmosphere which is almost unbearable to an Englishman. To
this cause, I am convinced, is to be attributed their thin faces,
the pale skins, the unenergetic temperament, unenergetic as
regards physical motion, and their early old age. The winters are
long and cold in America, and mechanical ingenuity is far
extended. The two facts together have created a system of stoves,
hot-air pipes, steam chambers, and heating apparatus, so extensive that from autumn till the end of spring all inhabited rooms
are filled with the atmosphere of a hot oven. An Englishman
fancies that he is to be baked, and for a while finds it almost
impossible to exist in the air prepared for him. How the heat is
engendered on board the river steamers I do not know, but it is
engendered to so great a degree that the sitting-cabins are
unendurable.

That is my first complaint. My second complaint is equally
unreasonable, and is quite as incapable of a remedy as the first.

Nine-tenths of the travellers carry children with them. They are not tourists engaged on pleasure excursions, but men and women intent on the business of life. They are moving up and down, looking for fortune, and in search of new homes. Of course they carry with them all their household gods. Do not let any critics say that I grudge these young travellers their right to locomotion. Neither their right to locomotion is grudged by me, nor any of those privileges which are accorded in America to the rising generation. The habits of their country and the choice of the parents give to them full dominion over all hours and over all places, and it would ill become a foreigner to make such habits and such choice a ground of serious complaint.

But nevertheless the uncontrolled energies of twenty children round one's legs do not convey comfort or happiness, when the passing events are producing noise and storm rather than peace and sunshine. I must protest that American babies are an unhappy race. They eat and drink just as they please; they are never punished; they are never banished, snubbed, and kept in the background as children are kept with us; and yet they are wretched and uncomfortable. My heart has bled for them as I have heard them squalling by the hour together in agonies of discontent and dyspepsia. Can it be, I wonder, that children are happier when they are made to obey orders and are sent to bed at six o'clock, than when allowed to regulate their own conduct; that bread and milk is more favourable to laughter and soft childish ways than beefsteaks and pickles three times a day; that an occasional whipping, even, will conduce to rosy cheeks?

But there was a third reason why travelling on these boats was not as pleasant as I had expected. I could not get my fellow-travellers to talk to me. It must be understood that our fellow-travellers were not generally of that class which we Englishmen, in our pride, designate as gentlemen and ladies. They were people, as I have said, in search of new homes and new fortunes. But I protest that as such they would have been in those parts much more agreeable as companions to me than any gentlemen or any ladies, if only they would have talked to me.

A western American man is not a talking man. He will sit for hours over a stove with his cigar in his mouth, and his hat over his eyes, chewing the cud of reflection. A dozen will sit together in the same way, and there shall not be a dozen words spoken between them in an hour. With the women one's chance of conversation is still worse. It seemed as though the cares of the world had been too much for them, and that all talking excepting as to business – demands for instance on the servants for pickles for their children – had gone by the board. They were generally hard, dry, and melancholy. I am speaking of course of aged females – from five and twenty perhaps to thirty, who had long since given up the amusements and levities of life. I very soon abandoned any attempt at drawing a word from these ancient mothers of families; but not the less did I ponder in my mind over the circumstances of their lives. Had things gone with them so sadly, was the struggle for independence so hard, that all the softness of existence had been trodden out of them? In the cities too it was much the same. It seemed to me that a future mother of a family in those parts had left all laughter behind her when she put out her finger for the wedding ring.

For these reasons I must say that life on board these steamboats was not as pleasant as I had hoped to find it, but for our discomfort in this respect we found great atonement in the scenery through which we passed. I protest that of all the river scenery that I know, that of the Upper Mississippi is by far the finest and the most continued. One thinks of course of the Rhine; but, according to my idea of beauty, the Rhine is nothing to the Upper Mississippi.

For miles upon miles, for hundreds of miles, the course of the river runs through low hills, which are there called bluffs. These bluffs rise in every imaginable form, looking sometimes like large straggling unwieldy castles, and then throwing themselves into sloping lawns which stretch back away from the river till the eye is lost in their twists and turnings. Landscape beauty, as I take it, consists mainly in four attributes: in water, in broken land, in scattered timber – timber scattered as opposed to continuous forest timber – and in the accident of colour. In all these particulars the banks of the Upper Mississippi can hardly be beaten. There are no high mountains, but there is a succession of hills which group themselves for ever without monotony. It is perhaps the ever-variegated forms of these bluffs which chiefly constitute the wonderful loveliness of this river.

To my taste the finest stretch of the river was that immediately above Lake Pepin; but then, at this point, we had all the glory of the setting sun. It was like fairy land, so bright were the golden hues, so fantastic were the shapes of the hills, so broken and twisted the course of the waters! But the noisy steamer went groaning up the narrow passages with almost unabated speed, and left the fairy land behind all too quickly. Then the bell would ring for tea, and the children with the beefsteaks, the pickled onions, and the light fixings would all come over again. The care-laden mothers would tuck the bibs under the chins of their tyrant children, and some embryo senator of four years old would listen with concentrated attention, while the Negro servant recapitulated to him the delicacies of the supper-table, in order that he might make his choice with due consideration. 'Beefsteak,' the embryo four-year-old senator would lisp, 'and stewed potato, and buttered toast, and corn cake, and coffee – and – and – and – mother, mind you get me the pickles.'

St Paul contains about fourteen thousand inhabitants, and, like all other American towns, is spread over a surface of ground adapted to the accommodation of a very extended population. As it is belted on one side by the river, and on the other by the bluffs which accompany the course of the river, the site is pretty, and almost romantic. Here also we found a great hotel – a huge square building, such as we in England might perhaps place near to a railway terminus, in such a city as Glasgow or Manchester, but on which no living Englishman would expend his money in a town even five times as big again as St Paul. Everything was sufficiently good, and much more than sufficiently plentiful. The whole thing went on exactly as hotels do down in Massachusetts, or the State of New York.

Look at the map, and see where St Paul is. Its distance from all known civilization – all civilization that has succeeded in obtaining acquaintance with the world at large – is very great. Even American travellers do not go up there in great numbers, excepting those who intend to settle there. A stray sportsman or two, American or English, as the case may be, makes his way into Minnesota for the sake of shooting, and pushes up through St Paul to the Red River.

Some few adventurous spirits visit the Indian settlements, and pass over into the unsettled regions of Dacotah and Washington territory. But there is no throng of travelling. Nevertheless, an hotel has been built there capable of holding three hundred guests, and other hotels exist in the neighbourhood, one of which is even larger than that at St Paul.

From St Paul there are two waterfalls to be seen, which we, of course, visited. We crossed the river at Fort Snelling, a rickety, ill-conditioned building, standing at the confluence of the Minnesota and Mississippi rivers, built there to repress the Indians. It is, I take it, very necessary, especially at the present moment, as the Indians seem to require repressing. They have learned that the attention of the Federal Government has been called to the war, and have become bold in consequence. When I was at St Paul I heard of a party of Englishmen who had been robbed of everything they possessed, and was informed that the farmers in the distant parts of the State were by no means secure. The Indians are more to be pitied than the farmers. They are turning against enemies who will neither forgive nor forget any injuries done. When the war is over, they will be improved, and polished, and annexed, till no Indian will hold an acre of land in Minnesota.

From Fort Snelling we went on to the Falls of Minnehaha. Minnehaha, laughing water. Such I believe is the interpretation. The name in this case is more imposing than the fall. It is a pretty little cascade, and might do for a picnic in fine weather, but it is not a waterfall of which a man can make much when found so far away from home. Going on from Minnehaha we came to Minneapolis, at which place there is a fine suspension bridge across the river, just above the falls of St Anthony and leading to the town of that name.

Till I got there I could hardly believe that in these days there should be a living village called Minneapolis by living men. I presume I should describe it as a town, for it has a municipality, and a post office, and of course, a large hotel.

There is very much in the mode of life adopted by the settlers in these regions which creates admiration. The people are all

intelligent. They are energetic and speculative, conceiving grand
ideas, and carrying them out almost with the rapidity of magic. A
suspension bridge half a mile long is erected, while in England
we should be fastening together a few planks for a foot passage.
Progress, mental as well as material, is the demand of the people
generally. Everybody understands everything, and everybody
intends sooner or later to do everything.

All this is very grand – but then there is a terrible drawback.
One hears on every side of intelligence, but one hears also on
every side of dishonesty. Talk to whom you will, of whom you
will, and you will hear some tale of successful or unsuccessful
swindling. It seems to be the recognized rule of commerce in the
Far West that men shall go into the world's markets prepared
to cheat and to be cheated. It may be said that as long as this is
acknowledged and understood on all sides, no harm will be done.
It is equally fair for all. When I was a child there used to be
certain games at which it was agreed in the beginning either
that there should be cheating or that there should not. It may be
said that out there in the western States, men agree to play the
cheating game; and that the cheating game has more of interest
in it than the other.

Unfortunately, however, they who agree to play this game on
a huge scale, do not keep outsiders altogether out of the play-
ground. Indeed outsiders become very welcome to them – and
then it is not pleasant to hear the tone in which such outsiders
speak of the peculiarities of the sport to which they have been
introduced. When a beginner in trade finds himself furnished
with a barrel of wooden nutmegs, the joke is not so good to him
as to the experienced merchant who supplies him. This dealing
in wooden nutmegs, this selling of things which do not exist, and
buying of goods for which no price is ever to be given, is an institution which is much honoured in the West. We call it swindling
– and so do they. But it seemed to me that in the western States the
word hardly seemed to leave the same impress on the mind that it
does elsewhere.

On our return down the river we passed La Crosse, at which
we had embarked, and went down as far as Dubuque in Iowa.
On our way down we came to grief and broke one of our paddle-

wheels to pieces. We had no special accident. We struck against nothing above or below water. But the wheel went to pieces, and we lay-to on the river side for the greater part of a day while the necessary repairs were being made. Delay in travelling is usually an annoyance, because it causes the unsettlement of a settled purpose. But the loss of the day did us no harm, and our accident had happened at a very pretty spot.

I climbed up to the top of the nearest bluff, and walked back till I came to the open country, and also went up and down the river banks, visiting the cabins of two settlers who live there by supplying wood to the river steamers. One of these was close to the spot at which we were lying; and yet though most of our passengers came on shore, I was the only one who spoke to the inmates of the cabin. There people must live almost in desolation from one year's end to another. Once in a fortnight or so they go up to a market town in their small boats, but beyond that they can have little intercourse with their fellow-creatures. Nevertheless none of these dwellers by the river side came out to speak to the men and women who were lounging about from eleven in the morning till four in the afternoon, nor did one of the passengers except myself knock at the door or enter the cabin, or exchange a word with those who lived there.

I could not then understand, nor can I now understand, why none of the numerous passengers out of the boat should have entered those cabins except myself and why the inmates of the cabins should not have come out to speak to anyone. Had they been surly, morose people, made silent by the specialties of their life, it would have been explicable but they were delighted to talk and to listen. The fact, I take it, is, that the people are all harsh to each other. They do not care to go out of their way to speak to anyone unless something is to be gained. They say that two Englishmen meeting in the desert would not speak unless they were introduced. The further I travel, the less true do I find this of Englishmen, and the more true of other people.

We stopped at the Julien House, Dubuque. Dubuque is a city in Iowa on the western shore of the Missisippi, and as the names both of the town and of the hotel sounded French in my ears, I asked for an explanation. I was then told that Julien Dubuque, a Canadian Frenchman, had been buried on one of the bluffs of the river within the precincts of the present town, that he had been the first white settler in Iowa, and had been the only man who had ever prevailed upon the Indians to work.

Iowa has a population of 674,000 souls, and in October 1861 had already mustered eighteen regiments of 1,000 men each. Such a population would give probably 170,000 men capable of bearing arms and therefore the number of soldiers sent had already amounted to more than a decimation of the available strength of the State.

When we were at Dubuque nothing was talked of but the Army. It seemed that mines, coal pits, and cornfields, were all of no account in comparison with the war. How many regiments could be squeezed out of the State, was the one question which filled all minds; and the general desire was that such regiments should be sent to the western army, to swell the triumph which was still expected for General Fremont, and to assist in sweeping slavery out into the Gulf of Mexico.

The patriotism of the West has been quite as keen as that of the North, and has produced results as memorable; but it has sprung from a different source, and been conducted and animated by a different sentiment. National greatness and support of the law have been the ideas of the North; national greatness and abolition of slavery have been those of the West. How they are to agree as to terms when between them they have crushed the South – that is the difficulty.

At Dubuque in Iowa, I ate the best apple that I ever encountered. I make that statement with the purpose of doing justice to the Americans on a matter which is to them one of considerable importance. Americans as a rule do not believe in English apples. They declare that there are none, and receive accounts of Devonshire cyder with manifest incredulity. 'But at any rate there are no apples in England equal to ours.' That is an assertion to which an Englishman is called upon to give an absolute assent; and I hereby give it.

'My great objection to your country, sir,' said another, 'is that you have got no vegetables.'

Had he told me that we had got no seaboard, or no coals, he

would not have surprised me more. No vegetables in England! No
vegetables! Had the gentleman told me that England did not suit
him because we had nothing but vegetables, I should have been
less surprised.

From Dubuque, on the western shore of the river, we passed
over to Dunleath in Illinois, and went on from thence by railway
to Dixon. I was induced to visit this not very flourishing town
by a desire to see the rolling prairie of Illinois, and to learn by
eyesight something of the crops of corn or Indian maize which
are produced upon the land. Had that gentleman told me that we
knew nothing of producing corn in England he would have been
nearer the mark; for of corn in the profusion in which it is
grown here we do not know much.

Better land than the prairies of Illinois for cereal crops the
world's surface probably cannot show. And here there has been
no necessity for the long previous labour of banishing the forest.
Enormous prairies stretch across the State, into which the plough
can be put at once. The earth is rich with the vegetation of
thousands of years, and the farmer's return is given to him without delay. The land bursts with its own produce and the plenty
is such that it creates wasteful carelessness in the gathering of
the crop. It is not worth a man's while to handle less than large
quantities. Up in Minnesota I had been grieved by the loose manner in which wheat was treated. I have seen bags of it upset, and
left upon the ground. The labour of collecting it was more than
it was worth. There wheat is the chief crop, and as the lands become cleared and cultivation spreads itself, the amount coming
down the Mississippi will be increased almost to infinity.

From Dixon we went to Chicago. Chicago is in many respects
the most remarkable city among all the remarkable cities of the
Union. Its growth has been the fastest and its success the most
assured. Twenty-five years ago there was no Chicago, and now it
contains 120,000 inhabitants. Cincinnati on the Ohio, and St
Louis at the junction of the Missouri and Mississippi, are larger
towns, but they have not grown large so quickly nor do they
now promise so excessive a development of commerce. Chicago
may be called the metropolis of American corn – the favourite

city haunt of the American Ceres. The goddess seats herself there amidst the dust of her full barns, and proclaims herself a goddess ruling over things political and philosophical as well as agricultural.

Not furrows only are in her thoughts, but free trade also, and brotherly love. And within her own bosom there is a boast that even yet she will be stronger than Mars. In Chicago there are great streets, and rows of houses fit to be the residences of a new Corn Exchange nobility. They look out on the wide lake which is now the highway for breadstuffs, and the merchant, as he shaves at his window, sees his rapid ventures as they pass away, one after the other, towards the East.

At Chicago the hotel was bigger than other hotels, and grander. There were pipes without end for cold water which ran hot, and for hot water which would not run at all. The Post Office also was grander and bigger than other Post Offices, though the postmaster confessed to me that the matter of the delivery of letters was one which could not be compassed. Just at that moment it was being done as a private speculation,. but it did not pay, and would be discontinued.

The theatre too was large, handsome, and convenient, but on the night of my attendance it seemed to lack an audience. A good comic actor it did not lack, and I never laughed more heartily in my life. There was something wrong too just at that time – I could not make out what – in the constitution of Illinois, and the present moment had been selected for voting a new constitution. To us in England such a necessity would be considered a matter of importance, but it did not seem to be much thought of here.

'Some slight alteration probably,' I suggested.

'No,' said my informant – one of the judges of their courts – 'it is to be a thorough radical change of the whole constitution. They are voting the delegates today.' I went to see them vote the delegates; but unfortunately got into a wrong place – by invitation – and was turned out, not without some slight tumult. I trust that the new constitution was carried through successfully.

From these little details it may perhaps be understood how a town like Chicago goes on and prospers, in spite of all the drawbacks which are incidental to newness. Men in those regions do not mind failures, and when they have failed, instantly begin again. They make their plans on a large scale, and they who come after them fill up what has been wanting at first. Those taps of hot and cold water will be made to run by the next owner of the hotel, if not by the present owner. In another ten years the letters, I do not doubt, will all be delivered. Long before that time the theatre will probably be full. The new constitution is no doubt already at work; and if found deficient, another will succeed to it without any trouble to the State or any talk on the subject through the Union. Chicago was intended as a town of export for corn, and, therefore, the corn stores have received first attention. When I was there, they were in perfect working order.

From Chicago we went on to Cleveland, a town in the State of Ohio on Lake Erie, again travelling by the sleeping-cars. I found that these cars were universally mentioned with great horror and disgust by Americans of the upper class. They always declared that they would not travel in them on any account. Noise and dirt were the two objections. They are very noisy, but to us belonged the happy power of sleeping down noise. I invariably slept all through the night, and knew nothing about the noise.

They are also very dirty – extremely dirty – dirty so as to cause much annoyance. But then they are not quite so dirty as the day cars. If dirt is to be a bar against travelling in America, men and women must stay at home. For myself I don't much care for dirt, having a strong reliance on soap and water and scrubbing brushes. No one regards poisons who carries antidotes in which he has perfect faith.

Cleveland is another pleasant town, pleasant as Milwaukee and Portland. The streets are handsome, and are shaded by grand avenues of trees. One of these streets is over a mile in length, and throughout the whole of it, there are trees on each side – not little paltry trees as are to be seen on the boulevards of Paris, but spreading elms – the beautiful American elm which not only spreads, but droops also, and makes more of its foliage than any other tree extant.

And there is a square in Cleveland, well sized, as large as Russell Square I should say, with open paths across it, and containing one or two handsome buildings. I cannot but think that all men and women in London would be great gainers if the iron rails of the squares were thrown down, and the grassy enclosures thrown open to the public. Of course the edges of the turf would be worn, and the paths would not keep their exact shapes. But the prison look would be banished and the sombre sadness of the squares would be relieved.

I was particularly struck by the size and comfort of the houses at Cleveland. All down that street of which I have spoken, they do not stand continuously together, but are detached and separate; houses which in England would require some fifteen or eighteen hundred a year for their maintenance. In the States, however, men commonly expend upon house rent a much greater proportion of their income than they do in England. With us it is, I believe, thought that a man should certainly not apportion more than a seventh of his spending income to his house rent, some say not more than a tenth.

But in many cities of the States a man is thought to live well within bounds if he so expends a fourth. There can be no doubt as to Americans living in better houses than Englishmen, making the comparison of course between men of equal incomes. But the Englishman has many more incidental expenses than the American. He spends more on wine, on entertainments, on horses, and on amusements. He has a more numerous establishment, and keeps up the adjuncts and outskirts of his residence with a more finished neatness.

These houses in Cleveland were very good, as indeed they are in most northern towns, but some of them have been erected with an amount of bad taste that is almost incredible. It is not uncommon to see in front of a square brick house a wooden quasi-Greek portico, with a pediment and Ionic columns, equally high with the house itself. Wooden columns with Greek capitals attached to the doorways, and wooden pediments over the windows, are very frequent. As a rule these are attached to houses which, without such ornamentation, would be simple, unpretentious, square, roomy residences. An Ionic or Corinthian capital stuck

on to a log of wood called a column, and then fixed promiscu-
ously to the outside of an ordinary house, is to my eye the vilest
of architectural pretences. Little turrets are better than this; or
even brown battlements made of mortar. Except in America I
do not remember to have seen these vicious bits of white timber,
timber painted white, plastered on to the fronts and sides of red-
brick houses.

Again we went on by rail to Buffalo. I have travelled some
thousands of miles by railway in the States, taking long journeys
by night and longer journeys by day; but I do not remember
that while doing so I ever made acquaintance with an American.
To an American lady in a railway car I should no more think
of speaking than I should to an unknown female in the next pew
to me at a London Church.

It is hard to understand from whence come the laws which
govern societies in this respect, but there are different laws in
different societies, which soon obtain recognition for themselves. American ladies are much given to talking, and are generally free from all *mauvaise honte*. They are collected in manner,
well instructed, and resolved to have their share of the social advantages of the world. In this phase of life they come out more
strongly than English women.

But on a railway journey, be it ever so long, they are never
seen speaking to a stranger. English women, however, on English
railways are generally willing to converse. They will do so if they
be on a journey, but will not open their mouths if they be simply
passing backwards and forwards between their homes and some
neighbouring town.

We soon learn the rules on these subjects, but who makes the
rules? If you cross the Atlantic with an American lady you invariably fall in love with her before the journey is over. Travel
with the same woman in a railway car for twelve hours, and you
will have written her down in your mind in quite other language
than that of love.

Over and beyond the grain elevators there is nothing specially
worthy of remark at Buffalo. It is a fine city, like all other American cities of its class. The streets are broad, the 'blocks' are high,
and cars on tramways run all day, and nearly all night as well.

Chapter 8

WHEN first the Americans of the northern States began to talk much of their country, their claims as to fine scenery were confined to Niagara and the Hudson River. Of Niagara I have spoken, and all the world has acknowledged that no claim made on that head can be regarded as exaggerated. As to the Hudson, I am not prepared to say so much generally, though there is one spot upon it which cannot be beaten for sweetness. I have been up and down the Hudson by water, and confess that the entire river is pretty. But the glory of the Hudson is at West Point itself, and thither on this occasion we went direct by railway, and there we remained for two days.

Of West Point there is something to be said independently of its scenery. It is the Sandhurst of the States. Here is their military school, from which officers are drafted to their regiments, and the tuition for military purposes is, I imagine, of a high order.

It must, of course, be borne in mind that West Point, even as at present arranged, is fitted to the wants of the old army, and not to that of the army now required. It can go but a little way to supply officers for 500,000 men, but would do much towards supplying them for 40,000. At the time of my visit to West Point the regular army of the northern States had not even then swelled itself to the latter number.

I found that there were 220 students at West Point, that about forty graduate every year, each of whom receives a commission in the army, that about 120 pupils are admitted every year and that in the course of every year about eighty either resign, or are called upon to leave on account of some deficiency, or fail in their final examination.

The result is simply this, that one third of those who enter succeeds, and that two thirds fail. The number of failures seemed to me to be terribly large – so large as to give great ground of hesitation to a parent in accepting a nomination for the college. I especially inquired into the particulars of these dismissals and resignations, and was assured that the majority of them take place in the first year of the pupilage. It is soon seen whether or no a lad has the mental and physical capacities necessary for the education and future life required of him, and care is taken that those shall be removed early as to whom it may be determined that the necessary capacity is clearly wanting.

If this is done – and I do not doubt it – the evil is much mitigated. The effect otherwise would be very injurious. The lads remain till they are perhaps one and twenty, and have then acquired aptitudes for military life, but no other aptitudes. At that age the education cannot be commenced anew, and, moreover, at that age the disgrace of failure is very injurious. The period of education used to be five years, but has now been reduced to four. This was done in order that a double class might be graduated in 1861 to supply the wants of the war. I believe it is considered that but for such necessity as that, the fifth year of education can be ill spared.

The discipline, to our English ideas, is very strict. In the first place no kind of beer, wine, or spirits is allowed at West Point. The law upon this point may be said to be very vehement, for it debars even the visitors at the hotel from the solace of a glass of beer. The hotel is within the bounds of the college, and as the lads might become purchasers at the bar, there is no bar allowed.

Any breach of this law leads to instant expulsion or, I should say rather, any detection of such breach. The officer who showed us over the college assured me that the presence of a glass of wine in a young man's room would secure his exclusion, even though there should be no evidence that he had tasted it. He was very firm as to this, but a little bird of West Point, whose information, though not official or probably accurate in words, seemed to me to be worthy of reliance in general, told me that eyes were wont to wink when such glasses of wine made themselves unnecessarily visible. Let us fancy an English mess of young men from seventeen to twenty-one, at which a mug of beer would be felony, and a glass of wine high treason !

But the whole management of the young with the Americans differs much from that in vogue with us. We do not require so much at so early an age, either in knowledge, in morals, or even in manliness. In America, if a lad be under control, as at West Point, he is called upon for an amount of labour, and a degree of conduct, which would be considered quite transcendental and out of the question in England. But if he be not under control, if at the age of eighteen he be living at home, or be from his circumstances exempt from professorial power, he is a full-fledged man with his pipe apparatus and his bar acquaintances.

And then I was told at West Point how needful and yet how painful it was that all should be removed who were in any way deficient in credit to the establishment.

'Our rules are very exact,' my informant told me; 'but the carrying out of our rules is a task not always very easy.' As to this also I had already heard something from that little bird of West Point, but of course I wisely assented to my informant, remarking that discipline in such an establishment was essentially necessary. The little bird had told me that discipline at West Point had been rendered terribly difficult by political interference.

'A young man will be dismissed by the unanimous voice of the Board, and will be sent away. And then, after a week or two, he will be sent back, with an order from Washington, that another trial shall be given him. The lad will march back into the college with all the honours of a victory, and will be conscious of a triumph over the superintendent and his officers.'

'And is that common?' I asked.

'Not at the present moment,' I was told. 'But it was common before the war. While Mr Buchanan, and Mr Pierce, and Mr Polk [15] were Presidents, no officer or board of officers then at West Point was able to dismiss a lad whose father was a Southerner, and who had friends among the Government.'

Not only was this true of West Point, but the same allegation is true as to all matters of patronage throughout the United States. During the three or four last Presidencies, and I believe back to the time of Jackson, there has been an organized system of dishonesty in the management of all beneficial places under the control of the Government. I doubt whether any despotic court of Europe has been so corrupt in the distribution of places – that is in the selection of public officers – as has been the assemblage of statesmen at Washington. And this is the evil which the country is now expiating with its blood and treasure. It has allowed its knaves to stand in the high places, and now it finds that knavish works have brought about evil results.

We went into all the schools of the college, and made ourselves fully aware that the amount of learning imparted was far above our comprehension. It always occurs to me in looking through the new schools of the present day, that I ought to be thankful to persons who know so much for condescending to speak to me at all in plain English.

I said a word to the gentleman who was with me about horses, seeing a lot of lads going to their riding lesson. But he was down upon me, and crushed me instantly beneath the weight of my own ignorance. He walked me up to the image of a horse, which he took to pieces bit by bit, taking off skin, muscle, flesh, nerves and bones, till the animal was a heap of atoms, and assured me that the anatomy of the horse throughout was one of the necessary studies of the place. We afterwards went to see the riding. The horses themselves were poor enough. This was accounted for by the fact that such of them as had been found fit for military service had been taken for the use of the army.

And then we were taken to the chapel, and there saw displayed as trophies, two of our own dear old English flags. I have seen many a banner hung up in token of past victory, and many a flag taken on the field of battle mouldering by degrees into dust on some chapel's wall, but they have not been the flags of England. Till this day I had never seen our own colours in any position but one of self-assertion and independent power. From the tone used by the gentleman who showed them to me, I could gather that he would have passed them by had he not foreseen that he could not do so without my notice.

'I don't know that we are right to put them there,' he said.

'Quite right,' was my reply, 'as long as the world does such things.'

In private life it is vulgar to triumph over one's friends, and malicious to triumph over one's enemies. We have not got so far yet in public life, but I hope we are advancing toward it. In the meantime I did not begrudge the Americans our two flags. If we keep flags and cannons taken from our enemies, and show them about as signs of our own prowess after those enemies have become friends, why should not others do so as regards us? It clearly would not be well for the world that we should always beat other nations and never be beaten. I did not begrudge that chapel our two flags. But nevertheless the sight of them made me sick in the stomach and uncomfortable.

As an Englishman I do not want to be ascendant over anyone. But it makes me very ill when anyone tries to be ascendant over me. I wish we could send back with our compliments all the trophies that we hold, carriage paid, and get back in return those two flags and any other flag or two of our own that may be doing similar duty about the world. I take it that the parcel sent away would be somewhat more bulky than that which would reach us in return.

The discipline at West Point seemed, as I have said, to be very severe but it seemed also that the severity could not in all cases be maintained. The hours of study also were long, being nearly continuous throughout the day.

'English lads of that age could not do it,' I said; thus confessing that English lads must have in them less power of sustained work than those of America.

'They must do it here,' said my informant, 'or else leave us.'

And then he took us off to one of the young gentlemen's quarters, in order that we might see the nature of their rooms. We found the young gentleman fast asleep on his bed, and felt uncommonly grieved that we should have thus intruded on him. As the hour was one of those allocated by my informant in the distribution of the day to private study, I could not but take the present occupation of the embryo warrior as an indication that the amount of labour required might be occasionally too much even for an American youth.

'The heat makes one so uncommonly drowsy,' said the young man.

I was not the least surprised at the exclamation. The air of the apartment had been warmed up to such a pitch by the hot-pipe apparatus of the building that prolonged life to me would, I should have thought, be out of the question in such an atmosphere.

'Do you always have it as hot as this?' I asked.

The young man swore that it was so, and with considerable energy expressed his opinion that all his health and spirits and vitality were being baked out of him. He seemed to have a strong opinion on the matter, for which I respected him; but it had never occurred to him, and did not then occur to him, that anything could be done to moderate the deathly flow of hot air which came up to him from the neighbouring infernal regions. He was pale in the face, and all the lads there were pale. American lads and lasses are all pale. Men at thirty and women at twenty-five have had all semblance of youth baked out of them. Infants even are not rosy, and the only shades known on the cheeks of children are those composed of brown, yellow, and white. All this comes of those damnable hot-air pipes with which every tenement in America is infested.

'We cannot do without them,' they say. 'Our cold is so intense that we must heat our houses throughout. Open fireplaces in a few rooms would not keep our toes and fingers from the frost.'

There is much in this. The assertion is no doubt true, and thereby a great difficulty is created. It is no doubt quite within the power of American ingenuity to moderate the heat of these stoves, and to produce such an atmosphere as may be most conducive to health. In hospitals no doubt this will be done; perhaps is done at present, though even in hospitals I have thought the air hotter than it should be. But hot-air-drinking is like dram-drinking. There is the machine within the house capable of supplying any quantity, and those who consume it unconsciously increase their draughts, and take their drams stronger and stronger, till a breath of fresh air is felt to be a blast direct from Boreas.

There is no intercourse by road between West Point and other towns and villages on the river side, and any such intercourse even by water is looked upon with jealousy by the authorities. The wish is that West Point should be isolated and kept apart for military instruction to the exclusion of all other purposes whatever, especially love-making purposes. The coming over from the other side of the water of young ladies by the ferry is regarded as a great hindrance. They will come, and then the military students will talk to them. We all know to what such talking leads!

A lad when I was there had been tempted to get out of barracks in plain clothes, in order that he might call on a young lady at the hotel and was in consequence obliged to abandon his commission and retire from the Academy. Will that young lady ever again sleep quietly in her bed? I should hope not.

An opinion was expressed to me that there should be no hotel in such a place, that there should be no ferry, no roads, no means by which the attention of the students should be distracted, that these military Rasselases should live in a happy military valley from which might be excluded both strong drinks and female charms – those two poisons from which youthful military ardour is supposed to suffer so much.

It always seems to me that such training begins at the wrong end. I will not say that nothing should be done to keep lads of eighteen from strong drinks. I will not even say that there should not be some line of moderation with reference to feminine allurements. But as a rule the restraint should come from the sense, good feeling, and education of him who is restrained. There is no embargo on the beer-shops either at Harrow or at Oxford – and certainly none upon the young ladies. Occasional damage may accrue from habits early depraved, or a heart too early and too easily susceptible; but the injury so done is not, I think, equal to that inflicted by a Draconian code of morals, which will probably be evaded, and will certainly create a desire for its evasion.

Nevertheless, I feel assured that West Point, taken as a whole, is an excellent military academy, and that young men have gone forth from it, and will go forth from it, fit for officers as far as training can make men fit. The fault, if fault there be, is that which is to be found in so many of the institutions of the United States and is one so allied to a virtue that no foreigner has a right to wonder that it is regarded in the light of a virtue by all Americans. There has been an attempt to make the place too perfect. In the desire to have the establishment self-sufficient at all points, more has been attempted than human nature can achieve.

The lad is taken to West Point, and it is presumed that from the moment of his reception, he shall expend every energy of his mind and body in making himself a soldier. At fifteen he is not to be a boy, at twenty he is not to be a young man. He is to be a gentleman, a soldier, and an officer. I believe that those who leave the College for the army are gentlemen, soldiers, and officers, and therefore the result is good. But they are also young men and it seems that they have become so, not in accordance with their training, but in spite of it.

But I have another complaint to make against the authorities of West Point, which they will not be able to answer so easily as that already preferred. What right can they have to take the very prettiest spot on the Hudson – the prettiest spot on the continent – one of the prettiest spots which Nature, with all her vagaries, ever formed – and shut it up from all the world for purposes of war? Would not any plain, however ugly, do for military exercises? Cannot broadsword, goose-step and double quick time be instilled into young hands and legs in any field of thirty, forty, or fifty acres? I wonder whether these lads appreciate the fact that they are studying fourteen hours a day amidst the sweetest river, rock, and mountain scenery that the imagination can conceive.

Of course it will be said that the world at large is not excluded from West Point, that the ferry to the place is open, and that there is even an hotel there, closed against no man or woman who will consent to become a teetotaller for the period of his visit. I must admit that this is so; but still one feels that one is only admitted as a guest. I want to go and live at West Point and why should I be prevented? The Government had a right to buy it of course, but Government should not buy up the prettiest spots on a country's surface. If I were an American I should make a grievance of this but Americans will suffer things from their Government which no Englishman would endure.

Chapter 9

SPEAKING of New York as a traveller I have two faults to find with it. In the first place there is nothing to see and in the second place there is no mode of getting about to see anything. Nevertheless New York is a most interesting city. It is the third biggest city in the known world – for those Chinese congregations of unwinged ants are not cities in the known world. In no other city is there a population so mixed and cosmopolitan in their modes of life. And yet in no other city that I have seen are there such strong and ever-visible characteristics of the social and political bearings of the nation to which it belongs.

New York appears to me as infinitely more American than Boston, Chicago, or Washington. It has no peculiar attribute of its own, as have those three cities, Boston in its literature and accomplished intelligence, Chicago in its internal trade, and Washington in its congressional and State politics. New York has its literary aspirations, its commercial grandeur, and – heaven knows – it has its politics also. But these do not strike the visitor as being specially characteristic of the city. That it is pre-eminently American is its glory or its disgrace, as men of different ways of thinking may decide upon it. Free institutions, general education, and the ascendancy of dollars are the words written on every paving-stone along Fifth Avenue, down Broadway, and up Wall Street. Every man can vote and values the privilege. Every man can read, and uses the privilege. Every man worships the dollar, and is down before his shrine from morning to night.

As regards voting and reading no American will be angry with me for saying so much of him, and no Englishman, whatever may be his ideas as to the franchise in his own country, will conceive that I have said aught to the dishonour of an American. But as to that dollar-worshipping, it will of course seem that I am abusing the New Yorkers. We all know what a wretchedly wicked thing money is! How it stands between us and heaven! How it hardens our hearts, and makes vulgar our thoughts! Dives has ever gone to the devil, while Lazarus has been laid up in heavenly lavender. The hand that employs itself in compelling gold to enter the service of man has always been stigmatized as the ravisher of things sacred.

The world is agreed about that, and therefore the New Yorker is in a bad way. There are very few citizens in any town known to me which under this dispensation are in a good way, but the New Yorker is in about the worst way of all. Other men, the world over, worship regularly at the shrine with matins and vespers, nones and complines, and whatever other daily services may be known to the religious houses; but the New Yorker is always on his knees.

This is the amount of the charge which I bring against New York; and now having laid on my paint thickly, I shall proceed, like an unskilful artist, to scrape a great deal of it off again. New York has been a leading commercial city in the world for not more than fifty or sixty years. As far as I can learn, its population at the close of the last century did not exceed 60,000, and ten years later it had not reached 100,000. In 1860 it had reached nearly 800,000 in the city of New York itself. To this number must be added the numbers of Brooklyn, Williamsburg, and the city of New Jersey, in order that a true conception may be had of the population of this American metropolis, seeing that those places are as much a part of New York as Southwark is of London. By this the total will be swelled to considerably above a million.

It will no doubt be admitted that this growth has been very fast, and that New York may well be proud of it. Increase of population is, I take it, the only trustworthy sign of a nation's success or of a city's success. We boast that London has beaten the other cities of the world, and think that the boast is enough to cover all the social sins for which London has to confess her guilt. New York beginning with 60,000 sixty years since has now a million souls – a million mouths, all of which eat a sufficiency of bread, all of which speak *ore rotundo*, and almost all of which can read. And this has come of its love of dollars.

The making of money is the work of man but he need not take

his work to bed with him, and have it ever by his side at table, amidst his family in church, while he disports himself, as he declares his passion to the girl of his heart, in the moments of his softest bliss, and at the periods of his most solemn ceremonies. That many do so elsewhere than in New York, in London, for instance, in Paris, among the mountains of Switzerland, and the steppes of Russia, I do not doubt. But there is generally a veil thrown over the object of the worshipper's idolatry. In New York one's ears are constantly filled with the fanatic's voice as he prays, one's eyes are always on the familiar altar. The frankincense from the temple is ever in one's nostrils. I have never walked down Fifth Avenue alone without thinking of money. I have never walked there with a companion without talking of it. I fancy that every man there, in order to maintain the spirit of the place, should bear on his forehead a label stating how many dollars he is worth, and that every label should be expected to assert a falsehood.

I do not think that New York has been less generous in the use of its money than other cities, or that the men of New York generally are so. Perhaps I might go farther and say that in no city has more been achieved for humanity by the munificence of its richest citizens than in New York. Its hospitals, asylums, and institutions for the relief of all ailments to which flesh is heir, are very numerous, and beyond praise in the excellence of their arrangements. And this has been achieved in a great degree by private liberality.

Men in America are not as a rule anxious to leave large fortunes to their children. The millionaire when making his will very generally gives back a considerable portion of the wealth which he has made to the city in which he made it. The rich citizen is always anxious that the poor citizen shall be relieved. It is a point of honour with him to raise the character of his municipality, and to provide that the deaf and dumb, the blind, the mad, the idiots, the old, and the incurable shall have such alleviation in their misfortune as skill and kindness can afford.

Nor is the New Yorker a hugger-mugger with his money. He does not hide up his dollars in old stockings and keep rolls of gold in hidden pots. He does not even invest it where it will not grow but only produce small though sure fruit. He builds houses, he speculates largely, he spreads himself in trade to the extent of his wings, and not seldom somewhat further. He scatters his wealth broadcast over strange fields, trusting that it may grow with an increase of an hundred-fold, but bold to bear the loss should the strange field prove itself barren. His regret at losing his money is by no means commensurate with his desire to make it. In this there is a living spirit which to me divests the dollar-worshipping idolatry of something of its ugliness. The hand when closed on the gold is instantly reopened. The idolator is anxious to get, but he is anxious also to spend. He is energetic to the last, and has no comfort with his stock unless it breeds with trans-atlantic rapidity of procreation.

No other American city is so intensely American as New York. It is generally considered that the inhabitants of New England, the Yankees properly so called, have the American characteristics of physiognomy in the fullest degree. The lantern jaws, the thin and lithe body, the dry face on which there has been no tint of the rose since the baby's long clothes were first abandoned, the harsh, thick hair, the thin lips, the intelligent eyes, the sharp voice with the nasal twang – not altogether harsh, though sharp and nasal – all these traits are supposed to belong especially to the Yankee. Perhaps it was so once, but at present they are, I think, more universally common in New York than in any other part of the States. Go to Wall Street, the front of the Astor House, and the regions about Trinity Church, and you will find them in their fullest perfection.

What circumstances of blood or food, of early habit or subsequent education, have created for the latter-day American his present physiognomy? It is as completely marked, as much his own, as is that of any race under the sun that has bred in and in for centuries. But the American owns a more mixed blood than any other race known. The chief stock is English, which is itself so mixed that no man can trace its ramifications. With this are mingled the bloods of Ireland, Holland, France, Sweden and Germany. All this has been done within but a few years, so that the American may be said to have no claims to any national type of face.

Nevertheless, no man has a type of face so clearly national as the American. He is acknowledged by it all over the continent of Europe, and on his own side of the water is gratified by knowing that he is never mistaken for his English visitor. I think it comes from the hot-air pipes and from dollar worship. In the Jesuit his mode of dealing with things divine has given a peculiar cast of countenance and why should not the American be similarly moulded by his special aspirations? As to the hot-air pipes, there can, I think, be no doubt that to them is to be charged the murder of all rosy cheeks throughout the States. If the effect was to be noticed simply in the dry faces of the men about Wall Street, I should be very indifferent to the matter. But the young ladies of Fifth Avenue are in the same category. The very pith and marrow of life is baked out of their young bones by the hot-air chambers to which they are accustomed. Hot air is the great destroyer of American beauty.

In saying that there is very little to be seen in New York, I have also said that there is no way of seeing that little. My assertion amounts to this – that there are no cabs. To the reading world at large this may not seem to be much, but let the reading world go to New York, and it will find out how much the deficiency means. In London, in Paris, in Florence, in Rome, in Havana, or at Grand Cairo, the cab-driver or attendant does not merely drive the cab or belabour the donkey, but he is the visitor's easiest and cheapest guide. In London, the Tower, Westminster Abbey, and Madame Tussaud, are found by the stranger without difficulty, and almost without a thought, because the cab-driver knows the whereabouts and the way. Space is moreover annihilated, and the huge distances of the English metropolis are brought within the scope of mortal power. But in New York there is no such institution.

In New York there are street omnibuses as we have – there are street cars such as last year we declined to have – and there are very excellent public carriages; but none of these give you the accommodation of a cab, nor can all of them combined do so. The omnibuses, though clean and excellent, were to me very unintelligible. They have no conductor to them. To know their different lines and usages a man should have made a scientific study of the city. To those going up and down Broadway I became accustomed, but in them I was never quite at my ease.

And then there are street cars – very long omnibuses – which run on rails but are dragged by horses. They are capable of holding forty passengers each, and as far as my experience goes carry an average load of sixty. The fare of the omnibus is six cents or threepence. That of the street car five cents or twopence halfpenny. They run along the different avenues, taking the length of the city. In the upper or new part of the town their course is simple enough, but as they descend to the Bowery, Peckslip and Peal Street, nothing can be conceived more difficult or devious than their courses. The Broadway omnibus, on the other hand, is a straightforward honest vehicle in the lower part of the town, becoming, however, dangerous and miscellaneous when it ascends to Union Square and the vicinities of fashionable life.

The street cars are manned with conductors and therefore are free from many of the perils of the omnibus, but they have perils of their own. They are always quite full. By that I mean that every seat is crowded, that there is a double row of men and women standing down the centre, and that the driver's platform in front is full, and also the conductor's platform behind.

I soon gave up all attempts at keeping a seat in one of these cars. It became my practice to sit down on the outside iron rail behind, and as the conductor generally sat in my lap I was in a measure protected. As for the inside of these vehicles, the women of New York were, I must confess, too much for me. I would no sooner place myself on a seat, than I would be called on by a mute, unexpressive, but still impressive stare into my face, to surrender my place. From cowardice if not from gallantry I would always obey; and as this led to discomfort and an irritated spirit, I preferred nursing the conductor on the hard bar in the rear.

And here if I seem to say a word against women in America, I beg that it may be understood that I say that word only against a certain class; and even as to that class I admit that they are respectable, intelligent, and, as I believe, industrious. Their manners, however, are to me more odious than those of any other human beings that I ever met elsewhere. Nor can I go on with that which I have to say without carrying my apology further, lest perchance I should be misunderstood by some American women whom I would not only exclude from my censure, but would include in the very warmest eulogium which words of mine could express as to those of the female sex whom I love and admire the most.

The happy privileges with which women are at present blessed, have come to them from the spirit of chivalry. That spirit has taught men to endure in order that women may be at their ease; and has generally taught women to accept the ease bestowed on them with grace and thankfulness. But in America the spirit of chivalry has sunk deeper among men than it has among women. It must be borne in mind that in that country material well-being and education are more extended than with us and that, therefore, men there have learned to be chivalrous who with us have hardly progressed so far.

The conduct of men to women throughout the States is always gracious. They have learned the lesson. But it seems to me that the women have not advanced as far as the men have done. They have acquired a sufficient perception of the privileges which chivalry gives them, but no perception of that return which chivalry demands from them. I have heard young Americans complain of it, swearing that they must change the whole tenor of their habits towards women.

In no position of life does an unfortunate man become more liable to anti-feminine atrocities than in the centre of one of these street cars. The woman, as she enters, drags after her a misshapen, dirty mass of battered wirework, which she calls her crinoline, and which adds as much to her grace and comfort as a log of wood does to a donkey when tied to the animal's leg in a paddock. Of this she takes much heed, not managing it so that it may be conveyed up the carriage with some decency, but striking it about against men's legs, and heaving it with violence over people's knees. The touch of a real woman's dress is in itself delicate but these blows from a harpy's fins are loathsome. If there be two of them they talk loudly together, having a theory that modesty has been put out of Court by women's rights.

But, though not modest, the woman I describe is ferocious in her propriety. She ignores the whole world around her, and as she sits with raised chin and face flattened by affectation, she pretends to declare aloud that she is positively not aware that any man is even near her. She speaks as though to her, in her womanhood, the neighbourhood of men was the same as that of dogs or cats. They are there, but she does not hear them, see them, or even acknowledge them by any courtesy of motion.

You will meet these women daily, hourly, everywhere in the streets. Now and again you will find them in society, making themselves even more odious there than elsewhere. Who they are, whence they come and why they are so unlike that other race of women of which I have spoken, you will settle for yourself. Do we not all say of our chance acquaintances after half an hour's conversation – nay, after half an hour spent in the same room without conversation – that this woman is a lady, and that that other woman is not? They jostle each other even among us, but never seem to mix. They are closely allied; but neither imbues the other with her attributes. Both shall be equally well-born, or both shall be equally ill-born; but still it is so. The contrast exists in England, but in America it is much stronger. In England women become ladylike or vulgar. In the States they are either charming or odious.

See that female walking down Broadway. She is not exactly such a one as her I have attempted to describe on her entrance into the street car for this lady is well-dressed, if fine clothes will make well-dressing. The machinery of her hoops is not battered, and altogether she is a personage much more distinguished in all her expenditures.

But yet she is a copy of the other woman. Look at the train which she drags behind her over the dirty pavement, where dogs have been, and chewers of tobacco, and everything concerned with filth except a scavenger. At every hundred yards some unhappy man treads upon the silken swab which she trails behind her – loosening it dreadfully at the girth one would say; and then see the style of face and the expression of features with which she accepts the sinner's half-muttered apology. The world, she supposes, owes her everything because of her silken train – even room enough in a crowded thoroughfare to drag it along unmolested. But, according to her theory, she owes the world nothing in return. She is a woman with perhaps a hundred dollars on her back, and having done the world the honour of wearing them in the world's presence, expects to be repaid by the world's homage and chivalry.

And now to continue with the street cars. They run, as I have said, the length of the town, taking parallel lines. They will take you from the Astor House, near the bottom of the town, for miles and miles northward – half way up the Hudson river – for, I believe, fivepence. They are very slow, averaging about five miles an hour; but they are very sure. For regular inhabitants, who have to travel five or six miles perhaps to their daily work, they are excellent. I have nothing really to say against the street cars. But they do not fill the place of cabs.

There are, however, public carriages, roomy vehicles dragged by two horses, clean and nice, and very well suited to ladies visiting the city. But they have none of the attributes of the cab. As a rule they are not to be found standing about. They are very slow. They are very dear. A dollar an hour is the regular charge but one cannot regulate one's motion by the hour. Going out to dinner and back costs two dollars, over a distance which in London would cost two shillings. As a rule, the cost is four times that of a cab and the rapidity half that of a cab. Under these circumstances I think I am justified in saying that there is no mode of getting about in New York to see anything.

Chapter 10

'HAVE you seen any of our great institootions, sir?' That of course is a question which is put to every Englishman who has visited New York, and the Englishman who intends to say that he has seen New York, should visit many of them. I went to schools, hospitals, lunatic asylums, institutes for deaf and dumb, water works, historical societies, telegraph offices, and large commercial establishments. I rather think that I did my work in a thorough and conscientious manner, and I owe much gratitude to those who guided me on such occasions.

In all such matters, New York is pre-eminently great. All through the States suffering humanity receives so much attention that humanity can hardly be said to suffer. The daily recurring boast of 'our glorious institootions, sir', always provokes the ridicule of an Englishman. The words have become ridiculous, and it would, I think, be well for the nation if the term 'Institution' could be excluded from its vocabulary.

But, in truth, they are glorious. The country in this respect boasts, but it has done that which justifies a boast. The arrangements for supplying New York with water are magnificent. The drainage of the new part of the city is excellent. The hospitals are almost alluring. The lunatic asylum which I saw was perfect – though I did not feel obliged to the resident physician for introducing me to all the worst patients as countrymen of my own.

'An English lady, Mr Trollope. I'll introduce you. Quite a hopeless case. Two old women. They've been here fifty years. They're English. Another gentleman from England, Mr Trollope. A very interesting case! Confirmed inebriety.'

And as to the schools, it is almost impossible to mention them with too high a praise. I am speaking here specially of New York, though I might say the same of Boston, or of all New England. I do not know any contrast that would be more surprising to an Englishman, up to that moment ignorant of the matter, than that which he would find by visiting first of all a free school in London, and then a free school in New York. If he would also learn the number of children that are educated gratuitously in each of the two cities, and also the number in each which altogether lack education, he would, if susceptible of statistics, be surprised also at that.

But seeing and hearing are always more effective than mere figures. The female pupil at a free school in London is, as a rule, either a ragged pauper, or a charity girl, if not degraded at least stigmatized by the badges and dress of the Charity. We Englishmen know well the type of each, and have a fairly correct idea of the amount of education which is imparted to them. We see the result afterwards when the same girls become our servants, and the wives of our grooms and porters.

The female pupil at a free school in New York is neither a pauper nor a charity girl. She is dressed with the utmost decency. She is perfectly cleanly. In speaking to her, you cannot in any degree guess whether her father has a dollar a day, or three thousand dollars a year. Nor will you be enabled to guess by the manner in which her associates treat her. As regards her own manner to you, it is always the same as though her father were in all respects your equal.

As to the amount of her knowledge, I fairly confess that it is terrific. When, in the first room which I visited, a slight slim creature was had up before me to explain to me the properties of the hypotenuse I fairly confess that, as regards education, I backed down, and that I resolved to confine my criticisms to manner, dress, and general behaviour. In the next room I was more at my ease, finding that ancient Roman history was on the tapis.

'Why did the Romans run away with the Sabine women?' asked the mistress, herself a young woman of about three-and-twenty.

'Because they were pretty,' simpered out a little girl with a cherry mouth.

The answer did not give complete satisfaction and then followed a somewhat abstruse explanation on the subject of population. It was all done with good faith and a serious intent, and showed what it was intended to show – that the girls there educated had in truth reached the consideration of important subjects, and that they were leagues beyond that terrible repetition of A.B.C., to which, I fear, most of our free metropolitan schools are still necessarily confined.

You and I, reader, were we called on to superintend the education of girls of sixteen, might not select as favourite points either the hypotenuse, or the ancient methods of populating young colonies. There may be, and to us on the European side of the Atlantic there will be, a certain amount of absurdity in the transatlantic idea that all knowledge is knowledge, and that it should be imparted if it be not knowledge of evil.

But as to the general result, no fair-minded man or woman can have a doubt. That the lads and girls in these schools are excellently educated comes home as a fact to the mind of anyone who will look into the subject. The girl could not have got as far as the hypotenuse without a competent and abiding knowledge of much that is very far beyond the outside limits of what such girls know with us.

It was at least manifest in the other examination that the girls knew as well as I did who were the Romans, and who were the Sabine women. That all this is of use, was shown in the very gestures and bearings of the girl. *Emollit mores*, as Colonel Newcombe used to say. The young woman whom I had watched while she cooked her husband's dinner upon the banks of the Mississippi had doubtless learned all about the Sabine women, and I feel assured that she cooked her husband's dinner all the better for that knowledge and faced the hardships of the world with a better front than she would have done had she been ignorant on the subject.

In order to make a comparison between the schools of London and those of New York, I have called them both free schools. They are in fact more free in New York than they are in London, because in New York every boy and girl, let his parentage be what it may, can attend these schools without any payment. Thus an education as good as the American mind can compass, prepared with every care, carried on by highly paid tutors, under ample surveillance, provided with all that is most excellent in the way of rooms, desks, books, charts, maps, and implements, is brought actually within the reach of everybody.

I need not point out to Englishmen how different is the nature of schools in London. It must not, however, be supposed that these are charity schools. Such is not their nature. Let us say what we may as to the beauty of charity as a virtue, the recipient of charity in its customary sense among us is ever more or less degraded by the position. In the States that has been fully understood, and the schools to which I allude, are carefully preserved from any such taint. Throughout the States a separate tax is levied for the maintenance of these schools, and as the taxpayer supports them, he is of course entitled to the advantage which they confer. The child of the non-taxpayer is also entitled, and to him the boon, if strictly analysed, will come in the shape of a charity.

But under the system as it is arranged, this is not analysed. It is understood that the school is open to all in the ward to which it belongs, and no inquiry is made whether the pupil's parent has or has not paid anything towards the school's support. I found this theory carried out so far that at the deaf and dumb school, where some of the poorer children are wholly provided by the institution, care is taken to clothe them in dresses of different colours and different make, in order that nothing may attach to them which has the appearance of a badge. Political economists will see something of evil in this. But philanthropists will see very much that is good.

I saw some five or six hundred girls collected in one room, and heard them sing. The singing was very pretty, and it was all very nice; but I own that I was rather startled, and to tell the truth somewhat abashed, when I was invited to 'say a few words to them'. No idea of such a suggestion had dawned upon me, and I felt myself quite at a loss. To be called up before five hundred men is bad enough, but how much worse before that number of girls! What could I say but that they were all very pretty. As far as I can remember I did say that and nothing else. Very pretty they were, and neatly dressed, and attractive; but among them all there was not a pair of rosy cheeks. How should there be, when every room in the building was heated up to the condition of an oven by those damnable hot-air pipes!

In England a taste for very large shops has come up during the last twenty years. A firm is not doing a good business, or at any rate a distinguished business, unless he can assert in his trade card that he occupies at least half a dozen houses – Nos. 105, 106, 107, 108, 109, and 110. The old way of paying for what you want over the counter is gone; and when you buy a yard of tape or a new carriage – for either of which articles you will probably visit the same establishment – you go through about the same amount of ceremony as when you sell a thousand pounds out of the stocks *in propria persona*.

But all this is still further exaggerated in New York. Mr Stewart's store there is perhaps the handsomest institution in the city, and his hall of audience for new carpets is a magnificent saloon.

'You have nothing like that in England,' my friend said to me as he walked me through it in triumph.

'I wish we had nothing approaching to it,' I answered.

For I confess to a liking for the old-fashioned private shops. Harper's establishment for the manufacture and sale of books is also very wonderful. Everything is done on the premises, down to the very colouring of the paper which lines the covers, and places the gilding on their backs. The firm prints, engraves, electroplates, sews, binds, publishes, and sells wholesale and retail. I have no doubt that the authors have rooms in the attics where the other slight initiatory step is taken towards the production of literature.

New York is built upon an island, which is I believe about ten miles long, counting from the southern point at the Battery up to Carmansville, to which place the city is presumed to extend northwards. This island is called Manhattan – a name which I have always thought would have been more graceful for the city than that of New York. It is formed by the Sound or East river, which divides the continent from Long Island, by the Hudson river which joins the East river at the city foot, and by a small stream called the Harlem river which runs out of the Hudson and meanders away into the Sound at the north of the city, thus cutting the island off from the mainland.

The breadth of the island does not much exceed two miles,

and therefore the city is long, and not capable of extension in point of breadth. In its old days it clustered itself round about the Point, and stretched itself up from there along the quays of the two waters. The streets down in this part of the town are devious enough, twisting themselves about with delightful irregularity; but as the city grew there came the taste for parallelograms, and the upper streets are rectangular and numbered.

Broadway, the street of New York with which the world is generally best acquainted, begins at the southern point of the town and goes northward through it. For some two miles and a half it walks away in a straight line, and then it turns to the left towards the Hudson, and becomes in fact a continuation of another street called the Bowery, which comes up in a devious course from the south-east extremity of the island. From that time Broadway never again takes a straight course, but crosses the various Avenues in an oblique direction till it becomes the Bloomingdale road, and under that name takes itself out of town.

There are eleven so-called Avenues, which descend in absolutely straight lines from the northern, and at present unsettled, extremity of the new town, making their way southward till they lose themselves among the old streets. These are called First Avenue, Second Avenue, and so on. The town had already progressed two miles up northwards from the Battery before it had caught the parallelogrammic fever from Philadelphia, for at about that distance we find 'First Street'. First Street runs across the Avenues from water to water, and then Second Street. I will not name them all, seeing that they go up to 154th Street! They do so at least on the map, and I believe on the lamp-posts. But the houses are not yet built in order beyond 50th or 60th Street. The other hundred streets, each of two miles long, with the Avenues which are mostly unoccupied for four or five miles, is the ground over which the young New Yorkers are to spread themselves. I do not in the least doubt that they will occupy it all, and that 154th Street will find itself too narrow a boundary for the population.

The Fifth Avenue is the Belgrave Square, the Park Lane, and the Pall Mall of New York. It is certainly a very fine street. The houses in it are magnificent, not having that aristocratic look which some of our detached London residences enjoy, or the palatial appearance of an old-fashioned hotel in Paris, but an air of comfortable luxury and commercial wealth which is not excelled by the best houses of any other town that I know. They are houses, not hotels or palaces; but they are very roomy houses, with every luxury that complete finish can give them. Many of them cover large spaces of ground, and their rent will sometimes go up as high as 800l. and 1,000l. a year.

Generally the best of these houses are owned by those who live in them, and rent is not therefore paid. But this is not always the case, and the sums named above may be taken as expressing their value. In England a man should have a very large income indeed who could afford to pay 1,000l. a year for his house in London. Such a one would as a matter of course have an establishment in the country, and be an Earl or a Duke or a millionaire. But it is different in New York. The resident there shows his wealth chiefly by his house, and though he may probably have a villa at Newport or a box somewhere up the Hudson he has no second establishment. Such a house therefore will not represent a total expenditure of above 4,000l. a year.

There are churches on each side of Fifth Avenue – perhaps five or six within sight at one time, which add much to the beauty of the street. They are well-built, and in fairly good taste. These, added to the general well-being and splendid comfort of the place, give it an effect better than the architecture of the individual houses would seem to warrant. I own that I have enjoyed the vista as I have walked up and down Fifth Avenue, and have felt that the city had a right to be proud of its wealth.

But the greatness and beauty and glory of wealth have on such occasions been all in all with me. I know no great man, no celebrated statesman, no philanthropist of peculiar note who has lived in Fifth Avenue. That gentleman on the right made a million of dollars by inventing a shirt-collar; this one on the left electrified the world by a lotion; as to the gentleman at the corner there – there are rumours about him and the Cuban slave-trade but my informant by no means knows that they are true. Such are the aristocracy of Fifth Avenue. I can only say that if I could make a million dollars by a lotion, I should certainly be right to live in such a house as one of those.

The suburbs of New York are, by the nature of the localities, divided from the city by water. New Jersey and Hoboken are on the other side of the Hudson, and in another State. Williamsburg and Brooklyn are in Long Island, which is part of the State of New York. But these places are as easily reached as Lambeth is reached from Westminster. Steam ferries ply every three or four minutes, and into these boats, coaches, carts, and waggons of any size or weight are driven. In fact they make no other stoppage to the commerce than that occasioned by the payment of a few cents.

Such payment no doubt is a stoppage, and therefore it is that New Jersey, Brooklyn, and Williamsburg are, at any rate in appearance, very dull and uninviting. They are, however, very populous. Many of the quieter citizens prefer to live there; and I am told that the Brooklyn tea-parties consider themselves to be, in aesthetic feeling, very much ahead of anything of the kind in the more opulent centres of the city.

In beauty of scenery Staten Island is very much the prettiest of the suburbs of New York. The view from the hill side in Staten Island down upon New York harbour is very lovely. It is the only really good view of that magnificent harbour which I have been able to find.

But the glory of New York is the Central Park – its glory in the mind of all New Yorkers of the present day. The first question asked of you is whether you have seen the Central Park, and the second is as to what you think of it. It does not do to say simply that it is fine, grand, beautiful, and miraculous. You must swear by cock and pie that it is more fine, more grand, more beautiful, more miraculous than anything else of the kind anywhere. Here you encounter, in its most annoying form, that necessity for eulogium which presses you everywhere. For, in truth, taken as it is at present, the Central Park is not fine, nor grand, nor beautiful. As to the miracle, let that pass. It is perhaps as miraculous as some other great latter-day miracles.

But the Central Park is a very great fact, and affords a strong additional proof of the sense and energy of the people. It is very large, being over three miles long, and about three-quarters of a mile in breadth. When it was found that New York was extending itself, and becoming one of the largest cities of the world, a space was selected between Fifth and Seventh Avenues, immediately outside the limits of the city as then built, but nearly in the centre of the city as it is intended to be built. The ground around it became at once of great value; and I do not doubt that the present fashion of the Fifth Avenue about Twentieth Street will in course of time move itself up to the Fifth Avenue as it looks, or will look, over the Park at Seventieth, Eightieth, and Ninetieth Streets. The great waterworks of the city bring the Croton River, whence New York is supplied, by an aqueduct over the Harlem river into an enormous reservoir just above the Park; and hence it has come to pass that there will be water not only for sanitary and useful purposes, but also for ornament.

At present the Park, to English eyes, seems to be all road. The trees are not grown up, and the new embankments, and new lakes, and new ditches, and new paths give to the place anything but a picturesque appearance. The Central Park is good for what it will be, rather than for what it is. The summer heat is so very great that I doubt whether the people of New York will ever enjoy such verdure as our parks show. But there will be a pleasant assemblage of walks and waterworks, with fresh air and fine shrubs and flowers immediately within the reach of the citizens. All that art and energy can do will be done, and the Central Park doubtless will become one of the great glories of New York. When I was expected to declare that St James's Park, Green Park, Hyde Park, and Kensington Gardens, altogether, were nothing to it, I confess that I could only remain mute.

As I progress in my work I feel that duty will call upon me to write a separate chapter on hotels in general, and I will not, therefore, here say much about those in New York. I am inclined to think that few towns in the world, if any, afford on the whole better accommodation, but there are many in which the accommodation is cheaper.

Of the railways also I ought to say something. The fact respecting them which is most remarkable is that of their being continued into the centre of the town through the streets. The cars are not dragged through the city by locomotive engines, but by horses; the pace therefore is slow, but the convenience to travellers in being brought nearer to the centre of trade must be much felt. It is as though passengers from Liverpool and passengers from Bristol were carried on from Euston Square and Paddington along the New Road, Portland Place, and Regent Street to Pall Mall, or up the City Road to the Bank.

As a general rule, however, the railways, railway cars, and all about them are ill-managed. They are monopolies, and the public, through the press, has no restraining power upon them as it has in England. A parcel sent by express over a distance of forty miles will not be delivered within twenty-four hours. I once made my plaint on this subject at the bar or office of an hotel, and was told that no remonstrance was of avail.

'It is a monopoly,' the man told me, 'and if we say anything, we are told that if we do not like it we need not use it.'

In railway matters and postal matters time and punctuality are not valued in the States as they are with us, and the public seems to acknowledge that they must put up with defects – that they must grin and bear them in America, as the public no doubt do in Austria where such affairs are managed by a government bureau.

I cannot end this chapter without remarking that out of the population of New York more than one-eighth is composed of Germans. It is, I believe, computed that there are about 120,000 Germans in the city, and that only two other German cities in the world, Vienna and Berlin, have a larger German population than New York. The Germans are good citizens and thriving men, and are to be found prospering all over the northern and western parts of the Union. It seems that they are excellently well adapted to colonization, though they have in no instance become the dominant people in a colony, or carried with them their own language or their own laws. The French have done so in Algeria, in some of the West India islands, and quite as essentially into Lower Canada, where their language and laws still prevail. And yet it is, I think, beyond doubt that the French are not good colonists, as are the Germans.

Of the ultimate destiny of New York as one of the ruling

commercial cities of the world, it is, I think, impossible to doubt. Whether or no it will ever equal London in population I will not pretend to say. Even should it do so, should its numbers so increase as to enable it to say that it had done so, the question could not very well be settled. When it comes to pass that an assemblage of men in one so-called city have to be counted by millions, there arises the impossibility of defining the limits of that city, and of saying who belong to it and who do not. An arbitrary line may be drawn, but that arbitrary line, though perhaps false when drawn as including too much, soon becomes more false as including too little. Ealing, Acton, Fulham, Putney, Norwood, Sydenham, Blackheath, Woolwich, Greenwich, Stratford, Highgate, and Hampstead, are, in truth, component parts of London, and very shortly Brighton will be as much so.

Chapter 11

FROM New York we returned to Boston by Hartford, the capital, or one of the capitals of Connecticut. This proud little State is composed of two old provinces, of which Hartford and Newhaven were the two metropolitan towns.

Hartford is a pleasant little town, with English-looking houses, and an English-looking country around it. Here, as everywhere through the States, one is struck by the size and comfort of the residences. I sojourned there at the house of a friend, and could find no limit to the number of spacious sitting-rooms which it contained. The modest dining-room and drawing-room which suffice with us for men of seven or eight hundred a year would be regarded as very mean accommodation by persons of similar incomes in the States.

I found that Hartford was all alive with trade, and that wages were high, because there are there two factories for the manufacture of arms. Colt's pistols come over from Hartford, as do also Sharpe's rifles. Wherever arms can be prepared, or gunpowder, where clothes or blankets fit for soldiers can be made, or tents or standards, or things appertaining in any way to warfare, there trade was still brisk. No being is more costly in his requirements than a soldier, and no soldier so costly as the American. He must eat and drink of the best, and have good boots and warm bedding, and good shelter. There were during the Christmas of 1861 above half a million of soldiers so to be provided – the President, in his message made in December to Congress, declared the number to be above six hundred thousand – and therefore in such places as Hartford trade was very brisk.

Immediately on my arrival in Boston I heard that Mr Emerson[16] was going to lecture at the Tremont Hall on the subject of the war, and I resolved to go and hear him.

Mr Emerson is a Massachusetts man, very well known in Boston, and a great crowd was collected to hear him. I suppose there were some three thousand persons in the room. I confess that when he took his place before us my prejudices were against him. The matter in hand required no philosophy. It required common sense, and the very best of common sense. It demanded that he should be impassioned, for of what interest can any address be on a matter of public politics without passion? But it demanded that the passion should be winnowed, and free from all rhodomontade. I fancied what might be said on such a subject as that overlauded star-spangled banner, and how the star-spangled flag would look when wrapped in a mist of mystic Platonism.

But from the beginning to the end there was nothing mystic – no Platonism; and, if I remember rightly, the star-spangled banner was altogether omitted. To the national eagle he did allude.

'Your American eagle,' he said, 'is very well. Protect it here and abroad. But beware of the American peacock.'

He gave an account of the war from the beginning, showing how it had arisen, and how it had been conducted; and he did so with admirable simplicity and truth. He thought the North were right about the war and as I thought so also, I was not called upon to disagree with him. He was terse and perspicuous in his sentences, practical in his advice, and, above all things, true in what he said to his audience of themselves.

They who know America will understand how hard it is for a public man in the States to practise such truth in his addresses. Fluid compliments and high-flown national eulogium are expected. In this instance none were forthcoming. The North had risen with patriotism to make this effort, and it was now warned that in doing so it was simply doing its national duty.

And then came the subject of slavery. I had been told that Mr Emerson was an abolitionist, and knew that I must disagree with him on that head, if on no other. To me it has always seemed that to mix up the question of general abolition with this war must be the work of a man too ignorant to understand the real subject of the war, or too false to his country to regard it. Throughout the whole lecture I was waiting for Mr Emerson's abolition doctrine, but no abolition doctrine came. The words abolition and compensation were mentioned, and then there was an end of the subject. If Mr Emerson be an abolitionist he expressed his views very mildly on that occasion. On the whole the lecture was excellent, and that little advice about the pea-cock was in itself worth an hour's attention.

That practice of lecturing is 'quite an institution' in the States. So it is in England, my readers will say. But in England it is done in a different way, with a different object and with much less of result. With us, if I am not mistaken, lectures are mostly given gratuitously by the lecturer. They are got up here and there with some philanthropical object, and in the hope that an hour at the disposal of young men and women may be rescued from idleness. The subjects chosen are social, literary, philanthro-pic, romantic, geographical, scientific, religious, anything rather than political. The lecture-rooms are not usually filled to over-flowing, and there is often a question whether the real good achieved is worth the trouble taken. The most popular lectures are given by big people, whose presence is likely to be attractive; and the whole thing, I fear we must confess, is not pre-eminently successful.

In the northern States of America the matter stands on a very different footing. Lectures there are more popular than either theatres or concerts. Enormous halls are built for them. Tickets for long courses are taken with avidity. Very large sums are paid to popular lecturers, so that the profession is lucrative – more so, I am given to understand, than is the cognate profession of literature. The whole thing is done in great style. Music is intro-duced. The lecturer stands on a large raised platform, on which sit around him the bald and hoary-headed and superlatively wise. Ladies come in large numbers, especially those who aspire to soar above the frivolities of the world. Politics is the subject most popular, and most general.

The men and women of Boston could no more do without their lectures, than those of Paris could without their theatres. It is the decorous diversion of the best ordered of her citizens. The fast young men go to clubs, and the fast young women to dances, as fast young men and women do in other places that are wicked; but lecturing is the favourite diversion of the steady-minded Bostonian.

After all, I do not know that the result is very good. It does not seem that much will be gained by such lectures on either side of the Atlantic, except that respectable killing of an evening which might otherwise be killed less respectably.

I went to see a public library in the city, which, if not founded by Mr Bates[17] whose name is so well known in London as connected with the house of Messrs Baring, has been greatly enriched by him. It is by his money that it has been enabled to do its work. In this library there is a certain number of thousands of volumes – a great many volumes, as there are in most public libraries. There are books of all classes, from ponderous unreadable folios, of which learned men know the title-pages, down to the lightest literature. Novels are by no means eschewed – are rather, if I understand right, considered as one of the staples of the library.

From this library any book, excepting such rare volumes as in all libraries are considered holy, is given out to any inhabitant of Boston, without payment, on presentation of a simple request on a prepared form. In point of fact, it is a gratuitous circulating library open to all Boston, rich or poor, young or old. The books seemed in general to be confided to young children, who came as messengers from their fathers and mothers, or brothers and sisters. No question whatever is asked, if the applicant is known or the place of his residence undoubted. If there be no such knowledge, or there be any doubt as to the residence, the applicant is questioned, the object being to confine the use of the library to the bona fide inhabitants of the city. Practically the books are given to those who ask for them, whoever they may be.

Boston contains over 200,000 inhabitants, and all those 200,000 are entitled to them. Some twenty men and women are kept employed from morning to night in carrying on this circulating library; and there is, moreover, attached to the establishment a large reading-room supplied with papers and magazines, open to the public of Boston on the same terms.

I shall always look back to social life in Boston with great pleasure. I met there many men and women whom to know is a distinction, and with whom to be intimate is a great delight. It was a Puritan city, in which strict old Roundhead sentiments and laws used to prevail; but nowadays ginger is hot in the mouth there, and in spite of the war there were cakes and ale.

There was a law passed in Massachusetts in the old days that any girl should be fined and imprisoned who allowed a young man to kiss her. That law has now, I think, fallen into abeyance, and such matters are regulated in Boston much as they are in other large towns further eastward. It still, I conceive, calls itself a Puritan city, but it has divested its Puritanism of austerity, and clings rather to the politics and public bearing of its old fathers than to their social manners and pristine severity of intercourse. The young girls are, no doubt, much more comfortable under the new dispensation – and the elderly men also, as I fancy.

Sunday, as regards the outer streets, is sabbatical. But Sunday evenings within doors I always found to be, what my friends in that country call 'quite a good time'. It is not the thing in Boston to smoke in the streets during the day; but the wisest, the sagest, and the most holy – even those holy men whom the lecturer saw around him – seldom refuse a cigar in the dining-room as soon as the ladies have gone. Perhaps even the wicked weed would make its appearance before that sad eclipse, thereby postponing, or perhaps absolutely annihilating, the melancholy period of widowhood to both parties, and would light itself under the very eyes of those who in sterner cities will lend no countenance to such lightings.

Ah me, it was very pleasant ! I confess I like this abandonment of the stricter rules of the more decorous world. I fear that there is within me an aptitude to the milder debaucheries which make such deviations pleasant. I like to drink and I like to smoke, but I do not like to turn women out of the room. Then comes the question whether one can have all that one likes together. In some small circles in New England I found people simple enough to fancy that they could. In Massachusetts the Maine Liquor Law [18] is still the law of the land, but, like that other law to which I have alluded, it has fallen very much out of use. At any rate it had not reached the houses of the gentlemen with whom I had the pleasure of making acquaintance. But here I must guard myself from being misunderstood. I saw but one drunken man through all New England, and he was very respectable. He was, however, so uncommonly drunk that he might be allowed to count for two or three.

The Puritans of Boston are, of course, simple in their habits and simple in their expenses. Champagne and canvas-back ducks I found to be the provisions most in vogue among those who desired to adhere closely to the manners of their forefathers. Upon the whole I found the ways of life which had been brought over in the *Mayflower* from the stern sects of England, and preserved through the revolutionary war for liberty, to be very pleasant ways, and I made up my mind that a Yankee Puritan can be an uncommonly pleasant fellow. I wish that some of them did not dine so early; for when a man sits down at half past two, that keeping up of the after-dinner recreations till bedtime becomes hard work.

In Boston the houses are very spacious and excellent, and they are always furnished with those luxuries which it is so difficult to introduce into an old house. They have hot and cold pipes into every room, and baths attached to the bedchambers. It is not only that comfort is increased by such arrangements, but that much labour is saved. In an old English house it will occupy a servant the best part of the day to carry water up and down for a large family.

Everything also is spacious, commodious, and well lighted. I certainly think that in house building the Americans have gone beyond us for even our new houses are not commodious as are theirs.

I found the spirit for the war quite as hot at Boston now (in November), if not hotter than it was when I was there ten weeks earlier; and I found also, to my grief, that the feeling against England was as strong. I can easily understand how difficult it must have been, and still must be, to Englishmen at home to understand this, and see how it has come to pass. It has not arisen, as I think, from the old jealousy of England. It has not sprung from that source which for years had induced certain newspapers, especially the *New York Herald* to vilify England. I do not think that the men of New England have ever been, as regards this matter, in the same boat with the *New York Herald*.

But when this war between the North and South first broke out, even before there was as yet a war, the northern men had taught themselves to expect what they called British sympathy, meaning British encouragement. They regarded, and properly regarded, the action of the South as a rebellion, and said among themselves that so staid and conservative a nation as Great Britain would surely countenance them in quelling rebels. If not – should it come to pass that Great Britain should show no such countenance and sympathy for northern law, if Great Britain did not respond to her friend as she was expected to respond – then it would appear that cotton was king, at least in British eyes.

The war did come, and Great Britain regarded the two parties as belligerents, standing, as far as she was concerned, on equal grounds. This it was that first gave rise to that fretful anger against England which has gone so far towards ruining the northern cause. We know how such passions are swelled by being ventilated, and how they are communicated from mind to mind till they become national. Politicians – American politicians I here mean – have their own future careers ever before their eyes, and are driven to make capital where they can.

Hence it is that such men as Mr Seward [19] in the cabinet, and Mr Everett out of it, can reconcile it to themselves to speak as they have done of England. It was but the other day that Mr Everett spoke in one of his orations of the hope that still existed that the flag of the United States might still float over the whole continent of North America. What would he say of an English statesman who should speak of putting up the Union Jack on the State House in Boston? Such words tell for the moment on the hearers, and help to gain some slight popularity; but they tell for more than a moment on those who read them and remember them.

And then came the capture of Messrs Slidell and Mason.[20] I was at Boston when those men were taken out of the *Trent* by the *San Jacinto*, and brought to Fort Warren in Boston Harbour. Captain Wilkes was the officer who had made the capture, and he immediately was recognized as a hero. He was invited to banquets and fêted. Speeches were made to him as speeches are commonly made to high officers who come home after many perils victorious from the wars. His health was drunk with great applause, and thanks were voted to him by one of the Houses of Congress. It was said that a sword was to be given to him, but I do not think that the gift was consummated. Should it not have been a policeman's truncheon? Had he at the best done anything beyond a policeman's work?

Of Captain Wilkes no one would complain for doing a policeman's duty. If his country were satisfied with the manner in which he did it, England, if she quarrelled at all, would not quarrel with him. It may now and again become the duty of a brave officer to do work of so low a calibre. It is a pity that an ambitious sailor should find himself told off for so mean a task, but the world would know that it is not his fault. No one could blame Captain Wilkes for acting policeman on the seas.

But who ever before heard of giving a man glory for achievements so little glorious? How Captain Wilkes must have blushed when those speeches were made to him, when that talk about the sword came up, when the thanks arrived to him from Congress! An officer receives his country's thanks when he has been in great peril, and has borne himself gallantly through his danger; when he has endured the brunt of war, and come through it with victory; and when he has exposed himself on behalf of his country and singed his epaulets with an enemy's fire. Captain Wilkes tapped a merchantman on the shoulder in the high seas, and told him that his passengers were wanted. In doing this he showed no lack of spirit, for it might be his duty; but where was his spirit when he submitted to be thanked for such work?

And then there arose a clamour of justification among the lawyers. Before twenty-four hours were over, every man and every woman in Boston were armed with precedents.

It was pretty to hear the charming women of Boston, as they became learned in the law of nations: 'Wheaton is quite clear about it,' one young girl said to me. It was the first I had ever heard of Wheaton,[21] and so far was obliged to knock under. All the world, ladies and lawyers, expressed the utmost confidence in the justice of the seizure, but it was clear that all the world was in a state of the profoundest nervous anxiety on the subject.

To me it seemed to be the most suicidal act that any party in a life-and-death struggle ever committed. All Americans on both sides had felt, from the beginning of the war, that any assistance given by England to one or the other would turn the scale. The Government of Mr Lincoln must have learned by this time that England was at least true in her neutrality; that no desire for cotton would compel her to give aid to the South as long as she herself was not ill-treated by the North.

But it seemed as though Mr Seward, the President's prime minister, had no better work on hand than that of showing in every way his indifference as to courtesy with England. Insults offered to England would, he seemed to think, strengthen his hands. He would let England know that he did not care for her. When our minister, Lord Lyons,[22] appealed to him regarding the suspension of the Habeas Corpus, Mr Seward not only answered him with insolence, but instantly published his answer in the papers. He instituted a system of passports, especially constructed so as to incommode Englishmen proceeding from the States across the Atlantic. He resolved to make every Englishman in America feel himself in some way punished because England had not assisted the North. And now came the arrest of Slidell and Mason out of an English mail-steamer; and Mr Seward took care to let it be understood that, happen what might, those two men should not be given up.

From the 1st of November, 1861, till the day on which I left the States, I do not think that I heard a good word spoken of Mr Seward as a Minister even by one of his own party. The radical or abolitionist Republicans all abused him. The Conservative or anti-abolition Republicans, to whose party he would consider himself as belonging, spoke of him as a mistake. He had been prominent as Senator from New York, and had been Governor of the State of New York, but had none of the aptitudes of a statesman. He was there, and it was a pity. He was not so bad as Mr Cameron,[23] the Minister for War; that was the best his own party could say for him, even in his own State of New York.

As to the Democrats, their language respecting him was as harsh as any that I have heard used towards the southern leaders. He seemed to have no friend, no one who trusted him – and yet he was the President's chief minister, and seemed to have in his own hands the power of mismanaging all foreign relations as he pleased. But, in truth, the States of America, great as they are, and much as they have done, have not produced statesmen. That theory of governing by the little men rather than by the great, has not been found to answer, and such follies as those of Mr Seward have been the consequence.

At Boston, and indeed elsewhere, I found that there was even then – at the time of the capture of Mason and Slidell – no true conception of the neutrality of England with reference to the two parties. When any argument was made, showing that England who had carried those messengers from the South, would undoubtedly have also carried messengers from the North, the answer always was, 'But the Southerners are all rebels. Will England regard us who are by treaty her friend, as she does a people that is in rebellion against its own Government?'

We, forsooth, who carry passengers about the world, from China and Australia, round to Chili and Peru, who have the charge of the world's passengers and letters, and as a nation incur out of our pocket annually a loss of some half-million of pounds sterling for the privilege of doing so, are to inquire the business of every American traveller before we let him on board, and be stopped in our work if we take anybody on one side whose journeyings may be conceived by the other side to be to them prejudicial! Not on such terms will Englishmen be willing to spread civilization across the ocean!

I do not pretend to have read a single word of any international law. I have refused to read any such, knowing that it would only confuse and mislead me. But I have my common sense to guide me. Two men living in one street, quarrel and shy brickbats at each other, and make the whole street very uncomfortable. Not only is no one to interfere with them, but they are to have the privilege of deciding that their brickbats have the right of way, rather than the ordinary intercourse of the neighbourhood! If that be national law, national law must be changed. It might do for some centuries back, but it cannot do now. Up to this period my sympathies had been with the North. I thought, and still think, that the North had no alternative, that the war had been forced upon them, and that they had gone about their work with patriotic energy. But this stopping of an English mail-steamer was too much for me.

What will they do in England? was now the question. But for any knowledge as to that, I had to wait till I reached Washington.[24]

Chapter 12

THE two places of most general interest in the vicinity of Boston are Cambridge and Lowell. Cambridge is to Massachusetts, and, I may almost say, is to all the northern States, what Cambridge and Oxford are to England. It is the seat of the University which gives the highest education to be attained by the highest classes in that country. Lowell also is in little to Massachusetts and to New England what Manchester is to us in so great a degree. It is the largest and most prosperous cotton-manufacturing town in the States.

Cambridge is not above three or four miles from Boston. Indeed, the town of Cambridge properly so called begins where Boston ceases. The Harvard College – that is its name, taken from one of its original founders – is reached by horse-cars in twenty minutes from the city. An Englishman feels inclined to regard the place as a suburb of Boston but if he so expresses himself, he will not find favour in the eyes of the men of Cambridge.

The University is not so large as I had expected to find it. It consists of Harvard College, as the undergraduates' department, and of professional schools of law, medicine, divinity, and science. In the few words that I will say about it I will confine myself to Harvard College proper, conceiving that the professional schools connected with it have not in themselves any special interest.

The average number of undergraduates does not exceed 450, and these are divided into four classes. The average number of degrees taken annually by bachelors of art is something under 100. Four years' residence is required for a degree, and at the end of that period a degree is given as a matter of course if the candidate's conduct has been satisfactory. When a young man has pursued his studies for that period, going through the required examinations and lectures, he is not subjected to any final examination as is the case with a candidate for a degree at Oxford and Cambridge.

It is, perhaps, in this respect that the greatest difference exists between the English universities and Harvard College. With us a young man may, I take it, still go through his three or four years with a small amount of study. But his doing so does not insure him his degree. If he have utterly wasted his time he is plucked, and late but heavy punishment comes upon him. At Cambridge in Massachusetts the daily work of the men is made more obligatory; but if this be gone through with such diligence as to enable the student to hold his own during the four years, he has his degree as a matter of course.

There are no degrees conferring special honour. A man cannot go out 'in honours' as he does with us. There are no 'firsts' or 'double firsts'; no 'wranglers'; no 'senior opts' or 'junior opts'. Nor are there prizes of fellowship and livings to be obtained. It is, I think, evident from this that the greatest incentives to high excellence are wanting at Harvard College. There is neither the reward of honour nor of money. There is none of that great competition which exists at our Cambridge for the high place of Senior Wrangler; and, consequently, the degree of excellence attained is no doubt lower than with us.

But I conceive that the general level of the university education is higher there than with us, that a young man is more sure of getting his education, and that a smaller percentage of men leaves Harvard College utterly uneducated than goes in that condition out of Oxford or Cambridge. The education at Harvard College is more diversified in its nature, and study is more absolutely the business of the place than it is at our universities.

The expense of education at Harvard College is not much lower than at our colleges; with us there are, no doubt, more men who are absolutely extravagant than at Cambridge, Massachusetts. The actual authorized expenditure in accordance with the rules is only 50l. per annum, i.e. 249 dollars; but this does not, by any means, include everything. Some of the richer young men may spend as much as 300l. per annum, but the largest number vary their expenditure from 100l. to 180l. per annum; and I take it the same thing may be said of our universities.

There are many young men at Harvard College of very small means. They will live on 70l. per annum, and will earn a great portion of that by teaching in the vacations. There are thirty-six scholarships attached to the University varying in value from 20*l*. to 60*l*. per annum and there is also a beneficiary fund for supplying poor scholars with assistance during their collegiate education. Many are thus brought up at Cambridge who have no means of their own, and I think I may say that the consideration in which they are held among their brother students is in no degree affected by their position. I doubt whether we can say so much of the sizars and bible clerks at our universities.

At Harvard College there is, of course, none of that old-fashioned, time-honoured, delicious, medieval life which lends so much grace and beauty to our colleges. There are no gates, no porters' lodges, no butteries, no halls, no battels, and no common rooms. There are no proctors, no bulldogs, no bursars, no deans, no morning and evening chapel, no quads, no surplices, no caps and gowns. I have already said that there are no examinations for degrees and no honours; and I can easily conceive that in the absence of all these essentials many an Englishman will ask what right Harvard College has to call itself a university.

I have said that there are no honours – and in our sense there are none. But I should give offence to my American friends if I did not explain that there are prizes given – I think, all in money, and that they vary from fifty to ten dollars. These are called deturs. The degrees are given on Commencement Day, at which occasion certain of the expectant graduates are selected to take part in a public literary exhibition. To be so selected seems to be tantamount to taking a degree in honours. There is also a dinner on Commencement Day – at which, however, 'no wine or other intoxicating drink shall be served'.

It is required that every student shall attend some place of Christian worship on Sundays; but he, or his parents for him, may elect what denomination of church he shall attend. There is a university chapel on the university grounds which belongs, if I remember right, to the Episcopalian Church. The young men for the most part live in college, have rooms in the college buildings but they do not board in those rooms. There are establishments in the town under the patronage of the university, at which dinner, breakfast, and supper are provided and the young men frequent one of these houses or another as they, or their friends for them, may arrange.

Every young man not belonging to a family resident within a hundred miles of Cambridge, and whose parents are desirous to obtain the protection thus provided, is placed, as regards his pecuniary management, under the care of a patron, and this patron acts by him as a father does in England by a boy at school. He pays out his money for him and keeps him out of debt. The arrangement will not recommend itself to young men at Oxford quite so powerfully as it may do to the fathers of some young men who have been there. The rules with regard to the lodging- and boarding-houses are very stringent. No wine or spirituous liquors may be used, etc. It is not a picturesque system, this; but it has its advantages.

There is a handsome library attached to the college, which the young men can use but it is not as extensive as I had expected. The university is not well off for funds by which to increase it. The new museum on the college is also a handsome building. The edifices used for the undergraduates' chambers and for the lecture-rooms are by no means handsome. They are very ugly red-brick houses standing here and there without order. There are seven such, and they are called Brattle House, College House, Divinity Hall, Hollis Hall, Holsworthy Hall, Massachusetts Hall, and Stoughton Hall. It is almost astonishing that buildings so ugly should have been erected for such a purpose. These, together with the library, the museum, and the chapel, stand on a large green, which might be made pretty enough if it were kept well mown like the gardens of our Cambridge colleges, but it is much neglected. Here, again, the want of funds – the *res angusta domi* – must be pleaded as an excuse. On the same green, but at some little distance from any other building, stands the President's pleasant house.

Taking the University of Harvard College as a whole, I should say that it is most remarkable in this – that it does really give to its pupils that education which it professes to give. Of our own universities other good things may be said, but that one special good thing cannot always be said.

That which most surprises an English visitor on going

through the mills at Lowell is the personal appearance of the men and women who work at them. As there are twice as many women as there are men, it is to them that the attention is chiefly called. They are not only better dressed, cleaner, and better mounted in every respect than the girls employed at manufactories in England, but they are so infinitely superior as to make a stranger immediately perceive that some very strong cause must have created the difference.

We all know the class of young women whom we generally see serving behind counters in the shops of our larger cities. They are neat, well dressed, careful, especially about their hair, composed in their manner, and sometimes a little supercilious in the propriety of their demeanour. It is exactly the same class of young women that one sees in the factories at Lowell. They are not sallow, nor dirty, nor ragged, nor rough. They have about them no signs of want, or of low culture. Many of us also know the appearance of those girls who work in the factories in England and I think it will be allowed that a second glance at them is not wanting to show that they are in every respect inferior to the young women who attend our shops. The matter, indeed, requires no argument. Any young woman at a shop would be insulted by being asked whether she had worked at a factory. The difference with regard to the men at Lowell is quite as strong, though not so striking. Working men do not show their status in the world by their outside appearance as readily as women.

One would of course be disposed to say that the superior condition of the workers must have been occasioned by superior wages and this, to a certain extent, has been the cause. But the higher payment is not the chief cause. Women's wages, including all that they receive at the Lowell factories, average about 14s. a week, which is, I take it, fully a third more than women can earn in Manchester, or did earn before the loss of the American cotton began to tell upon them. But if wages at Manchester were raised to the Lowell standard, the Manchester women would not be clothed, fed, cared for, and educated like the Lowell women. The fact is, that the workmen and workwomen at Lowell are not exposed to the chances of an open labour market. They are taken in, as it were, to a philanthropical manufacturing college, and then looked after and regulated more as girls and lads at a great seminary, than as hands by whose industry profit is to be made out of capital. This is all very nice and pretty at Lowell, but I am afraid it could not be done at Manchester.

The following is taken from the hand-book to Lowell:

Mr F. C. Lowell [25] had in his travels abroad observed the effect of large manufacturing establishments on the character of the people, and in the establishment at Waltham the founders looked for a remedy for these defects. They thought that education and good morals would even enhance the profit, and that they could compete with Great Britain by introducing a more cultivated class of operatives. For this purpose they built boarding-houses, which, under the direct supervision of the agent, were kept by discreet matrons

— I can answer for the discreet matrons at Lowell —

mostly widows, no boarders being allowed except operatives. Agents and overseers of high moral character were selected; regulations were adopted at the mills and boarding-houses, by which only respectable girls were employed. The mills were nicely painted and swept

— I can also answer for the painting and sweeping at Lowell —

trees set out in the yards and along the streets, habits of neatness and cleanliness encouraged; and the result justified the expenditure. At Lowell the same policy has been adopted and extended; more spacious mills and elegant boarding-houses have been erected

— as to the elegance, it may be a matter of taste, but as to the comfort there is no question —

the same care as to the classes employed; more capital has been expended for cleanliness and decoration; a hospital has been established for the sick, where, for a small price, they have an experienced physician and skilful nurses. An institute, with an extensive library, for the use of the mechanics, has been endowed. The agents have stood forward in the support of schools, churches, lectures and lyceums, and their influence contributed highly to the elevation of the moral and intellectual character of the operatives.

Talent has been encouraged, brought forward, and recommended.

For some considerable time the young women wrote, edited, and published a newspaper among themselves, called the *Lowell Offering*.

And Lowell has supplied agents and mechanics for the later manufacturing places who have given tone to society, and extended the beneficial influence of Lowell through the United States. Girls from the country, with a true Yankee spirit of independence, and confident in their own powers, pass a few years here, and then return to get married with a dower secured by their exertions, with more enlarged ideas and extended means of information, and their places are supplied by younger relatives. A larger proportion of the female population of New England has been employed at some time in manufacturing establishments, and they are not on this account less good wives, mothers, or educators of families.

Then the account goes on to tell how the health of the girls has been improved by their attendance at the mills, how they put money into the savings-banks, and buy railway shares and farms; how there are thirty churches at Lowell, a library, banks, and insurance offices; how there is a cemetery and a park, and how everything is beautiful, philanthropic, profitable, and magnificent.

Thus Lowell is the realization of a commercial Utopia. Of all the statements made in the little book which I have quoted I cannot point out one which is exaggerated, much less false. I should not call the place elegant; in other respects I am disposed to stand by the book. Before I had made any inquiry into the cause of the apparent comfort, it struck me at once that some great effort at excellence was being made.

I went into one of the discreet matrons' residences; and perhaps may give but an indifferent idea of her discretion when I say that she allowed me to go into the bedrooms. If you want to ascertain the inner ways or habits of life of any man, woman, or child, see, if it be practicable to do so, his or her bedroom. You will learn more by a minute's glance round that holy of holies, than by any conversation. Looking-glasses and such like, suspended dresses, and toilet-belongings, if taken without notice, cannot lie or even exaggerate. The discreet matron at first showed me rooms only prepared for use, for at the period of my visit

Lowell was by no means full; but she soon became more intimate with me, and I went through the upper part of the house.

My report must be altogether in her favour and in that of Lowell. Everything was cleanly, well-ordered, and feminine. There was not a bed on which any woman need have hesitated to lay herself if occasion required it. I fear that this cannot be said of the lodgings of the manufacturing classes at Manchester. The boarders all take their meals together. As a rule, they have meat twice a day. Hot meat for dinner is with them as much a matter of course, or probably more so, than with any English man or woman who may read this book. For in the States of America regulations on this matter are much more rigid than with us. Cold meat is rarely seen, and to live a day without meat would be as great a privation as to pass a night without bed.

The rules for the guidance of these boarding-houses are very rigid. The houses themselves belong to the corporations or different manufacturing establishments, and the tenants are altogether in the power of the managers. None but operatives are to be taken in. The tenants are answerable for improper conduct. The doors are to be closed at ten o'clock. Any boarders who do not attend divine worship are to be reported to the managers. The yards and walks are to be kept clean, and snow removed at once; and the inmates must be vaccinated, etc., etc., etc. It is expressly stated by the Hamilton Company – and I believe by all the companies – that no one shall be employed who is habitually absent from public worship on Sunday, or who is known to be guilty of immorality.

It is stated that the average wages of the women are two dollars, or eight shillings, a week, besides their board. I found when I was there that from three dollars to three and a half a week were paid to the women, of which they paid one dollar and twenty-five cents for the board. As this would not fully cover the expense of their keep, twenty-five cents a week for each was also paid to the boarding-house keepers by the mill agents. This substantially came to the same thing, as it left the two dollars a week, or eight shillings, with the girls over and above their cost of living. The board included washing, lights, food, bed, and attendance, leaving a surplus of eight shillings a week for clothes and saving. Now let me ask any one acquainted with Manchester and its operatives, whether that is not Utopia realized. Factory girls, for whom every comfort of life is secured, with 21l. a year over for saving and dress !

One sees the failing, however, at a moment. It is Utopia. Any Lady Bountiful can tutor three or four peasants and make them luxuriously comfortable. But no Lady Bountiful can give luxurious comfort to half a dozen parishes. Lowell is now nearly forty years old, and contains but 40,000 inhabitants. From the very nature of its corporations it cannot spread itself. Chicago, which has grown out of nothing in a much shorter period, and which has no factories, has now 120,000 inhabitants. Lowell is a very wonderful place and shows what philanthropy can do; but I fear it also shows what philanthropy cannot do.

On my return from Lowell in the smoking car, an old man came and squeezed in next to me. The place was terribly crowded, and as the old man was thin and clean and quiet I willingly made room for him, so as to avoid the contiguity of a neighbour who might be neither thin, nor clean, nor quiet. He began talking to me in whispers about the war, and I was suspicious that he was a Southerner and a Secessionist. Under such circumstances his company might not be agreeable, unless he could be induced to hold his tongue.

At last he said, 'I come from Canada, you know, and you – you're an Englishman; and therefore I can speak to you openly;' and he gave me an affectionate grip on the knee with his old skinny hand. I suppose I do look more like an Englishman than an American, but I was surprised at his knowing me with such certainty.

'There is no mistaking you,' he said, 'with your round face and your red cheeks. They don't look like that here,' and he gave me another grip. I felt quite fond of the old man, and offered him a cigar.

Chapter 13

I [26] WENT through New York to Philadelphia and made a short visit to the latter town. Philadelphia seems to me to have thrown off its Quaker garb, and to present itself to the world in the garments ordinarily assumed by large cities; by which I intend to express my opinion that the Philadelphians are not in these latter days any better than their neighbours. I am not sure whether in some respects they may not perhaps be worse. Quakers – Quakers absolutely in the very flesh of close bonnets and brown knee-breeches – are still to be seen there; but they are not numerous, and would not strike the eye if one did not specially look for a Quaker in Philadelphia. It is a large town with a very large hotel – there are no doubt half a dozen large hotels, but one of them is specially great – with long straight streets, good shops and markets, and decent comfortable-looking houses. The houses of Philadelphia generally are not so large as those of other great cities in the States. They are more modest than those of New York, and less commodious than those of Boston.

The city of Philadelphia lies between the two rivers, the Delaware and the Schuylkill. Eight chief streets run from river to river, and twenty-four cross streets bisect the eight at right angles. The long streets are, with the exception of Market Street, called by the names of trees – chestnut, walnut, pine, spruce, mulberry, vine and so on.

The cross streets are all called by their numbers. In the long streets the numbers of the houses are not consecutive, but follow the numbers of the cross-streets; so that a person living in Chestnut Street between Tenth Street and Eleventh Street, and ten doors from Tenth Street, would live at No. 1010. The opposite house would be No. 1011. It thus follows that the number of the house indicates the exact block of houses in which it is situated. I do not like the right-angled building of these towns, nor do I like the sound of Twentieth Street and Thirtieth

Street; but I must acknowledge that the arrangement in Philadelphia has its convenience. In New York I found it by no means an easy thing to arrive at the desired locality.

They boast in Philadelphia that they have half a million inhabitants. If this be taken as a true calculation, Philadelphia is in size the fourth city of the world – putting out of the question the cities of China, as to which we have heard so much and believe so little. But in making this calculation the citizens include the population of a district on some sides ten miles distant from Philadelphia. It takes in other towns connected to it by railway, but separated by large stretches of open country. American cities are very proud of their population, but if they all counted in this way, there would be no rural population left at all. There is a very fine bank at Philadelphia – and Philadelphia is a town somewhat celebrated in its banking history. My remarks here, however, apply simply to the external building, and not to its internal honesty and wisdom, or to its commercial credit.

The railway from Philadelphia to Baltimore passes along the top of Chesapeake Bay and across the Susquehanna river; at least the railway cars do. On one side of that river they are run on to a huge ferryboat, and are again run off at the other side. Such an operation would seem to be one of difficulty to us under any circumstances; but as the Susquehanna is a tidal river, rising and falling a considerable number of feet, the natural impediment in the way of such an enterprise would, I think, have staggered us. We should have built a bridge costing two or three million sterling, on which no conceivable amount of traffic would pay a fair dividend. Here, in crossing the Susquehanna, the boat is so constructed that its deck shall be level with the line of railway at half tide, so that the inclined plane from the shore down to the boat, or from the shore up to the boat, shall never exceed half the amount of the rise or fall. One would suppose that the most intricate machinery would have been necessary for such an arrangement, but it was all rough and simple, and apparently managed by two Negroes.

Regarding railways in America generally, as to the relative safety of which, when compared with our own, we have not in England a high opinion, I must say that I never saw any accident

or in any way became conversant with one. It is said that large
numbers of men and women are slaughtered from time to time
on different lines, but if it be so, the newspapers make very light
of such cases. I myself have seen no such slaughter, nor have I
even found myself in the vicinity of a broken bone.

Nature has done a great deal for Maryland; and fortune also
has done much for it in these latter days in directing the war
from its territory. Maryland is a slave State lying immediately
south of Mason and Dixon's line. Small portions of Virginia and
of Delaware do run north of Maryland, but practically Maryland
is the frontier State of the slave States. It was therefore of much
importance to know which way Maryland would go in the event
of secession among the slave States becoming general; and of
much also to ascertain whether it would secede if desirous of
doing so. I am inclined to think that as a State it was desirous
of following Virginia, though there are many in Maryland who
deny this very stoutly. But it was at once evident that if loyalty
to the North could not be had in Maryland of its own free will,
adherence to the North must be enforced upon Maryland. Otherwise the city of Washington could not be maintained as the
existing capital of the nation.

The question of the fidelity of the State to the Union was first
tried by the arrival at Baltimore of a certain Commissioner from
the State of Mississippi, who visited that city with the object of
inducing secession. It must be understood that Baltimore is the
commercial capital of Maryland, whereas Annapolis is the seat
of Government and the legislature – or is, in other terms, the
political capital. Baltimore is a city containing 230,000 inhabitants, and is considered to have as strong and perhaps as
violent a mob as any city in the Union. Of the above number
30,000 are Negroes and 2,000 are slaves.

The Commissioner made his appeal, telling his tale of southern
grievances, declaring, among other things, that secession was
not intended to break up the Government but to perpetuate it,
and asked for the assistance and sympathy of Maryland. The
Commissioner was answered by Governor Hicks,[27] who was placed
in a somewhat difficult position. The existing legislature of the

State was presumed to be secessionist, but the legislature was not sitting, nor in the ordinary course of things would that legislature have been called to sit again. The existing legislature was therefore exempt from further work – unless specially summoned for an extraordinary session. To do this was within the power of the Governor. But Governor Hicks, who seems to have been mainly anxious to keep things quiet, and whose individual politics did not come out strongly, was not inclined to issue the summons. 'Let us show moderation as well as firmness,' he said; and that was about all he did say to the Commissioner from Mississippi.

On the 18th of April Governor Hicks issued a proclamation to the people of Maryland, begging them to be quiet, the chief object of which, however, was that of promising that no troops should be sent out from their State, unless with the object of guarding the neighbouring city of Washington – a promise which he had no means of fulfilling. This proclamation was immediately backed up by one from the Mayor of Baltimore to the city, in which he congratulates the citizens on the Governor's promise that none of their troops are to be sent to another State; and then he tells them that they shall be preserved from the horrors of civil war.

But on the very next day the horrors of civil war began in Baltimore. But this time President Lincoln was collecting troops at Washington for the protection of the capital; and that army of the Potomac, which has ever since occupied the Virginian side of the river, was in course of construction. To join this, certain troops from Massachusetts were sent down by the usual route via New York, Philadelphia, and Baltimore; but on their reaching Baltimore by railway, the mob of that town refused to allow them to pass through – and a fight began. Nine citizens were killed and two soldiers, and as many more were wounded. This, I think, was the first blood spilt in the Civil War; and the attack was first made by the mob of the first slave city reached by the northern soldiers. This goes far to show, not that the border States desired secession, but that, when compelled to choose between secession and union – when not allowed by circumstances to remain neutral – their sympathies were with their sister slave States rather than with the North.

The President was besieged with entreaties that no troops should be sent through Baltimore. Now this was hard enough on President Lincoln, seeing that he was bound to defend his capital, that he could get no troops from the South, and that Baltimore is on the high road from Washington, both to the West and to the North; but, nevertheless, he gave way. Had he not done so all Baltimore would have been in a blaze of rebellion, and the scene of the coming contest must have been removed from Virginia to Maryland, and Congress and the Government must have travelled from Washington north to Philadelphia. 'They shall not come through Baltimore,' said Mr Lincoln. 'But they shall come through the State of Maryland. They shall be passed over Chesapeake Bay by water to Annapolis, and shall come up by rail from thence.' This arrangement was as distasteful to the State of Maryland as the other; but Annapolis is a small town without a mob, and the Marylanders had no means of preventing the passage of the troops.

On the 27th of April, Governor Hicks, having now had a sufficiency of individual responsibility, summoned the legislature, and submitted his views in very proper terms to the wisdom of the senators and the representatives. He entertained, as he said, an honest conviction that the safety of Maryland lay in preserving a neutral position between the North and the South. Certainly, Governor Hicks, if it were possible! The legislature again went to work to prevent, if it might be prevented, the passage of troops through their State; but luckily for them, they failed. The President was bound to defend Washington, and the Marylanders were denied their wish of having their own fields made the fighting ground of the Civil War.

On the 10th of May the Maryland legislature passed the following resolution: [28]

Resolved – that Maryland implore the President, in the name of God, to cease this unholy war, at least until Congress assembles, – a period of above six months.
That Maryland desires and consents to the recognition of the independence of the Confederate States. The military occupation of Maryland is unconstitutional and she protests against it, though the violent interference with the Federal troops is discountenanced.

That the vindication of her rights be left to time and reason, and that a convention under existing circumstances is expedient.

From which it is plain that Maryland would have seceded as effectually as Georgia seceded, had she not been prevented by the interposition of Washington between her and the confederate States – the happy intervention seeing that she has thus been saved from becoming the battleground of the contest. But the legislature had to pay for its rashness. On the 13th September thirteen of its members were arrested, as were also the editors of newspapers presumed to be secessionists. A member of Congress was also arrested at the same time, and a candidate for Governor Hicks's place, who belonged to the secessionist party. Previously, in the last days of June and the beginning of July, the chief of the police at Baltimore and the member of the Board of Police had been arrested by General Banks,[29] who then held Baltimore in his power.

I reached that city just seven months later,[30] and its condition was considerably altered. There was no question then whether troops should pass through Baltimore, or by an awkward round through Annapolis, or not pass at all through Maryland. General Dix,[31] who had succeeded General Banks, was holding the city in his grip, and martial law prevailed. In such times as those, it was bootless to inquire as to that promise that no troops should pass southward through Baltimore. What have such assurances been worth in such days! Baltimore was now a military depot in the hands of the northern army, and General Dix was not a man to stand any trifling. He did me the honour to take me to the top of Federal Hill, a suburb of the city, on which he had raised great earth works and planted mighty cannons, and built tents and barracks for his soldiery, and to show me how instantaneously he could destroy the town from his exalted position.

'This hill was made for the very purpose,' said General Dix; and no doubt he thought so. Generals when they have fine positions and big guns and prostrate people lying under their thumbs, are inclined to think that God's providence has specially ordained them and their points of vantage. Previously to the days of secession Baltimore had been guarded by Fort MacHenry, which lies on a spit of land running out into the bay just below the town. Hither I went with General Dix, and he explained to me how the cannon had heretofore been pointed solely towards the sea; that, however, now was all changed, and the mouths of his bombs and his great artillery were turned all the other way. The commandant of the fort was with us, and other officers, and they all spoke of this martial tenure as a great blessing. Hearing them, one could hardly fail to suppose that they had lived their forty, fifty, or sixty years of life in full reliance on the powers of a military despotism. But not the less were they American Republicans, who, twelve months since, would have dilated on the all-sufficiency of their republican institutions, and on the absence of any military restraint in their country, with that peculiar pride which characterizes the citizens of the States. There are, however, some lessons which may be learned with singular rapidity !

Such was the state of Baltimore when I visited that city. I found, nevertheless, that cakes and ale still prevailed there. I am inclined to think that cakes and ale prevail most freely in times that are perilous, and when sources of sorrow abound. I have seen more reckless joviality in a town stricken by pestilence than I ever encountered elsewhere. There was General Dix seated on Federal Hill with his cannon; and there, beneath the artillery, were gentlemen hotly professing themselves to be secessionists, men whose sons and brothers were in the southern army, and women ! – alas whose brothers would be in one army and their sons in another. That was the part of it which was most heart-rending in the border land. In New England and New York men's minds at any rate were bent all in the same direction – as doubtless they were also in Georgia and Alabama. But here fathers were divided from sons, and mothers from daughters. Terrible tales were told of threats uttered by one member of a family against another. Old ties of friendship were broken up. Society had so divided itself, that one side could hold no terms of courtesy with another.

'When this is over,' one gentleman said to me, 'every man in Baltimore will have a quarrel to the death on his hands with some friend whom he used to love.' The complaints made on both sides were eager and open-mouthed against the other.

Baltimore is, or at any rate was, an aspiring city proud of its commerce and proud of its society. It has regarded itself as the New York of the South, and to some extent has forced others so to regard it also. In many respects it is more like an English town than most of its transatlantic brethren, and the ways of its inhabitants are English. In old days a pack of foxhounds was kept here – or indeed in days that are not yet very old, for I was told of their doings by a gentleman who had long been a member of the hunt. The country looks as a hunting country should look, whereas no man that ever crossed a field after a pack of hounds would feel the slightest wish to attempt that in New England or New York. There is in Baltimore an inn with an old sign, standing at the corner of Eutaw and Franklin Streets, just as may still be seen in the towns of Somersetshire, and before it are to be seen old wagons, covered and soiled and battered, about to return from the city to the country, just as the wagons do in our own agricultural counties. I have found nothing so thoroughly English in any other parts of the Union.

But canvas-back ducks and terrapins are the great glory of Baltimore. Of the nature of the former bird I believe all the world knows something. It is a wild duck which obtains the peculiarity of its flavour from the wild celery on which it feeds. This celery grows on the Chesapeake Bay only. At any rate Baltimore is the headquarters of the canvas-backs, and it is on the Chesapeake Bay that they are shot. I was kindly invited to go down on a shooting-party; but when I learned that I should have to ensconce myself alone for hours in a wet wooden box on the water's edge, waiting there for the chance of a duck to come, I declined. The fact of my never having as yet been successful in shooting a bird of any kind conduced somewhat perhaps to my decision. I must acknowledge that the canvas-back duck fully deserves all the reputation it has acquired.

As to the terrapin, I have not so much to say. The terrapin is a small turtle, found on the shores of Maryland and Virginia, out of which a very rich soup is made. It is cooked with wines and spices, and is served in the shape of a hash, with heaps of little bones mixed through it. It is held in great repute, and the guest is expected as a matter of course to be helped twice. The man who did not eat twice of terrapin would be held in small repute, as the Londoner would be held who at a city banquet does not partake of both thick and thin turtle. I must confess, however, that the terrapin for me had no surpassing charms.

Maryland was so called from Henrietta Maria, the wife of Charles I, by which king in 1632 the territory was conceded to the Roman Catholic Lord Baltimore. It was chiefly peopled by Roman Catholics, but I do not think that there is now any such speciality attaching to the State. There are in it two or three old Roman Catholic families, but the people have come down from the North, and have no peculiar religious tendencies. Some of Lord Baltimore's descendants remained in the State up to the time of the revolution. From Baltimore I went on to Washington.

Chapter 14

THE site of the present city of Washington was chosen with three special views; firstly, that being on the Potomac it might have the full advantage of water carriage and a sea port; secondly, that it might be so far removed from the seaboard as to be safe from invasion; and, thirdly, that it might be central alike to all the States. It was presumed when Washington was founded that these three advantages would be secured by the selected position.

As regards the first, the Potomac affords to the city but few of the advantages of a sea port. Ships can come up, but not ships of large burthen. The river seems to have dwindled since the site was chosen and at present it is, I think, evident that Washington can never be great in its shipping. *Statio benefida carinis* can never be its motto. As regards the second point, singularly enough Washington is the only city of the Union that has been in an enemy's possession since the United States became a nation. In the war of 1812 it fell into our hands, and we burnt it. As regards the third point, Washington, from the lie of the land, can hardly have been said to be centrical at any time. Owing to the irregularities of the coast it is not easy of access by railways from different sides. Baltimore would have been far better. But as far as we can now see, and as well as we can now judge, Washington will soon be on the borders of the nation to which it belongs, instead of at its centre. I fear, therefore, that we must acknowledge that the site chosen for his country's capital by George Washington has not been fortunate.

I have a strong idea, which I expressed before in speaking of the capital of the Canadas, that no man can ordain that on such a spot shall be built a great and thriving city. No man can ordain even though he leave behind him, as was the case with Washington, a prestige sufficient to bind his successors to his wishes. The political leaders of the country have done what they could for Washington. The pride of the nation has endeavoured to sustain the character of its chosen metropolis. There has been no rival, soliciting favour on the strength of other charms. The country has all been agreed on the point since the father of the country first commenced the work. Florence and Rome in Italy have each their pretensions but in the States no other city has put itself forward for the honour of entertaining Congress.

And yet Washington has been a failure. It is commerce that makes great cities, and commerce has refused to back the General's choice. New York and Philadelphia, without any political power, have become great among the cities of the earth. They are beaten by none except by London and Paris. But Washington is but a ragged, unfinished collection of unbuilt broad streets, as to the completion of which there can now, I imagine, be but little hope. Of all places that I know it is the most ungainly and most unsatisfactory — I fear I must also say the most presumptuous in its pretensions. There is a map of Washington accurately laid down; and taking that map with him in his journeyings a man may lose himself in the streets, not as one loses oneself in London between Shoreditch and Russell Square, but as one does so in the deserts of the Holy Land, between Emmaus and Arimathea.

In the first place no one knows where the places are, or is sure of their existence, and then between their presumed localities the country is wild, trackless, unbridged, uninhabited, and desolate. Massachusetts Avenue runs the whole length of the city, and is inserted on the maps as a full-blown street, about four miles in length. Go there, and you will find yourself not only out of town, away from the fields, but you will find yourself beyond the fields, in an uncultivated, undrained wilderness. Tucking your trousers up to your knees you will wade through the bogs, you will lose yourself among rude hillocks, you will be out of the reach of humanity. The unfinished dome of the Capitol will loom before you in the distance, and you will think that you approach the ruins of some western Palmyra. If you are a sportsman, you will desire to shoot snipe within sight of the President's house. There is much unsettled land within the States of America, but I think none so desolate in its state of nature as

three-fourths of the ground on which is supposed to stand the
city of Washington.

The city of Washington is something more than four miles
long, and is something more than two miles broad. The land
apportioned to it is nearly as compact as may be, and it exceeds
in area the size of a parallelogram four miles long by two broad.
These dimensions are adequate for a noble city, for a city to
contain a million of inhabitants. It is impossible to state with
accuracy the actual population of Washington, for it fluctuates
exceedingly. The place is very full during Congress, and very
empty during the recess. By which I mean it to be understood
that those streets, which are blessed with houses, are full when
Congress meets. I do not think that Congress makes much difference to Massachusetts Avenue. I believe that the city never
contains as many as eighty thousand, and that its permanent
residents are less than sixty thousand.

But, it will be said – was it not well to prepare for a growing
city? Is it not true that London is choked by its own fatness,
not having been endowed at its birth or during its growth, with
proper means for accommodating its own increasing proportions? Was it not well to lay down fine avenues and broad
streets, so that future citizens might find a city well prepared to
their hand?

There is no doubt much in such an argument, but its correct-
ness must be tested by its success. When a man marries it is
well that he should make provision for a coming family. But a
Benedict, who early in his career shall have carried his friends
with considerable self-applause through half a dozen nurseries
and at the end of twelve years shall still be the father of one
rickety baby, will incur a certain amount of ridicule. It is very
well to be prepared for good fortune, but one should limit one's
preparation within a reasonable scope. Two miles by one might
perhaps have done for the skeleton sketch of a new city. Less
than half that would contain much more than the present population of Washington; and there are, I fear, few towns in the
Union so little likely to enjoy any speedy increase.

Three avenues sweep the whole length of Washington –
Virginia Avenue, Pennsylvania Avenue, and Massachusetts

Avenue. But Pennsylvania Avenue is the only one known to ordinary men, and the half of that only is so known. This avenue is the backbone of the city, and those streets which are really inhabited cluster round that half of it which runs westward from the Capitol. The eastern end, running from the front of the Capitol, is again a desert.

The plan of the city is somewhat complicated. It may truly be called a 'mighty maze, but not without a plan'. The Capitol was intended to be the centre of the city. It faces eastward, away from the Potomac – or rather from the main branch of the Potomac, and also unfortunately from the main body of the town. It turns its back upon the chief thoroughfare, upon the Treasury buildings, and upon the President's house and indeed upon the whole place. It was, I suppose, intended that the streets to the eastward should be noble and populous, but hitherto they have come to nothing. The building therefore is wrong side foremost, and all mankind who enter it, senators, representatives, and judges included, go in at the backdoor.

Of course it is generally known that in the Capitol is the Chamber of the Senate, that of the House of Representatives, and the Supreme Judicial Court of the Union. It may be said that there are two centres in Washington, this being one and the President's house the other. At these centres the main avenues are supposed to cross each other, which avenues are called by the names of the respective States. At the Capitol, Pennsylvania Avenue, New Jersey Avenue, Delaware Avenue, and Maryland Avenue converge. They come from one extremity of the city to the square of the Capitol on one side, and run out from the other side of it to the other extremity of the city. Pennsylvania Avenue, New York Avenue, Vermont Avenue, and Connecticut Avenue do the same at what is generally called President's Square.

In theory, or on paper, this seems to be a clear and intelligible arrangement; but it does not work well. These centre depots are large spaces, and consequently one portion of a street is removed a considerable distance from the other. It is as though the same name should be given to two streets, one of which entered St James's Park at Buckingham Gate, while the other started from the Park at Marlborough House. To inhabitants the matter probably is not of much moment, as it is well known that this portion of such an avenue and that portion of such another avenue are merely myths – unknown lands away in the wilds. But a stranger finds himself in the position of being sent across the country knee-deep into the mud, wading through snipe grounds, looking for civilization where none exists.

All these avenues have a slanting direction. They are so arranged that none of them run north and south or east and west; but the streets, so called, all run in accordance with the points of the compass. Those from east to west, are A Street, B Street, C Street, and so on – counting them away from the Capitol on each side, so that there are two A streets, and two B streets. On the map these streets run up to V Street, both right and left – V Street North and V Street South. Those really known to mankind are, E, F, G, H, I, and K Streets North. Then those streets which run from north to south are numbered First Street, Second Street, Third Street, and so on, on each front of the Capitol, running to Twenty-Fourth or Twenty-Fifth Street on each side. Not very many of these have any existence, or I might perhaps more properly say, any vitality in their existence.

Such is the plan of the city, that being the arrangement and those the dimensions intended by the original architects and founders of Washington; but the inhabitants have hitherto confined themselves to Pennsylvania Avenue West, and to the streets abutting from it or near to it. Whatever address a stranger may receive, however perplexing it may seem to him, he may be sure that the house indicated is near Pennsylvania Avenue. If it be not, I should recommend him to pay no attention to the summons. Even in those streets with which he will become best acquainted, the houses are not continuous. There will be a house, and then a blank, then two houses, and then a double blank. After that a hut or two, and then probably an excellent, roomy, handsome family mansion.

Taken altogether, Washington as a city is most unsatisfactory, and falls more grievously short of the thing attempted than any other of the great undertakings of which I have seen anything in the States. San José, the capital of the republic of Costa Rica [32] in Central America, has been prepared and arranged as a new city in the same way. But even San José comes nearer to what was intended than does Washington.

For myself, I do not believe in cities made after this fashion. Commerce, I think, must select the site of all large congregations of mankind. In some mysterious way she ascertains what she wants, and having acquired that, draws men in thousands round her properties. Liverpool, New York, Lyons, Glasgow, Venice, Marseilles, Hamburg, Calcutta, Chicago, and Leghorn, have all become populous, and are or have been great, because trade found them to be convenient for its purposes. Trade seems to have ignored Washington altogether. Such being the case, the Legislative and the Executive of the country together have been unable to make of Washington anything better than a straggling congregation of buildings in a wilderness.

The streets of Washington, such as exist, are all broad. Throughout the town there are open spaces – spaces, I mean, intended to be open by the plan laid down for the city. At the present moment it is almost all open space. There is also a certain nobility about the proposed dimensions of the avenues and squares. Desirous of praising it in some degree, I can say that the design is grand. The thing done, however, falls so infinitely short of that design, that nothing but disappointment is felt. And I fear that there is no look-out into the future which can justify a hope that the design will be fulfilled. It is therefore a melancholy place.

The society into which one falls there consists mostly of persons who are not permanently resident in the capital; but of those who were permanent residents I found none who spoke of their city with affection. The men and women of Boston think that the sun shines nowhere else – and Boston Common is very pleasant. The New Yorkers believe in Fifth Avenue with an unswerving faith; and Fifth Avenue is calculated to inspire a faith. Philadelphia to a Philadelphian is the centre of the universe, and the progress of Philadelphia, perhaps, justifies the partiality. The same thing may be said of Chicago, of Buffalo, and of Baltimore. But the same thing cannot be said in any degree of Washington. They who belong to it turn up their noses at it. They feel that they live surrounded by a failure. Its grand names are as yet false, and none of the efforts made have hitherto been successful. Even in winter, when Congress is sitting, Washington is melancholy – but Washington in summer must surely be the saddest spot on earth.

There are six principal public buildings in Washington, as to which no expense seems to have been spared, and in the construction of which a certain amount of success has been obtained. In most of these success has been more or less marred by an independent deviation from recognized rules of architectural taste. These are the Capitol, the Post Office, the Patent Office, the Treasury, the President's house, and the Smithsonian Institute. The five first are Grecian, and the last in Washington is called Romanesque. Had I been left to classify it by my own unaided lights, I should have called it bastard Gothic.

The Capitol is by far the most imposing and though there is much about it with which I cannot but find fault, it certainly is imposing. The present building was, I think, commenced in 1815, the former Capitol having been destroyed by the English in the war of 1812–13.

The front of the original building is certainly grand. The architect who designed it must have had skill, taste, and nobility of conception; but even this was spoilt, or rather wasted, by the fact that the front is made to look upon nothing, and is turned from the city. It is as though the façade of the London Post Office had been made to face the Goldsmiths' Hall. The Capitol stands upon the side of a hill, the front occupying a much higher position than the back; consequently they who enter it from the back – and everybody does so enter it – are first called on to rise to the level of the lower floor by a stiff ascent of exterior steps, which are in no way grand or imposing, and then, having entered by a mean back door, are instantly obliged to ascend again by another flight – by stairs sufficiently appropriate to a back entrance, but altogether unfitted for the chief approach to such a building. It may, of course, be said that persons who are particular in such matters should go in at the front door and not at the back; but one must take these things as one finds them.

Nevertheless, and in spite of all that I have said, I have had pleasure in walking backwards and forwards, and through the grounds which lie before the eastern front of the Capitol. The space for the view is ample, and the thing to be seen has points which are very grand. If the Capitol were finished and all Washington were built around it, no man would say that the house in which Congress sat disgraced the city.

The President's House – or the White House as it is now called all the world over – is a handsome mansion fitted for the chief officer of a great Republic, and nothing more. I think I may say that we have private houses in London considerably larger. It is neat and pretty, and with all its immediate outside belongings calls down no adverse criticism. It faces on to a small garden, which seems to be always accessible to the public, and opens out upon that everlasting Pennsylvania Avenue, which has now made another turn. Here in front of the White House is President's Square, as it is generally called. The technical name is, I believe, La Fayette Square. The houses round it are few in number – not exceeding three or four on each side, but they are among the best in Washington, and the whole place is neat and well kept. President's Square is certainly the most attractive part of the city. The garden of the square is always open, and does not seem to suffer from any public ill-usage; by which circumstance I am again led to suggest that the gardens of our London squares might be thrown open in the same way.

In the centre of this one at Washington, immediately facing the President's House, is an equestrian statue of General Jackson. It is very bad but that it is not nearly as bad as it might be is proved by another equestrian statue, of General Washington, erected in the centre of a small garden-plot at the end of Pennsylvania Avenue, near the bridge leading to Georgetown. Of all the statues on horseback which I ever saw, either in marble or bronze, this is by far the worst and most ridiculous. The horse is most absurd, but the man sitting on the horse is manifestly drunk. I should think the time must come when this figure at any rate will be removed.[33]

I did not go inside the President's house, not having had while at Washington an opportunity of paying my personal respects to Mr Lincoln. I had been told that this was to be done without trouble, but when I inquired on the subject I found that this was not exactly the case. I believe there are times when anybody may walk into the President's house without an introduction but that, I take it, is not considered to be the proper way of doing the work. I found that something like a favour would be incurred, or that some disagreeable trouble would be given, if I made a request to be presented, and therefore I left Washington without seeing the great man.

The President's house is nice to look at, but it is built on marshy ground, not much above the level of the Potomac, and is very unhealthy. I was told that all who live there become subject to fever and ague, and that few who now live there have escaped it altogether. This comes of choosing the site of a new city, and decreeing that it shall be built on this or on that spot. Large cities, especially in these latter days, do not collect themselves in unhealthy places. Men desert such localities, or at least do not congregate at them when their character is once known. But the poor President cannot desert the White House. He must make the most of the residence which the nation has prepared for him.

Of the other considerable public building of Washington, called the Smithsonian Institution, I have said that its style was bastard Gothic; by this, I mean that its main attributes are Gothic, but that liberties have been taken with it, which, whether they may injure its beauty or no, certainly are subversive of architectural purity. It is built of red stone, and is not ugly in itself. There is a very nice Norman porch to it, and little bits of Lombard Gothic have been well copied from Cologne. But windows have been fitted in with stilted arches, of which the stilts seem to crack and bend, so narrow are they and so high. And then the towers with high pinnacled roofs are a mistake – unless indeed they be needed to give to the whole structure that name of Romanesque which it has assumed.

The building is used for museums and lectures, and was given to the city by one James Smithson,[34] an Englishman. I cannot say that the city of Washington seems to be grateful, for all to whom I spoke on the subject hinted that the Institution was a failure. It is to be remarked that nobody in Washington is proud of Washington, or of anything in it. If the Smithsonian Institution were at New York or at Boston, one would have a different story to tell.

There has been an attempt made to raise at Washington a vast obelisk to the memory of Washington – the first in war and first in peace, as the country is proud to call him. This obelisk is a fair type of the city. It is unfinished – not a third of it having as yet been erected – and in all human probability ever will remain so. If finished it would be the highest monument of its kind standing on the face of the globe – and yet, after all, what would it be even then as compared with one of the great pyramids?

Modern attempts cannot bear comparison with those of the old world in simple vastness. But in lieu of simple vastness, the modern world aims to achieve either beauty or utility. By the Washington monument, if completed, neither would be achieved. An obelisk with the proportions of a needle may be very graceful but an obelisk which requires an expanse of flat-roofed, sprawling buildings for its base, and of which the shaft shall be as big as a cathedral tower, cannot be graceful. At present some third portion of the shaft has been built, and there it stands. No one has a word to say for it. No one thinks that money will ever again be subscribed for its completion. I saw somewhere a box of plate-glass kept for contributions for this purpose, and looking in perceived that two half-dollar pieces had been given – but both of them were bad. I was told also that the absolute foundation of the edifice is bad – that the ground, which is near the river and swampy, would not bear the weight intended to be imposed on it.

For myself I have much faith in the American character, but I cannot believe either in Washington city or in the Washington monument.[35] The boast made has been too loud, and the fulfilment yet accomplished has been too small!

Chapter 15

On the Virginian side of the Potomac stands a country-house called Arlington Heights, from which there is a fine view down upon the city. Arlington Heights is a beautiful spot – having all the attractions of a fine park in our country. It is covered with grand timber. The ground is varied and broken, and the private roads about sweep here into a dell and then up a brae-side, as roads should do in such a domain. Below it is the Potomac, and immediately on the other side stands the city of Washington. Any city seen thus is graceful; and the white stones of the big buildings when the sun gleams on them, showing the distant rows of columns, seem to tell something of great endeavour and success. It is the place from whence Washington should be seen by those who want to think well of the present city and of its future prosperity. But is it not the case that every city is beautiful from a distance?

The house at Arlington Heights is picturesque, but neither large nor good. It has before it a high Greek colonnade, which seems to be almost bigger than the house itself. The place did belong, and I think still does belong, to the family of Lees – if not already confiscated. General Lee [36] who is or would be the present owner, bears high command in the army of the Confederalists, and knows well by what tenure he holds, or is likely to hold, his family property. The family were friends of General Washington, whose seat, Mount Vernon, stands about twelve miles lower down the river; and here, no doubt, Washington often stood, looking on the site he had chosen. If his spirit could stand there now and look around upon the masses of soldiers by which his capital is surrounded, how could it address the city of his hopes? When he saw that every foot of the neighbouring soil was desecrated by a camp, or torn into loathsome furrows of mud by cannons and army waggons – that agriculture was gone, and that every effort both of North and South was concentrated on the art of killing; when he saw that this was done on the very spot chosen by himself for the centre temple of an everlasting union, what would he then say as to that boast made on his behalf by his countrymen that he was first in war and first in peace?

Mount Vernon, Washington's own residence, stands close over the Potomac, above six miles below Alexandria. When I first made inquiry on the subject I was told that Mount Vernon at that time was not to be reached; that though it was not in the hands of the rebels, neither was it in the hands of the North-erners, and that therefore strangers could not go there; but this, though it was told to me and others by those who should have known the facts, was not the case. I had gone down the river with a party of ladies, and we were opposite to Mount Vernon; but on that occasion we were assured we could not land. The rebels, we were told, would certainly seize the ladies, and carry them off into Secessia. On hearing which the ladies were of course doubly anxious to be landed. But our stern commander, for we were on a Government boat, would not listen to their prayers, but carried us instead on board the *Pensacola*, a sloop-of-war which was now lying in the river, ready to go to sea, and ready also to run the gauntlet of the rebel batteries which lined the Vir-ginian shore of the river for many miles. A sloop-of-war in these days means a large man-of-war, the guns of which are so big that they only stand on one deck, whereas a frigate would have them on two decks, and a line-of-battle ship on three. We went over the *Pensacola* and I must say she was very nice, pretty and clean. I have always found American sailors on their men-of-war to be clean and nice-looking – as much so I should say as our own; but nothing can be dirtier, more untidy, or apparently more ill-pre-served than all the appurtenances of their soldiers.

We landed also on this occasion at Alexandria, and saw as melancholy and miserable a town as the mind of man can con-ceive. Its ordinary male population, counting by the voters, is 1,500, and of these 700 were in the southern army. The place had been made a hospital for northern soldiers, and no doubt the site for that purpose had been well chosen. But let any woman imagine what would be the feelings of her life while living in a town used as a hospital for the enemies against whom her absent husband was then fighting! Her own man would be away ill –

wounded, dying, for what she knew, without the comfort of any
hospital attendance, without physic, with no one to comfort him;
but those she hated, with a hatred much keener than his, were
close to her hand, using some friend's house that had been forcibly
taken, crawling out into the sun under her eyes, taking the bread
from her mouth ! Life in Alexandria at this time must have been
sad enough. The people were all secessionists, but the town was
held by the northern party. Through the lines, into Virginia
they could not go at all. Up to Washington they could not go
without a military pass, not to be obtained without some cause
given. All trade was at an end. In no town at that time was trade
very flourishing; but here it was killed altogether – except that
absolutely necessary trade of bread. Who would buy boots or
coats, or want new saddles, or waste money on books, in such
days as these, in such a town as Alexandria : and then out of
1,500 men, one half had gone to fight the southern battles !
Among the women of Alexandria secession would have found
but few opponents.

I found afterwards that Mount Vernon was accessible, and I
rode thither with some officers from the staff of General Heintzelman,[37] whose outside pickets were stationed beyond the old place.
I certainly should not have been well pleased had I been forced
to leave the country without seeing the house in which Washington had lived and died. There is nothing very special about the
house. Indeed, as a house, it would have been found comfortless
and inconvenient. But the ground falls well down to the river,
and the timber, if not fine, is plentiful and picturesque. The chief
interest of the place, however, is in the tomb of Washington and
his wife. At Mount Vernon there is now a cemetery of the
Washington family; and there, in an open vault – a vault open,
but guarded by iron grating – is the great man's tomb, and by his
side the tomb of Martha his wife.

As I stood there alone, with no one to irritate me by assertions
of the man's absolute supremacy, I acknowledged that I had come
to find the final resting place of a great and good man – of a man
whose patriotism was, I believe, an honest feeling, untinged by
any personal ambition of a selfish nature. That he was pre-
eminently a successful man may have been due chiefly to the

excellence of his cause, and the blood and character of the people who put him forward as their right arm in their contest; but that he did not mar that success by arrogance, or destroy the brightness of his own name by personal aggrandisement, is due to a noble nature and the calm individual excellence of the man.

Considering the circumstances and history of the place, the position of Mount Vernon, as I saw it, was very remarkable. It lay exactly between the lines of the two armies. The pickets of the northern army had been extended beyond it, not improbably with the express intention of keeping a spot so hallowed within the power of the northern Government. But since the war began it had been in the hands of the seceders. In fact, it stood there in the middle of the battlefield, on the very line of division between loyalism and secession. And this was the spot which Washington had selected as the heart and centre, and safest rallying homestead of the united nation which he had left behind him. But Washington, when he resolved to found his capital on the banks of the Potomac, knew nothing of the glories of the Mississippi. He did not dream of the speedy addition to his already gathered constellations of those western stars, of Wisconsin, Illinois, Minnesota, and Iowa; nor did he dream of Texas conquered, Louisiana purchased, and Missouri and Kansas rescued from the wilderness.

Men whom one met in Washington were not unhappy about the state of things, as I had seen men unhappy in the North and in the West. They were mainly indifferent, but with that sort of indifference which arises from a breakdown of faith in anything. 'There was the Army! Yes, the Army! But what an Army! Nobody obeyed anybody! Nobody did anything! Nobody thought of advancing! There were, perhaps, two hundred thousand men assembled round Washington; and now the effort of supplying them with food and clothing was as much as could be accomplished! But the contractors, in the meantime, were becoming rich. And then as to the Government! Who trusted it? Who would put their faith in Seward and Cameron? Cameron was now gone, it was true; and in that way the whole of the Cabinet would soon be broken up. As to Congress, what could Congress do? Ask questions which no one would care to answer, and finally get itself packed up and sent home.' The President and the con-

stitution fared no better in men's mouths. The former did nothing
– neither harm nor good; and as for the latter, it had broken down
and shown itself to be inefficient. So men ate, and drank, and
laughed, waiting till chaos should come, secure in the belief that
the atoms into which their world would resolve itself, would con-
nect themselves again in some other form without trouble on their
part.

And at Washington I found no strong feeling against England
and English conduct towards America. 'We men of the world,
a Washington man might have said, 'know very well that everybody must take care of himself first. We are very good friends
with you – of course, and we are glad to see you at our table
whenever you come across the water, but as for rejoicing at your
joys, or expecting you to sympathize with our sorrows, we know
the world too well for that. We are splitting into pieces, and of
course that is gain to you. Take another cigar.'

This polite, fashionable, and certainly comfortable way of looking at the matter had never been attained at New York or Philadelphia, at Boston or Chicago. The northern provincial world
of the States had declared to itself that those who were not with
it were against it; that its neighbours should be either friends or
foes; that it would understand nothing of neutrality. This was
often mortifying to me, but I think I liked it better on the whole
than the *laissez-aller* indifference of Washington.

Everybody acknowledged that society in Washington had been
almost destroyed by the loss of the southern half of the usual
sojourners in the city. The senators and members of Government,
who heretofore had come from the southern States, had no doubt
spent more money in the capital than their northern brethren.
They and their families had been more addicted to social pleasures.
They are the descendants of the old English Cavaliers, whereas
the northern men have come from the old English Roundheads.
Or, if as may be the case, the blood of the races has now been too
well mixed to allow of this being said with absolute truth, yet
something of the manners of the old forefathers has been left.
The southern gentleman is more genial, less dry – I will not say
more hospitable, but more given to enjoy hospitality than his
northern brother; and this difference is quite as strong with the

women as with the men. It may therefore be understood that secession would be very fatal to the society of Washington.

In the interior of the Capitol much space is at present wasted, but this arises from the fact of great additions to the original plan having been made. The two chambers – that of the Senate and that of the Representatives, are in the two new wings, are on the middle, or what we call the first floor. The entrance is made under a dome, to a large circular hall, which is hung around with surely the worst pictures by which a nation ever sought to glorify its own deeds. There are yards of paintings at Versailles which are bad enough; but there is nothing at Versailles comparable in villainy to the huge daubs which are preserved in this hall at the Capitol. It is strange that even self-laudatory patriotism should desire the perpetuation of such rubbish. When I was there the new dome was still in progress, and an ugly column of woodwork, required for internal support and affording a staircase to the top, stood in this hall. This of course was a temporary and necessary evil; but even this was hung around with the vilest of portraits.

The Representative Chamber itself – which of course answers to our House of Commons – is a handsome, commodious room, admirably fitted for the purpose required. The Speaker sits opposite to the chief entrance, his desk being fitted against the opposite wall. He is thus brought nearer to the body of men before him than is the case with our Speaker. Every representative has his own armchair and his own desk before it. This may be done for a house consisting of about 240 members, but could hardly be contrived with us. A score or so of little boys are always running about the floor, ministering to the members' wishes, carrying up petitions to the chair, bringing water to the long-winded legislators, delivering and carrying out letters, and running with general messages. They do not seem to interrupt the course of business, and yet they are the liveliest little boys I ever saw. When a member claps his hands, indicating a desire for attendance, three or four will jockey for the honour. On the whole, I thought the little boys had a good time of it.

But not so the Speaker. It seemed to me that the amount of

work falling upon the Speaker's shoulders was cruelly heavy. His voice was always ringing in my ears, exactly as does the voice of a croupier at a gambling-table who goes on declaring and explaining the results of the game, and who generally does so in sharp, loud, ringing tones, from which all interest in the proceeding itself seems to have been excluded. It was just so with the Speaker in the House of Representatives. The debate was always full of interruptions; but on every interruption the Speaker asked the gentleman interrupted whether he would consent to be so treated. 'The gentleman from Indiana has the floor.' 'The gentleman from Ohio wishes to ask the gentleman from Indiana a question.' 'The gentleman from Indiana gives permission.' 'The gentleman from Ohio!' – these last words being a summons to him of Ohio to get up and ask his question. 'The gentleman from Pennsylvania rises to order.' 'The gentleman from Pennsylvania is in order.'

And then the House seems always to be voting, and the Speaker always putting the question. 'The gentlemen who agree to the amendment will say, "Ay".' Not a sound is heard. 'The gentlemen who oppose the amendment will say, "No".' Again not a sound. 'The Ayes have it,' says the Speaker, and then he goes on again. All this with amazing rapidity, and is always at it with the same, hard, quick, ringing, uninterested voice. The gentleman whom I saw in the chair was very clever, and quite up to the task. Perhaps it might be found that any great accession of dignity would impede the celerity of the work to be done, and that a closer copy of the British model might not on the whole increase the efficiency of the American machine.

The Senate House is in the opposite wing of the building, the position of one house answering exactly to the other. It is somewhat smaller, but is, as a matter of course, much less crowded. There are thirty-four States, and therefore sixty-eight seats and sixty-eight desks only are required. These are also arranged in a horseshoe form, and face the President; but there was a sad array of empty chairs when I was in Washington, nineteen or twenty seats being vacant in consequence of secession. In this house the Vice-President of the United States acts as President, but has by no means so hard a job of work as his brother on the other side of the way. Mr Hannibal Hamlin, from Maine, now fills this chair. I was driven, while in Washington, to observe something amounting almost to a peculiarity in the Christian names of the gentlemen who were then administering the Government of the country. Mr Abraham Lincoln was the President, Mr Hannibal Hamlin the Vice-President, Mr Galusha Grow the Speaker of the Representatives, Mr Salmon Chase the Secretary of the Treasury, Mr Caleb Smith the Attorney-General, Mr Simon Cameron the Secretary at War, and Mr Gideon Welles the Secretary of the Navy.

All the adjuncts of both these chambers are rich and in good keeping. The staircases are of marble, and the outside passages and lobbies are noble in size and in every way convenient. One knows very well the trouble of getting into the House of Lords and the House of Commons, and the want of comfort which attends one there; and an Englishman cannot fail to make comparisons injurious to his own country. It would not, perhaps, be possible to welcome all the world in London as is done in Washington, but there can be no good reason why the space given to the public by us should not equal that given in Washington. But so far are we from sheltering the public, that we have made our House of Commons so small, that it will not even hold its own members.

I had an opportunity of being present at one of their field-days in the Senate. Slidell and Mason had just then been sent from Fort Warren across to England in the *Rinaldo*. And here I may as well say what further there is for me to say about these two heroes. I was in Boston when they were taken, and all Boston was full of them. I was at Washington when they were surrendered, and at Washington for a time their names were the only household words in vogue. That, under all the circumstances, the States Government behaved well in the matter no one, I think, can deny; but the newspapers, taken as a whole, were not very consistent and, I think, not very dignified. They had declared with throats of brass that these men should never be surrendered to perfidious Albion; but when it came to be understood that in all probability they would be so surrendered, they veered round without an excuse, and spoke of their surrender as of a thing of course. And thus, in the course of about a week, the whole current of men's minds were turned. For myself, on my first arrival at Washington, I felt certain that there would be war, and was preparing myself for a quick return to England; but from the moment that the first whisper of England's message reached us, and that I began to hear how it was received and what men said about it, I knew that I need not hurry myself.

Lord Russell's [38] demand was worded in language so mild, was so devoid of threat, was so free from anger, that at the first reading it seemed to ask for nothing. It almost disappointed by its mildness. Mr Seward's reply, on the other hand, by its length of argumentation, by a certain sharpness of diction to which that gentleman is addicted in his State papers, and by a tone of satisfaction inherent through it all, seemed to demand more than he conceded. But, in truth, Lord Russell had demanded everything, and the United States Government had conceded everything.

The question of slavery in America cannot be handled fully and fairly by anyone who is afraid to go back upon the subject, and take its whole history since one man first claimed and exercised the right of forcing labour from another man. I certainly am afraid of any such task; but I believe that there has been no period yet, since the world's work began, when such a practice has not prevailed in a large portion, probably in the largest portion of the world's work fields. As civilization has made its progress, it has been the duty and the delight, as it has also been the interest of the men at the top of affairs, not to lighten the work of the men below, but so to teach them that they should recognize the necessity of working without coercion. Emancipation of serfs and thralls, of bondsmen and slaves, has always meant this – that men having been so taught, should then work without coercion. As men become educated and aware of the nature of the tenure on which they hold their life, they learn the fact that work is a necessity for them, and that it is better to work without coercion than with it. When men have learned this they are fit for emancipation, but they are hardly fit till they have learned so much.

It is vain to say that slavery has not caused secession, and that slavery has not caused the war. That, and that only has been the real cause of this conflict, though other small collateral issues may now be put forward to share the blame. Those other issues have arisen from this question of slavery, and are inclined to it and a part of it. Massachusetts, as we all know, is democratic in its tendencies, but South Carolina is essentially aristocratic. This difference has come of slavery. A slave country, which has progressed far in slavery, must be aristocratic in its nature – aristocratic and patriarchal. A large slave-owner from Georgia may call himself a Democrat – may think that he reverses republican institutions, and may talk with American horror of the thrones of Europe; but he must in his heart be an aristocrat. We, in England, are apt to speak of Republican institutions, and of universal suffrage which is perhaps the chief of them, as belonging equally to all the States. In South Carolina there is not and has not been any such thing. The electors for the President there are chosen not by the people, but by the legislature; and the votes for the legislature are limited by a high property qualification. Russia and England are not more unlike in their political and social feelings than are the real slave States and the real free-soil States.

The southern gentry have been 'Uncle-Tommed' into madness. It is no light thing to be told daily by your fellow citizens, by your fellow representatives, by your fellow senators, that you are guilty of the one damning sin that cannot be forgiven. All this they could partly moderate, partly rebuke, and partly bear as long as political power remained in their hands; but they have gradually felt that that was going, and were prepared to cut the rope and run as soon as it was gone.

But I cannot defend the South. As long as they could be successful in their schemes for holding the political power of the nation, they were prepared to hold by the nation. Immediately those schemes failed, they were prepared to throw the nation overboard. In this, there has undoubtedly been treachery as well as rebellion. Had these politicians been honest – though the political growth of Washington had hardly admitted of political honesty – but had these politicians been even ordinarily respectable in their dishonesty, they would have claimed secession openly before Congress, while yet their own President was at the White House. Congress would not have acceded under the constitution; but a way would have been found, had the southern States been persistent in their demand. A way indeed has been found; but it has lain through fire and water, through blood and ruin, through treason and theft, and the downfall of national greatness. Secession will, I think, be accomplished, and the southern Confederation of States will stand something higher in the world than Mexico and the republics of Central America. Her cotton monopoly will have vanished, and her wealth will have been wasted.

One cannot but ask what abolition means, and to what it would lead. Any ordinance of abolition now pronounced would not effect the emancipation of the slaves, but might probably effect a servile insurrection. I will not accuse those who are preaching this crusade of any desire for so fearful a scourge on the land. They probably calculate that an edict of abolition once given would be so much done towards the ultimate winning of the battle. They are making their hay while the sun shines. But if they could emancipate those four million slaves, in what way would they then treat them? How would they feed them? In what way would they treat the ruined owners of the slaves, and the acres of land which would lie uncultivated? Of all the subjects with which a man can be called on to deal, it is the most difficult.

In Maryland and Delaware are men who hate slavery, who would be only too happy to enfranchise their slaves; but the Negroes who have been slaves are not fit for freedom. In many cases, practically, they cannot be enfranchised. Give them their liberty, starting them well in the world at what expense you please, and at the end of six months they will come back upon your hands for the means of support. Everything must be done for them. They expect food and clothes, and instruction as to every simple act of life, as do children. The Negro domestic servant is handy at his own work; no servant more so; but he cannot go beyond that. He does not comprehend the object and purport of continued industry. If he have money he will play with it – will amuse himself with it. If he have none, he will amuse himself without it. His work is like a schoolboy's task; he knows it must be done, but never comprehends that the doing of it is the very end and essence of his life. He is a child in all things, and the extent of prudential wisdom to which he ever attains is to disdain emancipation, and to cling to the security of his bondage. It is true enough that slavery has been a curse. Whatever may have been its effect on the Negroes, it has been a deadly curse upon the white masters.

Abolition, in truth, is a political cry. It is the banner of defiance opposed to secession. As the differences between the North and South have grown with years, and have swelled to the proportions of national antipathy, southern nullification has amplified itself into secession, and northern free-soil principles have burst into this growth of abolition. Charming pictures are drawn for you of the Negro in a state of Utopian bliss, owning his own hoe and eating his own hog; in a paradise, where everything is bought and sold, except his wife, his little ones, and himself. But the enfranchised Negro has always thrown away his hoe and eaten any man's hog but his own – and has too often sold his daughter for a dollar when any such market has been open to him.

I confess that the cry of abolition has been made particularly displeasing to me, by the fact that the northern abolitionist is by no means willing to give even to the Negro who is already free that position in the world which alone might tend to raise him in the scale of human beings – if anything can so raise him and make him fit for freedom. The abolitionists hold that the Negro is the white man's equal. I do not. I see or think that I see, that the Negro is the white man's inferior through laws of nature. That he is not mentally fit to cope with white men – I speak of the full-blooded Negro – and that he must fill a position simply servile. But the abolitionist declares him to be the white man's equal. But yet, when he has him at his elbow, he treats him with a scorn which even the Negro can hardly endure.

I will give him his political equality, but not social equality, says the abolitionist. But even in this he is untrue. A black man may vote in New York, but he cannot vote under the same circumstances as a white man. He is subjected to qualifications which in truth debar him from the poll. But political equality is not what such men want, nor indeed is it social equality. It is social tolerance and social sympathy; and these are denied to the Negro. An American abolitionist would not sit at a table with a Negro. He might do so in England at the house of an English duchess; but in his own country the proposal of such a companion would be an insult to him. He will not sit with him in a public carriage if he can avoid it. In New York I have seen special street cars for coloured people. The abolitionist is struck with horror when he thinks that a man and brother should be a slave; but when the man and brother is made free, he is regarded with loathing and contempt.

All this I cannot see with equanimity. There is falsehood in it from the beginning to the end. The slave as a rule is well treated – he gets all he wants and almost all he desires. The free Negro as a rule is ill-treated and does not get that consideration which alone might put him in the worldly position for which his advocate declares him to be fit. It is false throughout – this preaching. The Negro is not the white man's equal by nature. But to the free Negro in the northern States this inequality is increased by the white man's hardness to him.

Every Englishman probably looks forward to the accomplishment of abolition of slavery at some future day. I feel as sure of it as I do of final judgement. When or how it shall come I will not attempt to foretell. The mode which seems to promise the surest success and the least present or future inconvenience, would be an edict enfranchising all female children born after a certain date, and all their children. Under such an argument the Negro population would probably die out slowly – very slowly. What might then be the fate of the cotton fields of the Gulf States, who shall dare say? It may be that coolies from India and from China will then have taken the place of the Negro there, as they will have done in Guiana and the West Indies.

Chapter 16

THOUGH I had felt Washington to be disagreeable as a city, yet I was almost sorry to leave it when the day of my departure came. I had allowed myself a month for my sojourn in the capital, and I had stayed a month to the day. Then came the trouble of packing up, the necessity of calling on a long list of acquaintances one after another, the feeling that bad as Washington might be, I might be going to places that were worse, a conviction that I should get beyond the reach of my letters, and a sort of affection which I had acquired for my rooms. My landlord, being a coloured man, told me that he was sorry I was going. Would I not remain? Would I come back to him? Had I been comfortable? Only for so and so and so and so, he would have done better for me. No white American citizen, occupying the position of landlord, would have condescended to such comfortable words. I knew the man did not in truth want me to stay, as a lady and gentleman were waiting to go in the moment I went out; but I did not the less value the assurance.

One hungers and thirsts after such civil words among American citizens in this class. The clerks and managers at hotels, the officials at railway stations, the cashiers at banks, the women in the shops – ah! they are the worst of all. An American woman who is bound by her position to serve you – who is paid in some shape to supply your wants, whether to sell you a bit of soap or bring you a towel in your bedroom at an hotel – is, I think, of all human creatures, the most insolent. I certainly had a feeling of regret at parting with my coloured friend – and some regret also as regards a few that are white.

As I drove down Pennsylvania Avenue, through this slush and mud, and saw, perhaps for the last time, those wretchedly dirty horse sentries, I almost wished that I could see more of them. How absurd they looked, with a whole kit of battletraps on their horses' backs behind them – blankets, coats, canteens, coils of rope, and always at the top of everything else, a tin pot! No doubt these things are all necessary to a mounted sentry, or they would not have been there; but it always seemed as though the horse had been loaded gipsy-fashion, in a manner that I may perhaps best describe as higgledy-piggledy, and that there was a want of military precision in the packing.

The man would have looked more graceful, and the soldier more warlike, had the pannikin been made to assume some rigidly fixed position, instead of dangling among the ropes. The drawn sabre, too, never consorted well with the dirty outside woollen wrapper which generally hung loose from the man's neck. Heaven knows, I did not begrudge him his comforter in that cold weather, or even his long, uncombed shock of hair; but I think he might have been made more spruce, and I am sure that he could not have looked more uncomfortable. As I went, however, I felt for him a sort of affection, and wished in my heart of hearts that he might soon be enabled to return to some more congenial employment.

My route lay over the Alleghenies by Pittsburgh and Cincinnati, and my first stopping-place was Harrisburg, the political capital of Pennsylvania. There is nothing special at Harrisburg to arrest any traveller; but the local legislature of the State was then sitting, and I was desirous of seeing the Senate and Representatives of at any rate one State, during its period of vitality.

The appearance of the members of the legislature of Pennsylvania did not impress me very favourably. I do not know why we should wish a legislator to be neat in his dress, and comely, in some degree, in his personal appearance. There is no good reason, perhaps, why they should have cleaner shirts than their outside brethren, or have been more particular in the use of soap and water, and brush and comb. But I have an idea that if ever our own Parliament becomes dirty, it will lose its prestige and I cannot but think that the Parliament of Pennsylvania would gain an accession of dignity by some slightly increased devotion to the Graces. I saw in the two houses but one gentleman, a Quaker, who looked like a Quaker; but even he was a very untidy Quaker.

In running down the mountains to Pittsburgh an accident occurred which in any other country could have thrown the engine off the line, and have reduced the carriages behind the engine to a heap of ruins. But here it had no other effect than that of delaying us for three or four hours. The tire of one of the heavy driving wheels flew off, and in the shock the body of the wheel itself was broken, one spoke and a portion of the circumference of the wheel was carried away, and the steam-chamber was ripped open. Nevertheless the train was pulled up, neither the engine nor any of the carriages got off the line, and the men in charge of the train seemed to think very lightly of the matter.

I was amused to see how little was made of the affair by any of the passengers. In England a delay of three hours would in itself produce a great amount of grumbling, or at least many signs of discomfort and temporary unhappiness. But here no one said a word. Some of the younger men got out and looked at the ruined wheel; but most of the passengers kept their seats, chewed their tobacco, and went to sleep. In all such matters an American is much more patient than an Englishman. To sit quiet, without speech, and ruminate in some contorted position of body comes to him by nature. On this occasion I did not hear a word of complaint – nor yet a word of surprise or thankfulness that the accident had been attended with no serious result.

'I have got a furlough for ten days,' one soldier said to me. 'And I have missed every connection all through from Washington here. I shall have just time to turn round and go back when I get home.' But he did not seem to be in any way dissatisfied. He had not referred to his relatives when he spoke of 'missing his connections', but to his want of good fortune as regarded railway travelling. He had reached Baltimore too late for the train on to Pittsburgh. Now he must again reach Pittsburgh too late for his further journey. But nevertheless he seemed to be well pleased with his position.

Pittsburgh is the Merthyr-Tydfil of Pennsylvania – or perhaps I should better describe it as an amalgamation of Swansea, Merthyr-Tydfil and South Shields. It is without exception the blackest place I ever saw. The three English towns which I have named are very dirty, but all their combined soot and grease and dinginess do not equal that of Pittsburgh. As regards scenery it is beautifully situated, being at the foot of the Allegheny mountains, and at the juncture of the two rivers Monongahela and Allegheny. Here, at the town, they come together and form the river Ohio. Nothing can be more picturesque than the site; for the spurs of the mountains come down close round the town, and the rivers are broad and swift, and can be seen for miles from heights which may be reached in a short walk. Even the filth and wondrous blackness of the place are picturesque when looked down upon from above. I was never more in love with smoke and dirt when I watched the darkness of night close in upon the floating soot which hovered over the housetops of the city. I cannot say that I ever saw the sun set, for there was no sun. I should say that the sun never shone at Pittsburgh – as foreigners who visit London in November declare that the sun never shines there.

Everything at the hotel was black; not black to the eye, for the eye teaches itself to discriminate colours even when loaded with dirt, but black to the touch. On coming out of a tub of water my foot took an impress from the carpet exactly as it would have done had I trod barefooted on a path laid with soot. I thought that I was turning Negro upwards, till I put my wet hand on the carpet, and found that the result was the same. And yet the carpet was green to the eye – a dull dingy green, but still green. 'You shouldn't damp your feet,' a man said to me to whom I mentioned the catastrophe. Certainly Pittsburgh is the dirtiest place I ever saw, but it is, as I said before, very picturesque in its dirt when looked at from above the blanket.

From Pittsburgh I went on by train to Cincinnati, and was soon in the State of Ohio. I had some little personal feeling in visiting Cincinnati, because my mother had lived there for some time, and had there been concerned in a commercial enterprise, by which no one, I believe, made any great sum of money. Between thirty and forty years ago she built a bazaar [39] in Cincinnati, which I was assured by the present owner of the house, was at the time of its erection considered to be the great building of the town. It has been sadly eclipsed now, and by no means rears its head proudly among the great blocks around it. It had become a 'Physico-medical Institute' when I was there, and was under the dominion of a quack doctor on one side, and of a college of rights-of-women female medical professors on the other.

'I believe, sir, no man or woman ever yet made a dollar in that building; and as for rent I don't even expect it.' Such was the account given of the unfortunate bazaar by its present proprietor.

Cincinnati has long been known as a great town – conspicuous among all towns for the number of hogs which are there killed, salted and packed. It is the great hog metropolis of the western States. It seems to be an established fact, that in this portion of the world the porcine genus are all hogs. One never hears of a pig. With us a trade in hogs and pigs is subject to some contumely. There is a feeling, which has perhaps never been expressed in words, but which certainly exists, that these animals are not so honourable in their bearing as sheep and oxen. It is a prejudice which by no means exists in Cincinnati. There hog killing and salting and packing are very honourable, and the great men in the trade are the merchant princes of the city.

The town is well built, with good fronts to many of the houses, with large shops and larger stores; of course also with an enormous hotel, which has never paid anything like a proper dividend to the speculator who built it. It is always the same story. But these towns shame our provincial towns by their breadth and grandeur. I am afraid that speculators with us are tramelled by an 'ignorant impatience of ruin'. I should not myself like to live in Cincinnati or any of these towns. They are slow, dingy, and uninteresting; but they all possess an air of substantial, civic dignity. It must however be remembered that the Americans live much more in towns than we do. All with us that are rich and aristocratic and luxurious live in the country, frequenting the metropolis for only a portion of the year. But all that are rich and aristocratic and luxurious in the States live in the towns. Our provincial towns are not generally chosen as the residences of our higher classes.

Cincinnati has 170,000 inhabitants, and there are 14,000 children at the free schools – which is about one in twelve of the whole population. This number gives the average of scholars throughout the year ended 30th June, 1861. But there are other schools in Cincinnati – parish schools and private schools, and it is stated to me that there were in all 32,000 children attending school in the city throughout the year. The education at the State schools is very good. Thirty-four teachers are employed, at an average salary of 92l. each, ranging from 260l. to 60l. per annum. It is in this matter of education that the cities of the free States of America have done so much for the civilization and welfare of their population. This fact cannot be repeated in their praise too often. Those who have the management of affairs, who are at the top of the tree, are desirous of giving all an opportunity of raising themselves in the scale of human beings.

I dislike universal suffrage; I dislike vote by ballot; I dislike above all things the tyranny of democracy. But I do like the political feeling – for it is a political feeling – which induces every educated American to lend a hand to the education of his fellow citizens. It shows, if nothing else does so, a germ of truth in that doctrine of equality. It is a doctrine to be forgiven when he who preaches it is in truth striving to raise others to his own level – though utterly unpardonable when the preacher would pull down others to his own level.

I visited the little towns of Lexington and Frankfort, in Kentucky. At the former I found in the hotel to which I went seventy-five teamsters belonging to the army. They were hanging about the great hall when I entered, and clustering round the stove in the middle of the chamber – a dirty, rough, quaint set of men, clothed in a wonderful variety of garbs, but not disorderly or loud. The landlord apologized for their presence, alleging that other accommodation could not be found for them in the town. He received, he said, a dollar a day for feeding them, and for supplying them with a place in which they could lie down. It did not pay him – but what could he do? Such an apology from an American landlord was in itself a surprising fact. Such high functionaries are, as a rule, men inclined to tell a traveller that if he does not like the guests among whom he finds himself, he may go elsewhere. But this landlord had as yet filled the place for not more than two or three weeks, and was unused to the dignity of his position.

While I was at supper, the seventy-five teamsters were summoned into the common eating-room by a loud gong, and sat down to their meal at the public table. They were very dirty; I doubt whether I ever saw dirtier men; but they were orderly and well-behaved, and but for their extreme dirt might have passed as the ordinary occupants of a well-filled hotel in the West. Such men, in the States, are less clumsy with their knives and forks, less astray in an unused position, more intelligent to adapting themselves to a new life than are Englishmen of the same rank. It is always the same story. With us there is no level of society. Men stand on a long staircase, but the crowd congregates near the bottom, and the lower steps are very broad. In America men stand upon a common platform, but the platform is raised above the ground, though it does not approach in height the top of our staircase. If we take the average altitude of the two countries, we shall find that the American heads are the more elevated of the two. I conceived rather an affection for those dirty teamsters; they answered me civilly when I spoke to them, and sat in quietness, smoking their pipes, with a dull and dirty, but orderly demeanour.

The country around Lexington is called the Blue Grass Region, and boasts itself as of peculiar fecundity in the matter of pasturage. Why the grass is called blue, and in what way or at what period it becomes blue, I did not learn; but the country is very lovely and very fertile. Between Lexington and Frankfort a large stock farm, extending over three thousand acres, is kept by a gentleman, who is very well known as a breeder of horses, cattle and sheep. He has spent much money on it, and is making for himself a Kentucky elysium. He was kind enough to entertain me for a while, and showed me something of country life in Kentucky.

A farm in that part of the States depends, and must depend, on slave-labour. The slaves are a material part of the estate, and as they are regarded by the law as real property an inheritor of land has no alternative but to keep them. A gentleman in Kentucky does not sell his slaves. To do so is considered to be low and mean, and is opposed to the aristocratic conditions of the country. A man who does so willingly, puts himself beyond the pale of good fellowship with his neighbours. A sale of slaves is regarded as a sign almost of bankruptcy. When a man owns more slaves than he needs, he hires them out by the year; and when he requires more than he owns, he takes them on hire by the year. Care is taken in such hirings not to remove a married man away from his home. The price paid for a Negro's labour at the time of my visit was about a hundred dollars or twenty pounds, for the year; but this price was then extremely low in consequence of the war disturbances. The usual price has been fifty or sixty per cent above this. The man who takes the Negro on hire feeds him, clothes him, provides him with a bed, and supplies him with medical attention.

I went into some of their cottages on the estate which I visited, and was not in the least surprised to find them preferable in size, furniture, and all material comforts to the dwellings of most of our own agricultural labourers. Any comparison between the material comfort of a Kentucky slave and an English ditcher and delver would be preposterous. The Kentucky slave never wants for clothing fitted to the weather. He eats meat twice a day, and has three good meals; he knows no limit but his own appetite; his work is light; he has many varieties of amusement; he has instant medical attention at all periods of necessity for himself, his wife, and his children. Of course he pays no rent, fears no banker, and knows no hunger. I would not have it supposed that I conceive slavery with all these comforts to be equal to freedom without them; nor do I conceive that the Negro can be made equal to the white man. But in discussing the condition of the Negro, it is necessary that we should understand what are the advantages of which abolition would deprive him, and in what condition he has been placed by the daily receipt of such advantages. If a Negro slave wants new shoes, he asks for them, and receives them, with the undoubted simplicity of a child. Such a state of things has its picturesquely patriarchal side; but what would be the state of such a man if he were emancipated tomorrow?

Going from Louisville up to St Louis, I crossed the Ohio river and passed through parts of Indiana and Illinois, and striking the Mississippi opposite St Louis, crossed that river also, and then entered the State of Missouri. The Ohio was flooded, and we went over it at night. The boat had been moored at some unaccustomed place. There was no light. The road was deep in mud up to the axle-tree, and was crowded with waggons and carts, which in the darkness of the night seemed to have stuck there. But the man drove his four horses through it all, and into the ferry-boat, over its side. There were three or four such omnibuses, and as many waggons, as to each of which I predicted in my own mind some fatal catastrophe. But they were all driven on to the boat in the dark, the horses mixing in through each other in a chaos which would altogether incapacitate any English coachman. And then the vessel laboured across the flood, going sideways, and hardly keeping her own against the stream. But we did get over, and were all driven out again, up to the railway station in safety.

On reaching the Mississippi about the middle of the next day, we found it frozen over, or rather covered from side to side with blocks of ice which had forced its way down the river, so that the steam ferry could not reach its proper landing. I do not think that we in England would have attempted the feat of carrying over horses and carriages under stress of such circumstances. But it was done here. Huge plankings were laid down over the ice, and omnibuses and waggons were driven on. In getting out again, these vehicles, each with four horses, had to be twisted about, and driven in and across the vessels, and turned in spaces to look at which would have broken the heart of an English coachman. And then with a spring they were driven up a bank as steep as a ladder! Ah me! Under what mistaken illusions have I laboured all the days of my youth, in supposing that no man could drive four horses well but an English stage-coachman? I have seen performances in America – and in Italy and France also, but above all in America, which would have made the hair of any English professional driver stand on end.

And in this way I entered St Louis.

Chapter 17

St Louis is the great town of Missouri, and is considered by the Missourians to be the star of the West. It is not beaten in population, wealth, or natural advantages by any other city so far west; but it has not increased with such rapidity as Chicago, which is considerably to the north of it on Lake Michigan. Of the great western cities I regard Chicago as the most remarkable, seeing that St Louis was a large town before Chicago was founded.

The population of St Louis is 170,000. Of this number only 2,000 are slaves. I was told that a large proportion of the slaves of Missouri are employed near the Missouri river in breaking hemp. The growth of hemp is very profitably carried on in that valley, and the labour attached to it is one which white men do not like to encounter. Slaves are not generally employed in St Louis for domestic service, as is done almost universally in the towns of Kentucky. This work is chiefly in the hands of Irish and Germans. Considerably above one third of the population of the whole city is made up of these two nationalities. So much is confessed; but if I were to form an opinion of the language I heard in the streets of the town, I should say that nearly every man was either an Irishman or a German.

St Louis, and indeed the whole of the State of Missouri, was at the time of my visit under martial law. General Hallek[40] was in command, holding his headquarters at St Louis, and carrying out, at any rate as far as the city was concerned, what orders he chose to issue. I am disposed to think that, situated as Missouri then was, martial law was the best law. No other law could have had force in a town surrounded by soldiers, and in which half the inhabitants were loyal to the existing Government, and half of them were in favour of rebellion. The necessity for such power is terrible, and the power itself in the hands of one man must be full of danger; but even that is better than anarchy.

Up to the time at which I was at St Louis, martial law had chiefly been used for closing grog-shops and administering the oath of allegiance to suspected secessionists. Something had also been done in the way of raising money by selling the property of convicted secessionists, and while I was there eight men were condemned for destroying railway bridges.

'But will they be shot?' I asked one of the officers.

'Oh yes. It will be done quietly and no one will know anything about it. We shall get used to that kind of thing presently.'

St Louis martial law was quite popular. Why should not General Hallek be as well able to say what was good for the people as any law or any lawyer? He had no interest in the injury of the State, but every interest in its preservation.

'But what,' I asked, 'would be the effect were he to tell you to put out all your fires at eight o'clock?'

'If he were so to order, we should do it; but we know that he will not.'

But who does know to what General Hallek or other generals may come, or how soon a curfew-bell may be ringing in American towns? The winning of liberty is long and tedious, but the losing of it is a downhill, easy journey.

I went out twice to Benton barracks, as the camp of wooden huts was called, which General Fremont had erected near the fair-ground of the city. This fair-ground, I was told, had been a pleasant place. It had been constructed for the recreation of the city, and for the purpose of periodical agricultural exhibitions. There is still in it a pretty ornamental cottage, and in the little garden a solitary Cupid stood dismayed by the dirt and ruin around him. But Benton barracks are outside the fair-green. Here on an open space, some half-mile in length, two long rows of wooden sheds have been built, opposite to each other, and behind them are sheds used for stabling and cooking places. Those in front are divided, not into separate huts, but into chambers capable of containing nearly two hundred men each. They were surrounded on the inside by great wooden trays, in three tiers – and on each tray four men were supposed to sleep.

I went into one or two while the crowd of soldiers was in them, but found it inexpedient to stay there long. The stench of those places was foul beyond description. Never in my life had I been in a place so horrid to the eyes and nose as Benton barracks. The path along the front outside was deep in mud. The whole space between the two rows of sheds was one field of mud, so slippery that the foot could not stand. Inside and outside every spot was deep in mud. The soldiers were mud-stained from foot to sole. These volunteer soldiers are in their nature dirty, as must be all men brought together in numerous bodies without special appliances for cleanliness, or control or discipline as to their personal habits. But the dirt of the men in the Benton barracks surpassed any dirt that I had hitherto seen. Nor could it have been otherwise with them. They were surrounded by a sea of mud, and the foul hovels in which they were made to sleep and live were fetid with stench and reeking with filth.

I had at this time been joined by another Englishman, and we went through this place together. When we inquired as to the health of the men, we heard the saddest of tales – of three hundred men gone out of one regiment, of whole companies that had perished, of hospitals crowded with fever patients. Measles had been the great scourge of the soldiers here – as it had been in the army of the Potomac. I shall not soon forget my visits to Benton barracks. It may be that our own soldiers were as badly treated in the Crimea; or that French soldiers were treated worse on their march into Russia. It may be that dirt, and wretchedness, diseases and listless idleness, a descent from manhood to habits lower than those of the beasts, are necessary in warfare; but I am no military critic and will not say. This I say – that the degradation of men to the state in which I saw the American soldiers in Benton barracks, is disgraceful to humanity.

General Hallek was at this time commanding in Missouri, and was himself stationed at St Louis; but his active measures were going on to the right and to the left. On the left shore of the Mississippi, at Cairo in Illinois, a fleet of gun-boats was being prepared to go down the river, and on the right an army was advancing against Springfield, in the south-western district of Missouri, with the object of dislodging Price,[41] the rebel guerrilla leader there and, if possible, catching him. Price had been the opponent of poor General Lyon[42] who was killed at Wilson's Creek, near Springfield, and of General Fremont, who during his hundred days had failed to drive him out of the State. This duty had now been trusted to General Curtis,[43], who had for some time been holding his headquarters at Rolla, halfway between St Louis and Springfield. Fremont had built a fort at Rolla, and it had become a military station. Over 10,000 men had been there at one time, and now General Curtis was to advance from Rolla against Price with something above that number of men. Many of them, however, had already gone on, and others were daily being sent up from St Louis. Under these circumstances my friend and I, fortified with a letter of introduction to General Curtis, resolved to go and see the army at Rolla.

It was dark when we got into Rolla. Everything had been covered with snow, and everywhere the snow was frozen. We had heard that there was an hotel, and that possibly we might get a bedroom there. We were first taken to a wooden building which we were told was the headquarters of the army, and in one room we found a colonel with a lot of soldiers loafing about, and in another a provost-marshal attended by a newspaper correspondent. We were received with open arms, and a suggestion was made at once that we were no doubt picking up news for European newspapers.

'Are you a son of the Mrs Trollope?' said the correspondent. 'Then, sir, you are an accession to Rolla.'

Upon which I was made to sit down and invited to 'loaf about' at the headquarters as long as I might remain in Rolla. Shortly, however, there came on a violent discussion about waggons. A general had come in and wanted all the colonel's waggons, but the colonel swore that he had none, declared how bitterly he was impeded with sick men, and became indignant and reproachful. It was Brutus and Cassius again; and as we felt ourselves in the way, and anxious moreover to ascertain what might be the nature of a Rolla hotel, we took up our heavy portmanteaux – for they were heavy – and with a guide to show us the way, started off through the dark and over the hill to our inn.

I shall never forget that walk. It was up hill and down hill, with an occasional half-frozen stream across it. My friend was impeded with an enormous cloak lined with fur, which in itself of the colonel's office, carried an umbrella and a small dressing- was a burden for a coalheaver. Our guide, who was a clerk out bag, but we ourselves manfully shouldered our portmanteaux. Why is it that a stout Englishman bordering on fifty finds himself in such a predicament as that? No Frenchman, no Italian, no German, would so place himself, unless under the stress of insurmountable circumstances. No American would do so under any circumstances. As I slipped about on the ice and groaned with that terrible fardel on my back, burdened with a dozen shirts, and a suit of dress clothes, and three pairs of boots, and four or five thick volumes, and a set of maps, and a box of cigars, and a washing-tub, I confessed to myself that I was a fool. What was I doing in such a galley as that? Why had I brought all that useless lumber down to Rolla? Why had I come to Rolla, with no certain hope even of shelter for a night? But we did reach the hotel; we did get a room between us with two bedsteads. And, pondering over the matter in my mind, since that evening I have been inclined to think that the stout Englishman is in the right of it. No American of my age and weight will ever go through what I went through; but I am not sure that he does not in his accustomed career go through worse things even than that. However, if I go to Rolla again during the war, I will at any rate leave the books behind me.

What a night we spent at that inn! They who know America will be aware that in all hotels there is a free admixture of different classes. The traveller in Europe may sit down to dinner with his tailor and shoemaker; but if so, his tailor and shoemaker have dressed themselves as he dresses, and are prepared to carry themselves according to a certain standard, which in exterior does not differ from his own. In the large Eastern cities of the States, such as Boston, New York and Washington, a similar practice of life is gradually becoming prevalent. There are various hotels for various classes, and the ordinary traveller does not find himself at the same table with a butcher fresh from the shambles. But in the West there are no distinctions whatever. 'A man's a man for a' that' in the West, let the 'a' that' comprise what it may of coarse attire and unsophisticated manners.

One soon gets used to it. In that inn at Rolla was a public-room, heated in the middle by a stove, and round that we soon found ourselves seated in a company of soldiers, farmers, labourers, and teamsters. But there was among them a general — not a fighting, or would-be fighting general of the present time, but one of the old-fashioned local generals — men who held, or had once held, some fabulous generalship in the State militia. There we sat, cheek by jowl with our new friends, till nearly twelve o'clock, talking politics and discussing the war. The General was a staunch Unionist, having according to his own showing suffered dreadful things from secessionist persecutors since the rebellion commenced.

As a matter of course everybody present was for the Union. In such a place one very rarely encounters any differences of opinion. The General was very eager about the war, advocating the immediate abolition of slavery, not as a means of improving the condition of the southern slaves, but on the ground that it would ruin the southern masters. We all sat by, edging in a word now and then, but the General was the talker of the evening. He was very wrathy, and swore at every other word.

'It was pretty well time,' he said, 'to crush out this rebellion and by — it must be and should be crushed out; General Jim Lane[44] was the man to do it, and by — General Jim Lane would do it!' and so on. But the time passes by as other weeks and months have passed before it, and the new General is found to be no more successful than his brethren. Our friend was very angry against England.

'When we've polished off these accursed rebels, I guess we'll take a turn at you. You had your turn when you made us give up Mason and Slidell, and we'll have our turn by and by.'

But in spite of his dislike to our nation he invited us warmly to come and see him at his home on the Missouri river.

At such a house (viz: the inn) all the guests go in to their meals together. A gong is sounded on a sudden, close behind your ears; accustomed as you may be to the sound you jump up from your chair in the agony of the crash, and by the time that you have collected your thoughts the whole crowd is off in a general stampede into the eating-room. You may as well join them; if you hesitate as to feeding with so rough a lot of men, you will have to sit down afterwards with the women and children of the family, and your lot will be then worse. Among such classes in the western States the men are always better than the women. The men are dirty and civil, the women are dirty and uncivil.

On the following day we returned to St Louis. I stayed two days longer in that city, and then I thought that I had seen enough of Missouri – enough of Missouri at any rate under the present circumstances of frost and secession. As regards the people of the West, I must say that they were not such as I expected to find them. With the Northerns we are more or less intimately acquainted. Those Americans whom we meet in our own country, or on the Continent, are generally from the North, or if not so they have that type of American manners which has become familiar to us. They are talkative, intelligent, inclined to be social, though frequently not sympathetically social with ourselves; somewhat *soi-disant*, but almost invariably companionable. As the traveller goes south into Maryland and Washington, the type is not altered to any great extent. The hard intelligence of the Yankee gives place gradually to the softer, and perhaps more polished manner of the Southern. But the change thus experienced is not so great as that between the American of the western and the American of the Atlantic States.

In the West I found the men gloomy and silent – I might almost say sullen. A dozen of them will sit for hours round a stove, speechless. They chew tobacco and ruminate. They are not offended if you speak to them, but they are not pleased. They answer with monosyllables, or, if it be practicable, with a gesture of the head. They care nothing for the graces – or shall I say, for the decencies of life. They are essentially a dirty people. Dirt, untidiness, and noise, seem in nowise to afflict them. Things are constantly done before your eyes, which should be done and might be done behind your back. No doubt we daily come into the closest contact with matters which, if we saw all that pertains to them, would cause us to shake and shudder. In other countries we do not see all this, but in the western States we do. I have eaten in Bedouin tents, and have been ministered to by Turks and Arabs. I have sojourned in the hotels of old Spain, and of Spanish America. I have lived in Connaught, and have taken up my quarters with monks of different nations. I have, as it were, been educated to dirt, and taken out my degree in outward abominations. But my education had not reached a point which would enable me to live at my ease in the western States. A man or woman who can do that may be said to have graduated in the highest honours, and to have become absolutely invulnerable, either through the sense of touch, or by the eye, or by the nose.

No men love money with more eager love than these western men, but they bear the loss of it as an Indian bears his torture at the stake. They are energetic in trade; speculating deeply whenever speculation is possible; but nevertheless they are slow in motion, loving to loaf about. They are slow in speech, preferring to sit in silence, with the tobacco between their teeth. They drink, but are seldom drunk to the eye; they begin it early in the morning, and take it in a solemn, sullen, ugly manner, standing always at a bar; swallowing their spirits, and saying nothing as they swallow it. They drink often, and to great excess; but they carry it off without noise, sitting down and ruminating over it with the everlasting cud between their jaws. I believe that a stranger might go to the West, and passing from hotel to hotel through a dozen of them, might sit for hours at each in the large everlasting public hall, and never have a word addressed to him.

I cannot part from the West without saying in its favour that there is a certain manliness about its men, which gives them a dignity of their own. It is shown in that very difference of which I have spoken. Whatever turns up the man is still there – still unsophisticated and still unbroken. It has seemed to me that no race of men requires less outward assistance than these pioneers of civilization. They rarely amuse themselves. Food, newspapers, and brandy-smashes suffice for life; and while these last the man is still there in his manhood. The fury of the mob does not shake him, nor the stern countenance of his present martial tyrant. Alas! I cannot stick to my text by calling him a just man. Intelligence, energy, and endurance are his virtues. Dirt, dishonesty, and morning drinks are his vices.

All native American women are intelligent. It seems to be their birthright. In the eastern cities they have, in their upper classes, superadded womanly grace to this intelligence, and consequently they are charming as companions. They are beautiful too, and, as

I believe, lack nothing that a lover can desire in his love. But I cannot fancy myself much in love with a western lady, or rather with a lady in the West. They are as sharp as nails, but then they are also as hard. They know, doubtless, all that they ought to know, but then they know so much more than they ought to know. They are tyrants to their parents, and never practise the virtue of obedience till they have half-grown-up daughters of their own.

They have faith in the destiny of their country, if nothing else; but they believe that destiny is to be worked out by the spirit and talent of the young women. I confess for me Eve would have had no charms had she not recognized Adam as her lord. I can forgive her in that she tempted him to eat the apple. Had she come from the West country she would have ordered him to make his meal, and then I should not have forgiven her.

St Louis should be, and still will be, a town of great wealth. To no city can have been given more means of riches. She is the centre of an enormous mileage of water-communication. The country around her produces Indian corn, wheat, grasses, hemp, and tobacco. Coal is dug even within the boundaries of the city, and iron-mines are worked at a distance from it of a hundred miles. The iron is so pure, that it is broken off in solid blocks, almost free from alloy; and as the metal stands up on the earth's surface in the guise almost of a gigantic metal pillar, instead of lying low within its bowels, it is worked at a cheap rate and with great certainty. Nevertheless, at the present moment, the iron-works of Pilot Knob, as the place is called, do not pay. As far as I could learn, nothing did pay, except government contracts.

Chapter 18

TO whatever period of life my days may be prolonged, I do not think that I shall ever forget Cairo. I do not mean Grand Cairo, which is also memorable in its way, and a place not to be forgotten – but Cairo in the State of Illinois, which by native Americans is always called Caaro. An idea is prevalent in the States, and I think I have heard the same broached in England, that a popular British author had Cairo, State of Illinois, in his eye when under the name of Eden he depicted a chosen happy spot on the Mississippi river, and told us how certain English emigrants fixed themselves in that locality, and there made light of those little ills of life which are incident to humanity even in the garden of the valley of the Mississippi. But I doubt whether that author ever visited Cairo in mid-winter, and I am sure that he never visited Cairo when Cairo was the seat of the American army. Had he done so, his love of truth would have forbidden him to presume that even Mark Tapley could have enjoyed himself in such an Eden.[45]

I had no wish myself to go to Cairo, having heard it but indifferently spoken of by all men; but my friend with whom I was travelling was peremptory in the matter. He had heard of gunboats and mortar-boats, of forts built upon the river, of all the pomps and circumstances of glorious war, and entertained an idea that Cairo was the nucleus or pivot of all really strategic movements in this terrible national struggle. Under such circumstances I was forced as it were to go to Cairo, and bore myself, under the circumstances, as much like Mark Tapley as my nature would permit. I was not jolly while I was there certainly, but I did not absolutely break down and perish in its mud.

Cairo is the southern terminus of the Illinois central railway. There is but one daily arrival there, namely, at half past four in the morning, and but one despatch, which is at half past three in the morning. Everything is thus done to assist that view of life which Mark Tapley took when he resolved to ascertain under what possible worst circumstances of existence he could still maintain his jovial character. Why anybody should ever arrive at Cairo at half past four a.m., I cannot understand. The departure at any hour is easy of comprehension. The place is situated exactly at the point in which the Ohio and the Mississippi meet, and is, I should say, merely guessing on the matter, some ten or twelve feet lower than the winter level of the two rivers. Who were the founders of Cairo I have never ascertained. They are probably buried fathoms deep in mud, and their names will no doubt remain a mystery to the latest ages.

I cannot tell what was the existing population of Cairo. I asked one resident; but he only shook his head and said that the place was about 'played out'. As Cairo is of all towns in America the most desolate, so is its hotel the most forlorn and wretched. Not that it lacked custom. It was so full that no room was to be had on our first entry from the railway cars at 5 a.m., and we were reduced to the necessity of washing our hands and faces in the public wash-room. At length we got a room, one room for the two. I had become so depressed in spirits that I did not dare to object to this arrangement. My friend could not complain much, even to me, feeling that these miseries had been produced by his own obstinacy. 'It is a new phase of life,' he said. That, at any rate, was true.

Within a week of that time my friend was taking quinine, looking hollow about the eyes, and whispering to me of fever and ague. To say that there was nothing eatable or drinkable in that hotel, would be to tell that which will be understood without telling. My friend, however, was a cautious man, carrying with him comfortable tin pots, hermetically sealed, from Fortnum and Mason's;[46] and on the second day of our sojourn we were invited by two officers to join their dinner at a Cairo eating-house. We ploughed our way gallantly through the mud to a little shanty, at the door of which we were peremptorily demanded to scrub ourselves before we entered with the stump of an old broom. This we did, producing on our nether persons the appearance of the bread which has been carefully spread with treacle by an economical housekeeper. And the proprietor was right, for had we not done so, the treacle would have run off through the whole house. But after this we fared royally. Squirrel soup and prairie chickens regaled us. One of our new friends had laden his pockets with champagne and brandy; the other with glasses and a cork-screw; and as the bottle went round, I began to feel something of the spirit of Mark Tapley in my soul.

We found that two days at Cairo were quite enough for us. We had seen the gun-boats and the mortar-boats, and gone through the sheds of the soldiers. The latter were bad, comfortless, damp, and cold; and certain quarters of the officers, into which we were hospitably taken, were wretched abodes enough; but the sheds of Cairo did not stink like those of Benton barracks at St Louis, nor had illness been prevalent there to the same degree. I do not know why this should have been so, but such was the result of my observation.

We were thoroughly disgusted with the hotel, and retired on the second night to bed, giving positive orders that we might be called at half past two, with reference to that terrible start to be made at half past three. As a matter of course we kept waking and dozing till past one, in our fear less neglect on the part of the watcher should entail on us another day in this place; of course we went fast asleep about the time at which we should have roused ourselves; and of course we were called just fifteen minutes before the train started. Everybody knows how these things always go. And then the pair of us, jumping out of bed in that wretched chamber, went through the mockery of washing and packing which always takes place on such occasions – a mockery indeed of washing, for there was but one basin between us! And a mockery also of packing, for I left my hair-brushes behind me! And then, while we were in our agony, pulling at the straps of the portmanteaux and swearing at the faithlessness of the boots up came the clerk of the hotel – the great man from behind the bar – and scolded us prodigiously for our delay.

'Called! We had been called an hour ago!' Which statement, however, was decidedly untrue, as we remarked, not with extreme patience. 'We should certainly be late,' he said; 'it would take us five minutes to reach the train, and the cars would be off in four.'

Nobody who has not experienced them can understand the agony of such moments – of such moments as regards travelling in general; but none who have not been in Cairo can understand the extreme agony produced by the threat of a prolonged sojourn in that city.

At last we were out of the house, rushing through the mud, slush and half-melted snow, along the wooden track to the railway, laden with bags and coats, and deafened by that melancholy, wailing sound, as though of a huge polar she-bear in the pangs of travail upon an iceberg, which proceeds from an American railway-engine before it commences work. How we slipped and stumbled, and splashed and swore, rushing along in the dark night, with buttons loose, and our clothes half on! And how pitilessly we were treated! We gained our cars, and even succeeded in bringing with us our luggage; but we did not do so with the sympathy, but amidst the derision of the bystanders. And then the seats were all full, and we found that there was a lower depth even in the terrible deep of a railway train in a western State.

There was a second-class carriage, prepared, I presume, for those who esteemed themselves too dirty for association with the aristocracy of Cairo; and into this we flung ourselves. Even this was a joy to us, for we were being carried away from Eden. We had acknowledged ourselves to be no fitting colleagues for Mark Tapley, and would have been glad to escape from Cairo even had we worked our way out of the place as assistant-stokers to the engine-driver. Poor Cairo! Unfortunate Cairo! 'It is about played out!' said one citizen to me. But in truth the play was commenced a little too soon. Those players have played out; but another set will have their innings, and make a score that shall perhaps be talked of far and wide in the western world.

We remained a few days at Louisville, and were greatly struck with the natural beauty of the country around it. Indeed, as far as I was enabled to see, Kentucky has superior attractions as a place of rural residence for an English gentleman, to any other State of the Union. There is nothing of landscape there equal to the banks of the Upper Mississippi, or to some parts of the Hudson river. It has none of the wild grandeur of the White Mountains of New Hampshire, nor does it break itself into valleys equal to those of the Alleghenies in Pennsylvania. But all those are beauties for the tourist rather than for the resident. In Kentucky the land lies in knolls in soft sloping hills. The trees stand apart, forming forest openings. The herbage is rich, and the soil, though not fertile like the prairies of Illinois, or the river bottoms of the Mississippi and its tributaries, is good, steadfast, wholesome farming ground. It is a fine country for a resident gentleman farmer, and in its outward aspect reminds me more of England in its rural aspects, than any other State which I visited.

At the hotels in Cincinnati and St Louis you are served by white men, and are very badly served. At Louisville the ministration is black men 'bound to labour'. The difference in the comfort is very great. The white servants are noisy, dirty, forgetful, indifferent, and sometimes impudent. The Negroes are the very reverse of all this; you cannot hurry them; but in all other respects – and perhaps even in that respect also – they are good servants. This is the work for which they seem to have been intended. But nevertheless where they are life and energy seem to languish, and prosperity cannot make any true advance. They are symbols of the luxury of the white men who employ them, and as such are signs of decay and emblems of decreasing power.

There has been and is at this moment a terribly bitter feeling among Americans against England, and I have heard this expressed quite as loudly by men in the army as by civilians; but I think I may say that this has never been brought to bear upon individual intercourse. Certainly we have said some very sharp things of them – words which, whether true or false, whether deserved or undeserved, must have been offensive to them. I have known this feeling of offence to amount almost to an agony of anger. But nevertheless I have never seen any falling off in the hospitality and courtesy generally shown by a civilized people to passing visitors. I have argued the matter of England's course throughout the war, till I have been hoarse with asseverating the rectitude of her conduct and her national unselfishness. I have met very strong opponents on the subject, and have been coerced into loud strains of voice; but I have never yet met one American who was personally uncivil to me as an Englishman, or who seemed to be made personally angry by my remarks. I found no coldness in the hospitality to which as a stranger I was entitled, because of the national ill-feeling which circumstances have engendered.

And while on this subject I will remark, that when travelling I have found it expedient to let those with whom I might chance to talk know at once that I was an Englishman. In fault of such knowledge things would be said which could not but be disagreeable to me; but not even from any rough western enthusiast in a railway carriage have I ever heard a word spoken insolently to England, after I had made my nationality known. I have learned that Wellington was beaten at Waterloo; that Lord Palmerston was so unpopular that he could not walk alone in the streets; that the House of Commons was an acknowledged failure; that starvation was the normal condition of the British people, and that the Queen was a bloodthirsty tyrant. But these assertions were not made with the intention that they should be heard by an Englishman. To us as a nation they are at the present moment unjust almost beyond belief; but I do not think that the feeling has ever taken the guise of personal discourtesy.

Chapter 19

I PASSED through Pittsburgh, and over the Allegheny mountains by Altoona, and down to Baltimore – back into civilization, secession, conversation, and gastronomy. I never had secessionist sympathies and never expressed them. I always believed in the North as a people – discrediting, however, to the utmost the existing northern Government, or, as I should more properly say, the existing northern Cabinet; but nevertheless, with such feelings and such belief I found myself very happy at Baltimore. Putting aside Boston which must, I think, be generally preferred by Englishmen to any other city in the States, I should choose Baltimore as my residence if I were called upon to live in America.

I am not led to this opinion, if I know myself, solely by the canvas-back ducks; and as to the terrapins, I throw them to the winds. The madeira, which is still kept there with a reverence which I should call superstitious were it not that its free circulation among outside worshippers prohibits the just use of such a word, may have something to do with it; as may also the beauty of the women – to some extent. Trifles do bear upon our happiness in a manner that we do not ourselves understand, and of which we are unconscious. But there was an English look about the streets and houses which I think had as much to do with us as either the wine, the women, or the ducks; and it seemed to me as though the manners of the people of Maryland were more English than those of other Americans. I do not say that they were on this account better. My English hat is, I am well aware, less graceful, and I believe less comfortable, than a Turkish fez and turban; nevertheless I prefer my English hat. New York I regard as the most thoroughly American of all cities. It is by no means the one in which I should find myself the happiest, but I do not on that account condemn it.

During my second visit to Baltimore I went over to Washington for a day or two, and found the capital still under the empire of King Mud. How the élite of a nation – for the inhabitants of

Washington consider themselves to be an élite – can consent to live in such a state of thraldom, a foreigner cannot understand. Were I to say that it was intended to be typical of the condition of the government, I might be considered cynical; but undoubtedly the sloughs of despond which were deepest in their despondency were to be found in localities which gave an appearance of truth to such a surmise. Of dirt of all kinds it behoves Washington and those concerned in Washington to make themselves free. It is the Augean stables through which some American Hercules must turn a purifying river before the American people can justly boast either of their capital or of their government.

The leaders of the rebellion are hated in the North. The names of Jefferson Davis,[47] of Gobb, Tombes, and Floyd[48] are mentioned with execration by the very children. This has sprung from a true and noble feeling; from a patriotic love of national greatness and a hatred of those who, for small party purposes, have been willing to lessen the name of the United States. I have reverenced the feeling even when I have not shared it. But, in addition to this, the names of those also should be execrated who have robbed their country when pretending to serve it; who have taken its wages in the days of its great struggle, and at the same time have filched from its coffers; who have undertaken the task of steering the ship through the storm in order that their hands might be in the meal-tub and bread-basket, and that they might stuff their own sacks with the ship's provisions. These are the men who must be loathed by the nation – whose fate must be held up as a warning to others before good can come! Northern men and women talk of hanging Davis and his accomplices. I myself trust that there will be no hanging when the war is over. I believe there will be none, for the Americans are not a bloodthirsty people. But if punishment of any kind be meted out, the men of the North should understand that they have worse offenders among them than Davis and Floyd.

The United States has now created a great army and a great debt. They will soon also have created a great navy. Affairs of other nations will press upon them, and they will press against the affairs of other nations. In this way statecraft will become necessary to them; and by degrees their ministers will become habile, graceful, adroit – and perhaps crafty, as are the ministers of other nations.

And, moreover the United States have had no outlying colonies or dependencies, such as an India and Canada are to us, as Cuba is and Mexico was to Spain, and as were the provinces of the Roman empire. Territories she has had, but by the peculiar beneficence of her political arrangements, these territories have assumed the guise of sovereign States, and been admitted into federal partnership on equal terms, with a rapidity which has hardly left to the central Government the reality of any dominion of its own. The outlying populations have been encouraged to take upon themselves their own governance, and the power of the President and his cabinet has been kept within moderate limits.

But none the less is the position of the President very dominant in the eyes of us Englishmen by reason of the authority with which he is endowed. It is not that the scope of his power is great, but that he is so nearly irresponsible in the exercise of that power. We know that he can be impeached by the representatives and expelled from his office by the verdict of the Senate; but this, in fact, does not amount to much. Responsibility of this nature is doubtless very necessary, and prevents ebullitions of tyranny such as those in which a Sultan or an Emperor may indulge; but it is not that responsibility which especially recommends itself to the mind of free men. The President is placed at the head of the executive for four years, and while he there remains no man can question him. Our Prime Minister is doubtless more powerful – has a wider authority. But it is that within the scope of his power the President is free from all check. It is hardly necessary that I should point out the fundamental difference between our King or Queen, and the President of the United States. Our Sovereign, we all know, is not responsible. The President is nominally responsible. But from that everyday working responsibility, which to us is so invaluable, the President is in fact free.

I will give an instance of this. Now, at this very moment of my writing, news has reached us that President Lincoln has relieved General Maclellan[49] from the command of the whole army, that he has given separate commands to two other generals – to General Hallek, namely, and alas! to General Fremont, and that he has altogether altered the whole organization of the military command as it previously existed. This he did not only during the war, but with reference to a special battle, for the special fighting of which he, as ex-officio commander-in-chief of the forces, had given orders. I do not hereby intend to criticize this act of the President's or to point out that that has been done which had better have been left undone. The President, in a strategical point of view, may have been – very probably has been, quite right. I, at any rate, cannot say that he has been wrong. But then neither can anybody else say so with any power of making himself heard. Of this action of the President's, so terribly great in its importance to the nation, no one has the power of expressing any opinion to which the President is bound to listen.

For four years he has this sway, and at the end of four years he becomes so powerless that it is not then worth the while of any demagogue in a fourth-rate town to occupy his voice with that President's name. The anger of the country as to the things done both by Pierce and Buchanan is very bitter.[50] But who wastes a thought upon either of the men? A past President of the United States is of less consideration than a past Mayor in an English borough. Whatever evil he may have done during his office, when out of office he is not worth the powder which would be expended in an attack.

But the President has his ministers as our Queen has hers. In one sense he has such ministers. He has high state servants who under him take the control of various departments, and exercise among them a certain degree of patronage and executive power. But they are the President's ministers, and not the ministers of the people. Till lately there has been no chief minister among them, nor am I prepared to say that there is any such chief at present. It will probably come to pass before long that one special minister will be the avowed leader of the cabinet, and that he will be recognized as the chief servant of the State under the President. But a Prime Minister in the United States can never take the place there which is taken here by our Premier.

Over our Premier there is no one politically superior. The highest political responsibility of the nation rests on him.

In the States this must always rest on the President, and any minister, whatever may be his name or assumed position, can only be responsible through the President. But the President, on whom it is presumed that the whole of the responsibility of the United States Government rests, goes out at a certain day, and of him no more is heard. There is no future before him to urge him on to constancy; no hope of other things beyond, of greater honours and a wider fame, to keep him wakeful in his country's cause. He has already enrolled his name on the list of his country's rulers, and received what reward his country can give him. Conscience, duty, patriotism may make him true to his place. But ambition and hope of things still to come are the moving motives in the minds of most men.

In the old days, before democracy had prevailed in upsetting that system of Presidential election which the constitution had intended to fix as permanent, the Presidents were generally re-elected for a second term. But this has never been done since the days of General Jackson; nor will it be done, unless a stronger conservative reaction takes place than the country even as yet seems to promise. As things have lately ordered themselves, it may almost be said that no man in the Union would be so improbable a candidate for the Presidency as the outgoing President. And it has been only natural that it should be so. Looking at the men themselves who have lately been chosen, the fault has not consisted in their non-election, but in their original selection. There has been no desire for great men, no search after a man of such a nature, that when tried the people should be anxious to keep him. 'It will not be in my time,' says the expiring President. And so, without dismay, he sees the empire of his country slide away from him.

From Washington I journeyed back to Boston through the cities which I had visited in coming thither, and stayed again on my route for a few days at Baltimore, at Philadelphia, and at New York. At each there were those whom I now regarded almost as old friends, and as the time of my departure drew near I felt a sorrow that I was not to be allowed to stay longer. As the general result of my sojourn in the country, I must declare that I was always happy and comfortable in the eastern cities, and generally unhappy and uncomfortable in the West. I had previously been inclined to think that I should like the roughness of the West, and that in the East I should encounter an arrogance which would have kept me always on the verge of hot water; but in both these surmises I found myself wrong. And I think that most English travellers would come to the same conclusion. The western people do not mean to be harsh or uncivil, but they do not make themselves pleasant. In all the eastern cities – I speak of the eastern cities north of Washington – a society may be found which must be esteemed as agreeable by Englishmen who like clever genial men, and who love clever pretty women.

I was forced to pass twice again over the road between New York and Boston, as the packet by which I intended to leave America was fixed to sail from the former port. I had promised myself, and had promised others, that I would spend in Boston the last week of my sojourn in the States, and this was a promise which I was by no means inclined to break. I became enamoured of Boston at last. Beacon Street was very pleasant to me, and the view over Boston Common was dear to my eyes. Even the State House, with its great yellow-painted dome, became sightly; and the sunset over the western waters that encompass the city beats all other sunsets that I have seen.

Farewell to thee, thou western Athens! When I have forgotten thee my right hand shall have forgotten its cunning, and my heart forgotten its pulses. Let us look at the list of names with which Boston has honoured itself in our days, and then ask what other town of the same size has done more. Prescott, Motley, Longfellow, Lowell, Emerson, Dana, Agassiz, Holmes, Hawthorne.[51] Who is there among us in England who has not been the better for these men? Who does not owe to some of them a debt of gratitude? In whose ears are not their names familiar? It is a bright galaxy and far extended, for so small a city. All these men, save one, are now alive and in the full possession of their powers. What other town of the same size has done as well in the same short space of time? I am thankful that my steps have wandered thither at such a period.

Chapter 20

WHEN the snow went in Boston I went with it. The evening before I left I watched them as they carted away the dirty uncouth blocks which had been broken up with pickaxes in Washington Street, and was melancholy as I reflected that I too should no longer be known in the streets. My weeks in Boston had not been very many, but nevertheless there were haunts there which I knew as though my feet had trodden them for years. I know that I shall never again be at Boston, and that I have said that about the Americans which would make me unwelcome as a guest if I were there. They who will expect blessings from me, will say among themselves that I have cursed them. As I read the pages which I have written I feel that words which I intended for blessings when I prepared to utter them have gone nigh to turn themselves into curses.

I have ever admired the United States as a nation. I have loved their liberty, their prowess, their intelligence, and their progress. I have sympathized with a people who themselves have had no sympathy with passive security and inaction. I have felt confidence in them, and have known, as it were, that their industry must enable them to succeed as a people, while their freedom would ensure to them success as a nation. With these convictions I went among them wishing to write of them good words – words which might be pleasant for them to read, while they might assist perhaps in producing a true impression of them here at home. But among my good words there are so many which are bitter, that I fear that I shall have failed in my object as regards them.

O, my friends with thin skins – and here I protest that a thick skin is a fault not to be forgiven in a man or a nation, whereas a thin skin is in itself a merit, if only the wearer of it will be master and not the slave of his skin – O, my friends with thin skins, ye whom I call my cousins and love as brethren, will ye not forgive me these harsh words that I have spoken? They have been spoken in love – with a true brotherly love, a love that has never been absent from the heart while the brain was coining them. And yet ye will not forgive me; because your skins are thin, and because the praise of others is as the breath of your nostrils.

I do not know that an American as an individual is more thin-skinned than an Englishman; but as the representative of a nation it may almost be said of him that he has no skin at all. Any touch comes at once upon the network of his nerves and puts in operation all his organs of feeling with the violence of a blow. And for this peculiarity he has been made the mark of much ridicule. It shows itself in two ways; either by extreme displeasure when anything is said disrespectful of his country; or by the strong eulogy with which he is accustomed to speak of his own institutions and of those of his countrymen whom at the moment he may chance to hold in high esteem. The manner in which this is done is often ridiculous.

'Sir, what do you think of our Mr Jefferson Brick? Mr Jefferson Brick, sir, is one of our most remarkable men.' And again. 'Do you like our institutions, sir? Do you find that philanthropy, religion, philosophy, and the social virtues are cultivated on a scale commensurate with the unequalled liberty and political advancement of the nation?'

There is something absurd in such a mode of address when it is repeated often. But hero-worship and love of country are not absurd; and do not these addresses show capacity for hero-worship and an aptitude for the love of country? Jefferson Brick may not be a hero; but a capacity for such worship is something. Indeed, the capacity is everything, for the need of a hero will at last produce the hero needed. And it is the same with that love of country. A people that are proud of their country will see that there is something in their country to justify their pride. Do we not all of us feel assured by the intense nationality of an American that he will not desert his nation in the hour of her need? I feel that assurance respecting them; and at those moments in which I am moved to laughter by the absurdity of their addresses, I feel it the strongest.

I left Boston with the snow, and returning to New York found that the streets there were dry and that the winter was nearly over. As I had passed through New York to Boston the streets had been by no means dry. The snow had lain in small mountains over which the omnibuses made their way down Broadway, till at the bottom of that thoroughfare, between Trinity Church and Bowling Green, alp became piled upon alp, and all traffic was full of danger. The accursed love of gain still took men to Wall Street, but they had to fight their way thither through physical difficulties which must have made even the state of the money market a matter of almost indifference to them. They do not seem to me to manage the winter in New York so well as they do in Boston. But now, on my last return thither, the alps were gone, the roads were clear, and one could travel through the city with no other impediment than those of treading on women's dresses if one walked, or having to look after women's bandboxes and pay their fares and take their change, if one used the omnibuses.

And now had come the end of my adventures, and as I set my foot once more upon the deck of the Cunard steamer I felt that my work was done. Whether it were done ill or well, or indeed any approach to the doing of it had been attained, all had been done that I could accomplish. No further opportunity remained to me of seeing, hearing, or of speaking. I had come out thither, having resolved to learn a little that I might if possible teach that little to others; and now the lesson was learned, or must remain unlearned. But in carrying out my resolution I had gradually risen in my ambition, and had mounted from one stage of inquiry to another, till at last I had found myself burdened with the task of ascertaining whether or no the Americans were doing their work as a nation well or ill; and now, if ever, I must be prepared to put forth the result of my inquiry. As I walked up and down the deck of the steam-boat I confess I felt that I had been somewhat arrogant.

I had been a few days over six months in the States, and I was engaged in writing a book of such a nature that a man might well engage himself for six years, or perhaps for sixty, in obtaining the materials for it. There was nothing in the form of government, or legislature, or manners of the people, as to which I had not taken upon myself to say something. I was professing to understand their strength and their weakness; and was daring to censure their faults and to eulogize their virtues.

'Who is he,' an American would say, 'that he comes to judge us? His judgement is nothing.'

'Who is he,' an Englishman would say, 'that he comes and teaches us? His teaching is of no value.'

In answer to this I have but a small plea to make. I have done my best. I have nothing 'extenuated, and I have set down naught in malice.' I do feel that my volumes have blown themselves out into proportions greater than I had intended – greater not in mass of pages, but in the matter handled. I am frequently addressing my own muse, who I am well aware is not Clio, and asking her whither she is wending. 'Cease, thou wrong-headed one, to meddle with these mysteries.' I appeal to her frequently, but ever in vain. One cannot drive one's muse, nor yet always lead her. Of the various women with which a man is blessed, his muse is by no means the least difficult to manage.

On our return to Liverpool, we stayed for a few hours at Queenstown, taking in coal, and the passengers landed that they might stretch their legs and look about them. I also went ashore at the dear old place which I had known well in other days,[52] when the people were not too grand to call it Cove, and were contented to run down from Cork in river steamers, before the Passage railway was built. I spent a pleasant summer there once in those times – God be with the good old days! And now I went ashore at Queenstown, happy to feel that I should be again in a British isle, and happy also to know that I was once more in Ireland.[53]

Or rather I should have been happy if I had not found myself instantly disgraced by the importunities of my friends. A legion of women surrounded me, imploring alms, begging my honour to bestow my charity on them for the love of the virgin, using the most holy names in their adjurations for halfpence, clinging to me with that half joking, half lachrymose air of importunity which an Irish beggar has assumed as peculiarly her own. There were men too, who begged as well as women. And the women were sturdy and fat, and, not knowing me as well as I knew them, seemed resolved that their importunities should be successful. After all, I had an old world liking for them in their rags. They were endeared to me by certain memories and associations which I cannot define. But then what would those Americans think of them – and of the country which produced them? That was the reflection which troubled me. A legion of women in rags clamorous for bread, protesting to heaven that they are starving, importunate with voices and with hands, surrounding the stranger when he puts his foot on the soil that he cannot escape, does not afford to the cynical American who then first visits us – and they are all cynical when they visit us – a bad opportunity for his sarcasm. He can at any rate boast that he sees nothing of that at home. I myself am fond of Irish beggars. It is an acquired taste – which comes upon one as does that for smoked whisky, or Limerick tobacco. But I certainly did wish that there were not so many of them at Queenstown.

I tell all this here not to the disgrace of Ireland – not for the triumph of America. The Irishman or American who thinks rightly on the subject will know that the state of each country has risen from its opportunities. Beggary does not prevail in new countries, and but few old countries have managed to exist without it. As to Ireland we may rejoice to say that there is less of it now than there was twenty years ago. Things are mending there. But though such excuses may be truly made, although an Englishman when he sees this squalor and poverty on the quays at Queenstown, consoles himself with reflecting that the evil has been unavoidable, but will perhaps soon be avoided – nevertheless he cannot but remember that there is so much squalor and no such poverty in the land from which he has returned. I claim no credit for the new country. I impute no blame to the old country. But there is the fact. The Irishman when he expatriates himself to one of those American States loses much of that affectionate, confiding, master-worshipping nature which makes him so good a fellow when at home. But he becomes more of a man. He assumes a dignity which he never has known before. He learns to regard his labour as his own property. That which he earns he takes without thanks, but he desires to take no more than he earns. To me he has perhaps become less pleasant than he was. But to himself —! It seems to me that such a man must feel himself half a god, if he has the power of comparing what he is with what he was.

It is right that all this should be acknowledged by us. When we speak of America and her institutions we should remember that she has given to our increasing population rights and privileges which we could not give — which as an old country we probably can never give. That self-asserting, obtrusive independence which so often wounds us is, if viewed aright, but an outward sign of those good things which a new country has produced for its people. Men and women do not beg in the States — they do not often offend you with tattered rags; they do not complain to heaven of starvation; they do not crouch to the ground for halfpence. If they are poor they are not abject in their poverty. They read and write. They walk like human beings made in God's form. They know that they are men and women, owing it to themselves and to the world that they should earn their bread by their labour, but feeling that when earned it is their own. If this be so — if it be acknowledged that it is so — should not such knowledge in itself be sufficient testimony of the success of the country and of her institutions?

Notes

1. (p. 19) *Domestic Manners of the Americans*, by Frances Milton Trollope (1832).
2. (p. 29) Trollope was then 46. He had married Ruth Heseltine, a bank manager's daughter, in 1844 and they had two children.
3. (p. 40) He was misinformed. *The Great Eastern*, of 18,900 tons, a huge ship for her day, was originally intended for the route to Australia but the many delays in getting her to sea drove her owners to bankruptcy and she was purchased for use on the North Atlantic route for which she proved unsuitable.
4. (p. 41) Pounds sterling, equal to $3000 to $4000 with the $ worth 4/-.
5. (p. 41) Neal Dow (1804–97) of English Quaker descent, was Mayor of Portland and so-called 'Father of the Maine Law' which introduced prohibition to the State. He had a world-wide reputation as a temperance reformer. He ran for the Presidency as candidate of the Prohibition Party but won only 10,300 votes.
6. (p. 43) John Murray had published twenty-three guide books between 1836 and 1861 covering nearly every country in Europe and places as far afield as Madras and Bombay, but never produced one on America or Canada.
7. (p. 47) Mr Gladstone was Chancellor of the Exchequer from 1859 to 1865 and reduced almost to vanishing point the duty on French and other wines which were accordingly often referred to at that time as 'Gladstone wines'. Trollope seems to assume that the wines were re-exported to the United States from England, which may have been the case.
8. (p. 51) Edward Everett (1794–1865) was one of the most distinguished and versatile Americans of his generation. After graduating from Harvard he became a Unitarian Minister at the early age of 19. Little more than a year later he was appointed Professor of Greek Literature at Harvard. He then in turn became a member of Congress, Governor of Massachusetts, Minister to the Court of St James, Secretary of State, a Senator, and candidate for the Vice-Presidency. The most famous of his speeches was that delivered on the occasion of the dedication of the national cemetery at Gettysburg, although as he himself wrote to President Lincoln the next

day, 'I should be glad if I could flatter myself that I came as near to the central idea of the occasion in two hours as you did in ten minutes'.

9. (p. 53) From Halifax to Montreal. Railway development was in fact very rapid and by 1864 there was a link between the maritime provinces and Quebec.

10. (p. 53) By the British North America Act of 1867, only six years after Trollope's visit, the Dominion of Canada was brought into being by the amalgamation of Upper and Lower Canada, new Brunswick and Nova Scotia.

11. (p. 57) Trollope had joined the Post Office at the age of 19 and despite his many other activities had remained a civil servant. At the time of his North American tour he was on long unpaid leave.

12. (p. 58) When he was in Vermont, Trollope had asked a mail driver,

'Are you going this morning? I always thought you started in the evening.'

'Wa'll, I guess I do. But it rained last night so I just stayed at home.'

'I do not know that I ever felt more shocked in my life,' Trollope commented, 'and I could hardly keep my tongue off the man.'

13. (p. 61) Sir Edmund Head (1805-68) was Governor-General of Canada from 1854 to 1861.

14. (p. 77) John Charles Fremont (1813-90) was a controversial figure of the Civil War. He had won recognition as an explorer in Oregon, New Mexico, and California and particularly in exploring the southern pass of the Rockies and establishing the feasibility of an overland route. He was one of the earliest members of the Republican Party and on the outbreak of the Civil War rose rapidly in the Union Army. His fortunes fluctuated considerably and Trollope was not the only man to have misgivings about his capacity as a general.

15. (p. 105) Two of these three ex-Presidents, Franklin Pierce (1804-69), the fourteenth President, and James Buchanan (1791-1868), the fifteenth, were still alive. James Polk, the eleventh, had died in 1849.

16. (p. 131) Ralph Waldo Emerson (1803-82), poet and essayist, was a pupil of Edward Everett at Harvard and like him entered the ministry. His writings, and his poetry in particular, won him wide

acclaim. He was a friend and admirer of Carlyle and visited Britain several times. In his book, *English Traits* (1856) he praised British achievements in the arts, government and trade.

17. (p. 134) Joshua Bates (1788–1864) was born in Weymouth, Massachusetts, but went to England as a young man and became a partner in the banking firm of Baring and Company. He gave $100,000 to found a public library in Boston which was to be 'an ornament to the city'.

18. (p. 135) See note 5.

19. (p. 137) William Henry Seward (1801–72) was Governor of New York for four years and a strong abolitionist. He then went to the Senate where he became the embodiment of the anti-slavery sentiment of the North. He became Secretary of State in Lincoln's first cabinet.

20. (p. 137) In his *Autobiography* Trollope summarizes the case as follows:

There was a moment in which the Northern cause was in danger, and the danger certainly lay in the prospect of British interference. Messrs Slidell and Mason – two men insignificant in themselves – had been sent to Europe by the Southern party, and had managed to get on board a British mail-steamer called *The Trent*, at Havannah. Almost undue importance was attached to this mission by Mr Lincoln's government and efforts were made to stop them. A certain Commodore Wilkes, doing duty as policeman on the seas, did stop *The Trent* and took the men out. They were carried, one to Boston and one to New York, and were incarcerated, amidst the triumph of the nation. Commodore Wilkes, who had done nothing in which a brave man could take glory, was made a hero and received a prize sword. England of course demanded her passengers back, and the States for a while refused to surrender them. But Mr Seward was at the time Secretary of State, and Mr Seward, with many political faults, was a wise man. I was at Washington at the time, and it was known that there the contest among the leading Northerners was very sharp on the matter. . . . Mr Seward's counsels at last prevailed with the President, and England's declaration of war was prevented.

21. (p. 138) Henry Wheaton (1785–1848) a distinguished international lawyer and for many years publisher of *The Decisions of the Supreme Court*.

22. (p. 139) Richard Lyons (1817–87) the first and last Earl Lyons, was appointed British Minister at Washington in 1858 but the enormous difficulties of the post during the Civil War undermined

his health and he returned home in December 1864 and resigned his post shortly afterwards.

23. (p. 139) Simon Cameron (1799–1889) was a member of the Senate from 1845 until he was made Secretary of War in 1860. He was the subject of much criticism and to get rid of him Lincoln made him Minister to Russia. He became a member of the Senate again in 1867 and until his death was a power in Pennsylvania politics.

24. (p. 141) By the time he reached Washington, Trollope was pessimistic. In a letter of 17 December 1861, to his American friend Kate Field, he wrote: 'I am anxious to get out and see the people before war [between England and the United States] is declared.... There will be war if these two horrid men are not given up. I wish Wilkes and his whole cargo had gone to the bottom.'

25. (p. 147) Francis Cabot Lowell (1775–1817) graduated at Harvard. He studied cotton manufacture in Lancashire and on his return to America in 1812 set up his own cotton factory near Boston. He was not only a successful business man but a humane and liberal employer.

26. (p. 151) It had always been intended that Mrs Trollope should return to England for Christmas, leaving her husband to visit areas that were considered too dangerous for a woman. She left Boston at the end of November and, as Trollope wrote to Kate Field, 'was very unhappy on her voyage, having resolved that she would be so'.

27. (p. 153) Thomas Holliday Hicks (1798–1865) was Governor of Maryland at the outbreak of the Civil War and later a Senator.

28. (p. 155) Trollope gave the preamble which is omitted here.

29. (p. 156) Nathaniel Prentiss Banks (1816–94) had been a congressman and Governor of Massachusetts before Lincoln appointed him a major-general in the volunteers.

30. (p. 156) December 1861.

31. (p. 156) John Adams Dix (1798–1879) had had a varied career prior to the Civil War, having been among other things, President of the Chicago and Rock Island Railroad, a member of the New York City Bar, and Secretary of the Treasury. In recognition of his excellent work at the Treasury, Lincoln made him a major-general and he served in Baltimore and later in New York.

32. (p. 164) Trollope had visited Costa Rica in 1858 when he was on an official mission to the Caribbean on behalf of the Post Office.

33. (p. 167) It is still there. In the handbook currently issued by the National Capital Parks it is described as 'a fine equestrian statue of George Washington'.

34. (p. 168) James Smithson (1765–1821) was the illegitimate son of Sir

Hugh Smithson (who later assumed the name of Percy and became the Duke of Northumberland). Described as 'the best chemist and microbiologist of his year' at Oxford, Smithson became a distinguished natural philosopher. In his will he left the residue of his estate, some £100,000, to the United States 'to found at Washington an establishment for the increase and diffusion among men'.

35. (p. 169) Trollope was too pessimistic. More than one million dollars was raised from public subscriptions and Federal appropriations and the monument, 555 feet high, was dedicated in 1885 and opened to the public in 1888. It is, of course, one of the city's most famous landmarks.

36. (p. 170) Robert Edward Lee (1807–70), one of the great figures of the Civil War, was born in Virginia and educated at West Point. He married the granddaughter of Martha Washington's son. Although an opponent of secession, he felt obliged to support his native state and joined the Confederate Army where he rapidly rose to high rank. His house at Arlington Heights was, as Trollope surmised, expropriated.

37. (p. 172) Samuel Peter Heintzelman (1805–80) was another graduate of West Point. Although a man of great personal courage, he was not completely successful as a leader.

38. (p. 178) Lord John Russell (1792–1878). A son of the 6th Duke of Bedford, became Foreign Secretary in the Palmerston administration of 1859. He was created Earl Russell in 1861.

39. (p. 186) 1827 had seen the most fatuous of all Trollope's father's ventures. Carried away by an account he had read of the great opportunities that awaited the pioneer in America, he took his wife and two daughters, leaving the boys at home, to Cincinnati where he set up a large bargain store. It was a disastrous failure and after four ghastly years the Trollopes crawled back to England, more depressed and desperate than ever.

40. (p. 192) Henry Wager Halleck (1815–72) (not Hallek as Trollope spells it) graduated from West Point and was commissioned in the engineers. Seeing little prospect of promotion he resigned from the army in 1853 and had a successful career in business. At the beginning of the Civil War he was commissioned as a major-general and in July 1862 he became military adviser to the President.

41. (p. 194) Sterling Price (1809–67), Governor of Missouri, was originally a conditional Union man but joined the Confederate Army and for a time at least was successful and popular.

42. (p. 194) Nathaniel Lyon (1818–61), a graduate of West Point, was

in command of the Union forces at St Louis in May, 1861. He was killed at the head of his troops at the battle of Wilson's Creek in August 1861. He had done much to hold Missouri for the Union and on his death he was hailed by the North as a hero and martyr.

43. (p. 195) Samuel Ryan Curtis (1805–66) was a graduate of West Point and an engineer. He was a member of Congress for Iowa but resigned soon after the outbreak of the Civil War when he was appointed a brigadier-general.

44. (p. 197) James Henry Lane (1814–66) was elected to the Senate when Kansas was admitted in 1861, and became a close friend of Lincoln. He was made a brigadier-general in June 1861. A man of remarkable energy and personal magnetism he was immensely popular among the Northern men of Kansas who had great faith in his military genius.

45. (p. 201) Trollope was not quite fair to Dickens. Martin Chuzzlewit was as depressed by Eden as Trollope was by Cairo and Mark Tapley's happiest moment was when he and Martin decided to quit the place and return to England.

46. (p. 202) Although the first reference to food canning in Fortnum and Mason's records goes back to 1820, it is clear from Trollope's account that canned foods were still a considerable novelty in 1862. The cans Trollope sampled in Cairo probably included Scotch salmon and beef stew.

47. (p. 208) As all Americans, and not so many English readers know, Jefferson Davis (1808–89), who was the only President of the Confederation during the Civil War, was captured in May 1865. He was indicted for treason and was refused bail and harshly treated. He was finally admitted to bail in 1867 and after long and complicated legal processes the administration dismissed the case and Davis was released. He settled in Canada but returned to Mississippi under the general amnesty of 1868.

48. (p. 209) John Buchanan Floyd (1806–63) was Governor of Virginia from 1849 to 1852 and Secretary of War in President Buchanan's cabinet. He was at first opposed to secession but after Virginia seceded he joined the Confederate Army as a brigadier-general.

49. (p. 209) George Brinton McClellan (not spelt as Trollope has it) (1826–85) was, like so many of the generals on both sides, a graduate of West Point. At the time Trollope is writing about, he had been removed from his post of commander-in-chief of the Union armies but was recalled a year or so later. After a few months, however, Lincoln relieved him of his post once again. In the 1864 election

he was the Democratic candidate for President but was defeated by Lincoln.

50. (p. 210) See note 15.

51. (p. 212) Some of these names have been mentioned already and most of the others are familiar to readers on both sides of the Atlantic. Except for William Hickling Prescott, the Latin American historian, who died in 1859, the others were all active in various fields, mainly in Boston, and particularly Harvard. John Lothrop Motley, author of *The Rise of the Dutch Republic*, was a diplomat as well as a historian and about this time had been appointed Minister to Austria; Longfellow, who had been Professor of Modern Languages at Harvard until 1854, lived at Nahant, not far from Cambridge; Richard Henry Dana, an eminent authority on international law, was United States Attorney for Massachusetts; Jean Louis Rodolphe Agassiz, a close friend of Longfellow, was Professor of Natural History at Harvard; Oliver Wendell Holmes was Professor of Anatomy and Physiology at Harvard; and Nathaniel Hawthorn had just returned from seven years as American Consul in Liverpool and had settled at Concord a few miles from Cambridge.

52. (p. 216) The quotation from *Othello* goes on:

> ... then must you speak,
> Of one that loved, not wisely, but too well;
> Of one not easily jealous but, being wrought,
> Perplex'd in the extreme.

53. (p. 216) Trollope lived in Ireland in the employment of the Post Office from 1841 to 1857 and during this time, as Michael Sadleir puts it (*Trollope: a commentary*, Constable & Co., Ltd.): 'he came to know gaiety and good fellowship'.

MORE ABOUT PENGUINS

Penguin Book News, which appears every month, contains details of all the new books issued by Penguins as they are published. From time to time it is supplemented by *Penguins in Print*, which is a complete list of all books published by Penguins which are in print. (There are nearly three thousand of these.)

A specimen copy of *Penguin Book News* will be sent to you free on request, and you can become a subscriber for the price of the postage – 3s. for a year's issues (including the complete lists). Just write to Dept EP, Penguin Books Ltd, Harmondsworth, Middlesex, enclosing a cheque or postal order, and your name will be added to the mailing list.

Some other books published by Penguins are described on the following pages.

Note: *Penguin Book News* and *Penguins in Print* are not available in the U.S.A. or Canada

MARK TWAIN

THE ADVENTURES
OF HUCKLEBERRY FINN

Edited by Peter Coveney

Of all the contenders for the title of The Great American
Novel, none has a better claim than *The Adventures of
Huckleberry Finn*. This idyll, intended at first as 'a kind
of companion to *Tom Sawyer*', grew and matured under
Mark Twain's hand into a work of immeasurable richness and complexity. Critics have argued over the
symbolic significance of Huck's and Jim's voyage down
the Mississippi: none has disputed the greatness of the
book itself. It remains a work that can be enjoyed at
many levels: as an incomparable adventure story, as a
classic of American humour, and as a metaphor of the
American predicament.

A Pelican Book

THE AMERICAN PEOPLE

The History of a Society

OSCAR HANDLIN

This is the story of Americanization – the biography of a people recruited from the world to work in a wilderness. Oscar Handlin, winner of the Pulitzer Prize, follows the Americans through three centuries of their development, as they built the most powerful nation in history and moved on from the safe ideals of isolation to the hazards of glory.

Professor Handlin is enough of a novelist to make a brilliant social historian ... *The American People* should be in every library in the country' – *Spectator*

'Deserves to be read and re-read, its insights to be pondered and savoured. It will lead historians to think afresh about many aspects of the American experience' – *The Times Educational Supplement*

Also in the Penguin English Library

ANTHONY TROLLOPE
THE LAST CHRONICLE
OF BARSET

with an Introduction by Laurence Lerner

As the complacent chronicler of cathedral cities and mildly erring parsons, Trollope has charmed and repelled modern readers in about equal numbers. In recent years critics have discovered in his later novels a gloomier, more profound, less comfortable Trollope hitherto neglected by his most ardent admirers. Somewhere between the two moods lies *The Last Chronicle of Barset* (1867), which retains enough of the familiar Barsetshire figures to delight the Trollopian and offers enough hints of the darker side of life to satisfy more astringent tastes. In Laurence Lerner's words, 'The two extremes of Trollope's range meet in this novel, the finest he ever wrote'.